THE PURSUIT OF MUSIC

THE PURSUIT OF MUSIC

by

WALFORD DAVIES

THOMAS NELSON & SONS LTD
LONDON EDINBURGH PARIS
TORONTO NEW YORK

THOMAS NELSON AND SONS LTD

Parkside Works Edinburgh 9
3 Henrietta Street London WC2
312 Flinders Street Melbourne C1

THOMAS NELSON AND SONS (CANADA) LTD
91–93 Wellington Street West Toronto 1

THOMAS NELSON AND SONS
385 Madison Avenue New York 17

SOCIÉTÉ FRANÇAISE D'EDITIONS NELSON
25 rue Henri Barbusse Paris Ve

First published October 1935
Reprinted 1936, 1946, 1949

DEDICATED TO

KING GEORGE V

BY GRACIOUS PERMISSION

OF HIS MAJESTY

CONTENTS

PART 1

THE NATURE OF MUSIC

PART 2

MUSICAL MATERIAL

PART 3

THE MIND IN ACTION

PART 4

THE HARMONIC HIGHWAY OF THE WEST

PART 5

MUSIC IN DOUBLE HARNESS

All the music examples in this book were engraved by Messrs. Novello & Co., and the author and publishers wish gratefully to acknowledge their indebtedness to them and to their Director, Mr. H. H. Hanhart.

FOREWORD

THIS book is about music, and music only. That is to say, it can neither be a text-book on how to write music, nor a musical history ; neither does it attempt to describe the works or lives of composers who made history. It is true that Part 4 is specially, and of necessity, associated with one period in music's story, and with one composer in particular—Beethoven—but that is only because of the momentous happenings to music itself in one short span, especially revealed through the mind of this one man, who seems to have been more than a Shakespeare of his art and time.

Again, no attempt is here made to discuss the subject of musical performance. All the adventures, problems, and pleasures of the mastery of voice and instrument are set aside ; and even that greatest of joys in music-making, team-work *in excelsis*, has to be taken for granted. Whenever I have occasion to speak of a Symphony, or any other work, I speak of it as of music perfectly rendered.

At the height of the Great War I received a letter from a total stranger, a major at the front, asking me to write such a book, and saying, " If I come out of this, I shall want to know what music is about." Though countless good books are now available, I still share the thirst of my unknown correspondent ; and it is echoed by so many people that the desire to bring my thoughts to book, and the urge to do as I was asked, have become unbearable. The result is this attempt to face afresh the issues raised by the major's question. I only hope he came through, and that if he chances to see this book, I may receive his forgiveness for its disappointments.

My friendly publisher has asked that the book should be specially addressed to young people. Any one who has broadcast to schools has made the discovery that there are innumerable grown-up children listening at mental keyholes. They often write letters to say they "wish they were young," which, of course, only goes to show how young they are. Musically the world is surely very young. Is not music itself still an infant among the arts? In any case, let it be imagined, for the purpose of our present book, that all readers—including the author—range, let us say, from about fifteen to twenty-one years, in a promising and inquiring mood. He who feels himself to have come of age musically had perhaps better close the book; for he may find it annoying to read such well-known facts re-approached and re-stated in ways only fit for beginners, to be asked to take so little for granted, and to cover so little ground in thirty chapters—a fact very troubling to the writer himself.

One thing more. To read this book without any attempt to hear the musical illustrations given, would be like reading a book on engines or architecture without the interest of a single diagram or sketch—almost useless, and certainly dull. They should be heard, in their context in the book, several times over; and those which the reader cannot easily play for himself must needs be played for him by some obliging friend.

I desire to add most grateful acknowledgment of invaluable help, both by suggestions and criticisms, received in proof stages from Sir James Jeans, and through every stage of the book from Miss Anne Williams.

PART I

THE NATURE OF MUSIC

THE PURSUIT OF MUSIC

CHAPTER 1

DISCOVERY AND DELIGHT

" I love all beauteous things,
I seek and adore them."
BRIDGES.

MUSIC is a sensible and reasonable pursuit. But neither because you and I can sense it, nor even because we can reason about it and find it interesting, are you reading and I writing about it. It is, we will believe, because it can be brimful of a reality of delight, which *moves* us from where we are to where we have never been, as naturally as a breeze moves a sailing ship, or as a tide moves a stranded one. Bach is reported to have said: " Music ought to move the heart with sweet emotion." This remark comes the more strikingly from one whose Fugues are as full of reason as Euclid's propositions. I once heard Delius exclaim that in music he required to be " emotioned." Let us be careful, throughout our inquiry, not to trust this loosely used word *Emotion*. The experience to which we usually give this word surely is but the symptom that music has gripped us. Yet anything which grand, logical old Bach and the sentient Delius agree to demand, we may surely expect from music. We rightly look to be *moved* by it.

But of course we look to be *wholly* moved, or, if the longer word is helpful, *wholesomely* moved. If only part of us, say our ear, is "moved," we can only be partially satisfied. For this reason vapid, sensational music soon bores us, leaving our minds stranded and our imagination comatose; and similarly a very different kind of music—unneighbourly, learned, specialized, brainy music—is also boring, leaving the ear unpleased and the imagination stupefied. Indeed, it seems hardly correct to speak of a mere *part* of one's self being "moved." Is this not to suppose that a train should leave a station while some of its coaches—passengers and all—remain behind? The truth seems to be that we humans are rather like trains. The engine is like the mystery we call our *will* or our *choice.* Love seems the name for it after all, though we may call it by lesser names, such as liking or taste, when it seems to matter less. Our many faculties are like so many carriages that the will has in train. It seems likely that if ever you have felt thrilled for a great moment in a Symphony, when perhaps the fiddles were blazing richly away at some noble tune which exactly fitted your "wave-length," and when skill and exhilarating team-work of conductor and orchestra were showing at their height, your thrill registered the wholeness of your experience. You were *moved.* Something outside yourself met the whole of your conscious inside being, not only your engine-will but all your carriage-faculties—sensible, reasonable, and imaginable—so you were moved for good and all from where you were before hearing the Symphony to where you had never been and whence you can never return, ready for your next thrilling journey.

It is this responsive delight—better, perhaps, called the *creative response* discovered in us by the best music—which is our natural aim. Nothing less will satisfy us musically. To seek pleasant sensation for itself may be as natural in the musical world as in the world of everyday life; but along that line lies the ultimate fate of becoming gradually a poor bored musical sensation-monger. On the other hand, to concentrate all interest and attention upon solving musically intellectual problems, though not so enervating, is equally abnormal, and threatens an equally horrid fate—that of becoming a sort of musical "cross-chord-puzzler." All persistently partial views of the thing called music must at last fail us; and fitting penalties await all who forget, through one cause or another, that music is wholly as well as essentially human.

Let us test this by an example. Beethoven seems the right exemplary helper. Surely no composer is freer from partiality. Go to the keyboard and play this (or get a friend to do it for you) from the first page of the Waldstein:

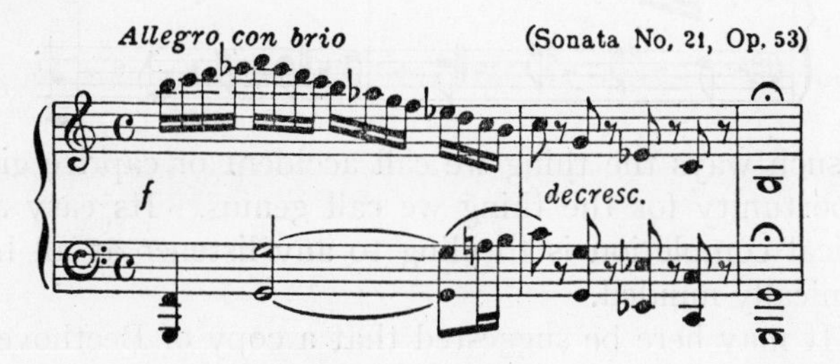

Play it twice or more, at a quick pace in high spirits. Now play it as it returns three or four minutes later in the Sonata:

The sudden turn of harmonic events on the last note introduces a very human touch of musical caprice. Sir Hubert Parry took the view that the composer's hand at this dashing moment had made a bad shot on the keyboard for the original note. However that may be, play on from this second example for six bars, to the restoration of the original key and subject, and you will hear the mind of the composer take absorbing command.

In such ways the thing we call accident or caprice gives opportunity for the thing we call genius. Its easy and logical completion is thrilling to any listener at all harmonically minded.

It may here be suggested that a copy of Beethoven's Sonatas, kept continually at hand, will provide the fullest treasure-house of such illustrations for any reader of these pages, if hands and mind are available to make the composer's thought audible. Turning over the pages, one finds working examples and tests of one's listening powers almost haphazard. For Beethoven is pre-eminently *communicative,* in the spontaneous sense of that word. Among all composers, the one who proves most fully aware of the "other fellow," the listener, and of his susceptibilities, is always the most likely to move men to hear exactly what moved him. He seems thoroughly concerned to put the delight he has discovered in such a way that it discovers itself to us at the moment of hearing. In other words, he seeks and gains our ear, and through our ear our mind, because he knows so well all the ways of the human ear and mind.

In using Beethoven or any other individual composer as exemplar and guide in our present pursuit, an inevitable fact must be taken into consideration—namely, that the composer who is not of our mind at a given moment is, of course, not our man at that moment. If, for example, through his or our shortcoming, or through any other circumstance, the chords he uses and dwells upon are in danger of meaning one thing to him and another thing (or nothing at all at present) to us, he is not, for the time at least, our composer at all. A very singular or ιδιωτης composer may reduce his audience to one. If he ultimately becomes pre-eminently human, he may increase it to a million.

This brings us to a point of some urgency. We shall hope to see more clearly in later chapters whether it is true that at the present time there is a wave (as some people think) of abnormal, unneighbourly, unpractical neglect on the part of many modern composers, of the sensible, reasonable claims of intelligent music-lovers, for whose delight writers to-day, as always, score and perform their music. The question must be in the minds of many readers of this book, and it is rendered more acute and interesting in that music neither pleasing to the senses nor satisfying to the reason of listeners, is frequently broadcast to innumerable puzzled ears.

Here it must be kept in mind that since 1905 or thereabouts, the range of music has widened to a bewildering extent. To gain some idea of what has happened in music recently, imagine for a moment the picture galleries of Europe filled, up to a certain date, with portraits and pictures of the most formal design according to given standards of beauty. Then imagine the stirring change if, in the course of a mere decade or so, pictures not only as beautiful as before, but of an exact realism, began to pour into these galleries—not only landscapes by such men as Constable, not only Turner's mists and flaming sunsets, but curious impressionist studies of seemingly negligible objects: a single flower, a hedgerow, a city street, a bird on the wing, a dead rabbit even—any detail of the universe in which an artist's eye had quickened interest. What questionings would result! What a challenge to new standards!

Has not this challenge been exactly paralleled in music? Not once but many times, and in our own generation surely, more acutely than ever before. Now imagine again not the picture galleries but the concert halls of Europe, filled with music of the most formal design. Composers, for a whole century, we know, continued to play the musical game according to rules suited to their not over-enterprising public; within those rules they were at the same time wonderfully and permanently widening the range of discovery and delight in music; Beethoven in particular bringing every human reality into the sphere of the Beautiful. Concurrently, however, outside these concert halls and their ever more exacting standards of beauty, another order of discovery and delight was developing. Music, in association with other arts, was finding its powers *to depict human life* in its bewildering variety. So there grew the demand, more and more urgent, for Music to become an interpreter of life, to be true to life whether beautiful or not. We in our day have realized, perhaps uniquely, even stunningly, that to shut our eyes to apparent truth in order to pursue apparent beauty of design as such, would be to create a cleavage which *cannot* exist between two issues, though it may often have appeared to do so. We may all humanly fear that in fashioning music to become an interpreter of what we call the real, it will be allowed to become less lovely; but to this fear there must be no yielding. For nothing can ever lessen the urgency of our intuitive demand that music *must* give us both truth and beauty; we shall continue to expect future symphonies as perfect in design as those of Mozart, as true to life as those of Beethoven, yet still true to the age and the hand by which they are forged. No doubt, until the day comes when angels and archangels are at home on this earth, making music to be interpreted by angelic choirs and orchestras, the problems of the perfect reconcilement of the two issues will continue to act as spurs to the mind of every vital composer. It is incentives such as these that quicken inspiration.

Our age is by no means unique in that it has been chosen by music as a forge whereon she may try to hammer out and to blend new joins of truth to beauty in the white heat of creative act, for this is normal and continually happening. But it *is* unique in the suddenness, the historic suddenness, with which this generation has had to realize that the range of music is as vast as the universe, and as limitless. The fact has not been allowed to dawn on us slowly, but has been almost forced upon us in the course of the last thirty or so years.

There is no known visible object—in earth or sea, in the starry heavens, and especially in "the sky's unresting cloudland"—which music cannot tonally interpret, finding for it an audibly imagined counterform. Nor is there any human motive or passion that the mind cannot imaginatively transmute into what may prove to be music. Moreover, to match this width of range you may, within any single octave of your present keyboard, spell out for yourself, if you choose and work hard enough, 2,049 different soundings or combinations of tones; and yet the complex symphony that puzzled your ears a day or two ago, probably leaves at least 2,009 of these unexplored!

Not all chords, of course, are aurally presentable; nor

are all objects worth musical regard ; nor are all motions of the musical mind worth the detaining of other men to dwell upon. But the above thoughts will help us to understand why the last thirty or so years have happened to bring such bewildering possibilities and such a crop of adventurous composers who write momentarily inscrutable and (to us) valueless music. They are our exploring pioneers ; all praise to them ; they will learn not to trouble us with *all* their present experiences and experiments, while we learn, for our part, to be more and more ready to listen—eagerly, imaginatively, and intelligently—to all they have to sound in public. For it is obvious that our first obligation in pursuit of music itself is eagerly to submit our own musical sensitivity and judgment of ear and mind to be quickened to the utmost; believing, incidentally, no music quite uninteresting, or quite unworth practised attention.

Listening to some music of the present moment (1935) is, it is true, like looking, not at chosen pictures, but at all sorts of promiscuous sights in life. A crowd in Fleet Street is not a work of art, yet it is a " sight," and as such can be full of interest to mindful observers with the leisure to give, and the imagination to descry, real, alive motives and deeds written in the lines of faces and in the way people move. The spectator may be the artist. Many a symphonic poem to-day is as realistic as Fleet Street. It is not music, in the hitherto accepted sense. It puts a new strain on the listener. But no imaginative listener, who goes to meet it, need ever be unentertained in the presence of a crowd of tones with so much bustle and novelty about them as we hear to-day. We need only be offended, and even insulted, if and when the composer fails to keep a promise—that is, fails to deliver certain musical goods, to fulfil expectations which he raised in vain. Now in music, as in all art, the only (tacit) promise made is duly to take and render delight in natural and loveable forms in a wholly loveable way. This is the normal expectation raised by normal music.

Discovery in the realm of music and subsequent Delight in the things discovered curiously enough both involve *Repetition.* There are three useful thoughts on this prosaic subject, which may be offered to any music-lover who desires, in such a bafflingly interesting time, to miss nothing he can grasp, and to gain the freedom of the kingdom of music for himself. But first the reader is asked to play, or to listen keenly once or twice, to any work of Mozart for at least a few moments—the E♭ Symphony, for example (heard on a good gramophone), or the F major piano Sonata that begins :

Having listened, let us recall the remarks of two unusually foolish and arrogant people of whom the reader may have heard : first, of the contemporary old gentleman (presumably in Vienna) who, on hearing Mozart, is said to have exclaimed, " If that is music, I have done with it." The other, the remark of the young and precious Victorian connoisseur who (in one of Du Maurier's best *Punch* sallies of sixty years ago) was heard to say : " I confess Mozart is too *tuney* for my taste." (Reply by Du Maurier's wise lady : " Really ! Now is that due to a defective ear, or is it lack of education ? ") If a composer so far forgets himself and his fellows as to write a work which shows no consideration either for the needs of the ear or of the mind—a work calculated only to astonish—he will get his reward. A composer's ultimate duty, like that of any other artist, includes the obligation to be intelligible to men possessing natural powers of ear and mind, of sense and reason; and if this is not his intention, if he has no aim but to astonish, he does well to say so beforehand, and to take his place frankly among the unmindful showmen of the world. But the music-lover can safely assume that such charlatans in music are rare enough to be ignored. Composers, as a class, are as human and rightheaded as most men, and therefore our musical journeys with all of them may almost invariably prove journeys of delight. We may travel safely with open ear and open mind to meet music everywhere, delight leading to discovery, and discovery leading in its turn to ampler delight.

Here are the three preliminary thoughts on the mere essential factor of Repetition, suggested for the reader's occasional pondering, while joining in the present pursuit of music:

1. (Falling naturally into question form.) *Is not repeated hearing necessary to all musical understanding?* The reply becomes a useful "yes," directly one recalls the natural difficulty with which the ear observes a work of art, as compared with the eye. For the latter can attend steadfastly to the parts of a picture just as it chooses, for as long as it chooses; but not so the ear to a "musical picture." The seen picture stands still in space complete, while the admiring eye moves from point to point, till it relates and comprehends the whole. Music, on the other hand, never stands still, but moves on ceaselessly, and is heard in process, a sound at a time. In this case, it is the ear that is still, standing to attention, as it were, and "watching" the music as it moves. A chord or a snatch of a tune is no sooner heard than it is gone, giving place to the next sound, which in its turn vanishes to give place to its successor. And this is a permanent condition of hearing. Hence the need, not only for concentration during the first hearing of a new musical work, but for

repeated hearings. Hence, also, the boon of gramophone and wireless to-day to all music-lovers who know how to use them.

2. *Repetition in Music must always be associated with the idea of perfecting.* This works in many ways. If the ear has received too light an impression, then repetition deepens it. If the mind has not caught the drift of the passage, repetition illumines it. Repetition, where not associated with such purpose, is dangerous, for it automatically dullens hearing and ceases to engage the mind. Music, however, is perhaps a particularly lucky art in this respect, since the ear and the mind of the acutest listener never can reach a point at which they cease to hear better and grasp more. So repetition need never bore listeners who are habitually intent on mastery. We are not, of course, concerned here with unmindful listeners, to whom a Sonata is a mass of notes, as a tree to a nonobservant eye is a mass of leaves, and a flock of sheep a mere mass of one sheep multiplied. To the artist's eye no two leaves hang alike in shape or poise on their stem. To the true shepherding eye and mind, every sheep of the flock is known from every other—even the passer-by may notice how different their funny faces really are. A Symphony is as full as Nature herself of subtle significances, which only alert and repeated glances (of the ear, in this instance) may detect.

3. *Repetition may be either vain or vital, and is most vital when applied to the music which lies next to, and just within, the listener's grasp at the moment.* As in reading books, so in listening to music, certain ideas may lie so far from our immediate interest and so far beyond our momentary equipment—or, in the opposite instance, so well within our customary round of thought—that it becomes of comparatively little use to spend time repeating them, however much in earnest we may be. A deadness may be induced by such repetition, where quickening of ear and

mind was our most innocent intention. Thought in music, as in everything else, is progressive; not only throughout one work, or one composer's output, but throughout the work of an age, through the works of a succession of composers. Does it not seem reasonable to expect the maximum delight and illumination from that particular music which lies neither far within nor far beyond your powers, but close to the *rim* of your mind, adjoining it, but just beyond it? Reach out and it is yours. It seems absurd to have to say it, but, if you take the *next* musical step from where you stand, you progress! To apply this truism simply: if Mozart gave you a thrill last week, then turn this week to early Beethoven, ignoring the remoter Beethoven of Opus 81 and onwards. If and when the dramatic turbulence of the Appassionata or the Seventh Symphony becomes a stirring experience to you, you are probably ready to grapple with such adventurous and stiff going as the Finale of Brahms's Fourth Symphony, and can even attack the later Beethoven Sonatas and the last Quartets, including the baffling Fugue itself. Should any movement prove particularly attractive, listen to it again. Should any prove particularly hard to grasp, the recipe is the same: listen to it again, and perhaps a third time. If it seems to remain outside your grasp, give it up for a while.

To sum up the above three hints:

In pursuit of music, we need to make use of repeated hearings; but repetition will be worse than useless, unless the result is to quicken sensitiveness and increase understanding.

Little of the music heard to-day really defies listening ears and attentive minds. There is possibly, as suggested already, a small *corpus* of music that is out merely to astonish us with the showy or monstrously sensational. But even this cannot hurt the healthy ear and mind; though it is not meant to please nor illumine, it may yet quicken our faculties of discernment. A deep lover of Nature can gaze to good purpose at a barren rock and see creation's story in it. So, not the stoniest music written by man can be entirely without human significance and an interest of its own; though to say this is expressly *not* to advise the reader to spend time over the seemingly inscrutable experiments of seemingly arrogant minds. Here "gumption" will come to the rescue. There is a measureless amount of music awaiting our eager attention. Cherish the music that lies nearest your comprehension, repeat it, and it will lead you to the next delight.

One final thought before we venture forth together. It is well to remember that from first to last all of us must needs discern for ourselves and in our own way melody and chords and all their inherent joys. As well expect to get the satisfaction and nourishment of a good meal from a cookery book, as to get musical joy from books about music. Both the ear and mind of every listener in the world must experience it for themselves. Each listener must "taste" the chord of C major, and know that taste, if he is ever to put his mind to the Jupiter Symphony. A description of the fragrance of an English garden would not mean much to one who had never smelt a rose! A theory of music which explained a chord and its uses would have no value whatever to one who had never known for himself the sound of the chord itself. Indeed, in the case of music, the futility would be much the more serious; for there is, as yet, no such thing as a symphony of fragrances. There may be, some day! Who knows but that the pleasures of a garden, and the relations of one fragrance with others, may prove to be vibrational experiences, comparable with the pleasures of the ear in beauty of tone, and capable of a sequel comparable to the joy of the mind in relating tones with other tones into recognizable and significant design?

Who knows but that fragrances at present pleasing only to the senses, may some day thus combine to quicken the mind ? So the moral clearly is : let each of us repeatedly taste tones and chords and rhythms for the ear's immediate delight and practice, and for the mind's mediate delight ; ultimately leading to the mind's immediate and delighted recognition of fine form. Beethoven is reported to have said that music " built a bridge " from the senses to the spirit. We may try to traverse such a bridge together.

CHAPTER 2

DISTINCTIONS AND LINES OF PURSUIT

THERE seem to be three lines of pursuit awaiting us. Let us try to distinguish them.

When we are in pursuit of some visual art, like Painting or Sculpture, we start with a good notion gained from experience from childhood onwards, as to the *appearance* of things beautiful ; and so, when in a picture by Corot or Rembrandt a tree or a face appears to us more heavenly than any our eyes have ever before seen, we are able to say confidently "That is beautiful !" We enter into communion with the wonderful painter who now quickens our *ready* eyes to share his vision ; and Beauty thus made visible is able to bring us instant delight.

Again, in pursuit of poetry, or any art conveyed in words, we start with a long experience of the medium used by the writer to bring his thoughts to our imagination. His language is our language. When Shakespeare uses words thus :

> " How sweet the moonlight sleeps upon this bank !
> Here will we sit, and let the sound of music
> Creep in our ears : soft stillness and the night
> Become the touches of sweet harmony,"

or when he says :

> " How far that little candle throws its beams !
> So shines a good deed in a naughty world. . . ."

we are able, by personal knowledge and use of the words he mobilizes (moonlight, sound, stillness, etc.), at once to apprehend the new thought, and love the inspiring image ;

and once again Beauty *imagined* brings us immediate delight.

But when we come to consider the art of Music, we find ourselves doubly handicapped at the outset: first, we are not daily surrounded from infancy by beautiful sounds, as we are by beautiful sights; secondly, we lack familiarity with the composer's language. Where the painter deepens vision through our already accustomed sense of sight; where the poet quickens thought through our age-old understanding of a mother-tongue, the musician finds us with ears unaccustomed by nature to the simple beauty of the chords which are the breath of life to music. Appealing to us in a speech of which we hardly even begin to know the elements, he discovers but slender daily experience of harmonious loveliness upon which he may base his utterance. What, then, is the position? Our ears, inexperienced in the most elementary harmonies, are yet aware of loveliness in tones; our imagination is stirred; we do somehow feel that the composer is doing for us, aurally, not only what the painter does visually, but also (if less intelligibly) what the poet does mentally. His chords *are* beautiful to the ear, as the colours of the artist to the eye, and at the same time should be as meaningful to our mind as the words of the poet. But are they?

Now (1) *if only* beautiful chords had been sounding familiarly about us from our infancy, and (2) *if only* our schools had educated us to recognize the easy alphabet of the composer's language (which, at that age, we should most certainly have grasped as quickly as we did that of our mother tongue), how much further on should we have been at this moment in our pursuit of music! Our gravest handicaps are that, lacking life-long familiarity with Beauty in audible form, and lacking practice in the actual speech of Beethoven and his peers, which we acquired naturally in the speech of Shakespeare, we are continually left only half comprehending, often wholly puzzled, and totally unable to fathom the classical composer's mind.

Wagner and Elgar tell us that they go to Nature and listen, and then having "heard" Beauty, write down what they heard. Or as much of it as they need. This is a welcome and impressive thing to know. Can *we* go to the same beauty spot and hear what they heard? How good if we can! But, while beauty made visible is all around us from the cradle to the grave, impressing itself on an unconsciously trained sense, beauty made audible is not. The latter seems only to come to us in music, and that *through the mind of man.* Therefore it has to be perpetually discovered and rediscovered by the mass of men, and the rudiments of its language have to be relearnt by succeeding generations.

And yet, just consider for a moment how all the world, from Wagner to the aboriginal native of mid-Australia to-day, happens to be waywardly composing melodies on the same five-note scale! * The pentatonic scale appears spontaneously put to melodic use in every quarter of the globe. It is a significant universal alphabet, not quite as easy as A B C, but as easy as any five letters of our alphabet of twenty-six, and a far simpler one for infants. Yet I myself once heard a world-famous modern composer exclaim, "What *is* the pentatonic scale?"

Our three lines of pursuit seem, then, fairly clear. We shall first discuss Music as audible beauty (apart, so far as possible, from its significance as human utterance). Secondly, we shall discuss its power to become an elemental expression of the mind of man—a *universal* language. Thirdly, we must discuss its equally incontestable power of expressing individual things in highly specialized ways—in short, of being a particular or *local* language.

* See page 41.

Chapter 3

BEAUTY HEARD

"Music, all dumb, hath trod
Into thine ear her one effectual way."

ALICE MEYNELL.

IN the last chapter crucial differences and distinctions were necessarily emphasized between the ways in which works of art are taken in by the imaginative mind, through the eye and ear respectively. But in this chapter we must try rather to grasp the deep resemblance between the two kinds of impression, and, as far as we may, to bring them into mental focus.

The senses to which the appeal is made vary, and work very differently; the appeal itself may possibly be in essence the same. For example, we may suppose that to an equally equipped man an equal rapture may be felt in five minutes spent listening to Mozart—beauty set forth in time—and in five minutes spent gazing at a Raphael cartoon—beauty set forth in space. Beauty heard and Beauty seen may not only have deep affinity;—let us boldly assume, for purposes of this inquiry, that they are at root one. And in doing this, let us remember that any of us may have such specialized physical quickness, either of eye *or* ear, together with such accuracy of visual *or* aural memory, as to apprehend beauty instantly with the one, but laboriously with the other sense. All of us, however, are able, with pains, to cultivate and quicken any weaker faculty, and in doing this we shall find the one impression confirm and even enrich the other.

Of course Beauty in Music, as in other forms, for ever defies description, analysis, and study. No book can teach it, no alchemist resolve it. We may pardonably exclaim, " Thank God for that ! " Beautiful music quickens wonder, not learning. Yet, though it be as elusive as love and life itself, it is as real. And anything real has *attributes* which may be searchingly contemplated. We cannot long for and be drawn to pursue it without discovering some of these. To consider the attributes of Beauty in music is more than merely worth our while. For as we ponder its many lovely qualities, as our study grows more comprehensive, Beauty itself naturally grows more comprehensible. It beckons us ever more alluringly to a life-long pursuit. Moreover, the discovery that the very same qualities are latent in a melody as in a picture, a word, a deed, a light, brings to our aid a crowd of independent witnesses, helping us to more confidence in our own joys.

For it is quite clear that in all forms and aspects of art, as indeed in life itself, we find certain vital attributes or qualities constantly recurring, such as Energy, Form, Curve, Balance, Change, Gradualness, Suddenness, and others (which, for a moment, let us make anonymous and label conveniently as (*a*), (*b*), (*c*), (*d*), (*e*), etc. Then, should we, on first looking into some work of art (which almost, but not quite, satisfies our thirst for Beauty), find that it has three of these qualities we love—perhaps (*a*), (*b*), and (*d*), but not a trace of (*c*), and very little of (*e*) or (*f*)—we immediately come (by this sort of analysis) nearer to discovering the essential attributes of creative delight in their due order. If we find some qualities in certain music, and miss others, comparisons are set up in our mind which eventually bring us to a far better comprehension of Beauty as a whole.

Supposing then, once more, that Beauty seen, Beauty heard, and Beauty conveyed in words are in vital ways and interests at one ; and supposing, too, that Dr. Henry Ley was not entirely mistaken when he said the other day, a little wistfully, "I confess I have no use for music that is not beautiful"—we may now try to discover such qualities in music as are common to other arts, and which seem so essential that we cannot conceive of being satisfied without them.

Undoubtedly the first of these qualities is Energy, the opposite of inertia, of all forms of deadness. When old Haydn was wheeled in a chair to hear his *Creation*, and the thrilling moment arrived :

he pointed upward and said, "Es kommt von oben."† I once heard a friend unforgettably describe the transfiguration on the faces of a choir of blind singers, as they flung out the word "Light" to Haydn's *fortissimo* chord of C major. That there is no manifestation of Beauty without Energy is clear. We all, in a million differing ways, seek fullness of life ; and, imagining the utter

* The small notes are instrumental.

† "It comes from above."

silence and darkness that would overwhelm us at the withdrawal of all signs of Energy, we are immediately aware of its significance for us, in art as in all existence. Energy in itself can, of course, be too slender to move us, or too terrific for human endurance. A well-known organist once took a very musical child to a cathedral, and thinking to please him, opened fire on the full organ. Turning to share the child's enjoyment, he was astonished to meet a look of such pathetic distress as filled his soul with repentance and compassion, and (as he later declared) completely changed his values for tonal energy.

Conceive a universe that is all Energy working at its maximum, proceeding from some imagined central generator. At once this picture of a fiery, irresistible sphere, rushing at top speed in any direction, for incalculable distances, is to us grim and appalling. No Beauty, no Art there! Yet what but such measureless Force burns controlledly through all Beauty and all Art? And though we shall never define Beauty, we know this Energy to be its primal attribute.

This leads us to discernment of a second vital attribute of Beauty; that power which, controlling or opposing Energy, is called FORM. Think again for a moment of mere Energy *without* Form! This means no swaying trees, no tender leaves as distinct from mere rugged growths, no rise and fall of tides; in music, no blending of semibreves played by a left hand against gently rippling quavers from the right hand—thus no "Moonlight Sonata." But what brings Form? It may come in two ways: either through a controlling, choosing "mind," working as it were in terms of Energy, shaping the leaves, ordering the rhythm of tides and bending trees, speeding or restraining semibreves or quavers. Or it may also be manifested through a strangely opposite cause, as when Energy meets Resistance or obstacle; which may be seen any day at such a place as Gurnards Head in Cornwall, or at any rocky point along the sea-coast, where the tide is the unexpressive, undetected Energy, till it reaches the rocks, the immobile obstacle. Here, Force and Resistance meet together in glorious activity; and curve of wave and dazzle of spray demonstrate, to the seeing eye, the urgency of our second attribute of Beauty, Form in all Art.

For Form, visible, audible, imaginable, or memorable, men will never cease to look and listen; and artists will ever strive to create it. Without it, Art is not. But how may we define it?

It is the name we casually give to any single impression made upon our mind—a curve, for example, or even a fleeting fragment of melody:

But every greatest or smallest impression *which our minds can take in as a unit of experience,* and distinguish from all other units of experience, and remember vividly enough to recognize again, is no longer mere Energy, but is manifestation of Energy in Form. We may use other words for it, such as *idea, shape,* even words like *quality* or *colour,* if we think of them as recognizable and memorable units of impression which have merely lost the definiteness we call *line*—that which was daringly described by Blake the poet in one place as "the line of the Almighty," and in another as "the hard and wiry line of rectitude." The reader may sometimes feel unable to conceive of Form *without* line. At other times, when regarding a sunset or hearing an orchestra, he may feel certain that colour or quality in sound is a deepened experience of Form. We may find it helpful to classify line as Form *emergent,* and colour, timbre, or quality as Form *immergent.*

Readers will now find it stimulating to try to determine for themselves what attribute they would put *third* in importance among all those factors in life which together make the mind exclaim of anything, "Beautiful—that's exactly right!" What shall it be?

Nature is our great guide here. In innumerable blades of grass, leaves of trees, trees of the forest, waves of the sea, she seems to show us *Repetition* as our most natural and necessary third attribute. But immediately a fourth attribute follows. For, as no two leaves are alike and no two waves on the shore leave the same impression, we are shown how often Repetition is inseparably associated with *Change*. An admittedly good portrait of a friend, for example, looked at steadily and long, may come to lack significance for us through its fixity of smile or expression; and the only possible semblance of life we can give it is to look fleetingly* at it and turn away; so an artist knows that the truly appreciative eye must ever move over the picture. His painting can only suggest movement that paused for a moment to be called a picture, leaving the on-looker to do the rest. This lively attribute, Change, working with Repetition, soon brings us to a fifth, also written large in Nature, certainly highly significant to Art—that which may be called *Gradualness*. Further, where Repetition and Change, working together, do *not* produce Gradualness, we find that they work up to a climax of reaction resulting in an eloquent sixth attribute, that of *Contrast*. We may also call it *Suddenness*, or Surprise.

Here then we have an imposing access of demands made by the Beauty-seeking mind:

1. Energy (limitless).
2. Form (chosen).
3. Repetition (natural).
4. Change, working alongside Repetition, becoming known as (4*a*) Gradualness. Opposed to Repetition, becoming known as (4*b*) Suddenness.

So far we have thought of the attributes of Beauty

* In all our responsive joy in form, it seems sound to say: look fleetingly at fixed form, and fixedly at fleeting form.

apparent in musical processes (taking reverent note of the way in which creative impulse works and manifests itself). But we should observe here that even *without* the creative urge, these things can be demanded and revelled in by our *creaturely* faculties of enjoyment alone. This "creaturely delight" in all things, and in their all-embracing attribute of Purpose, man actually shares with the animals, as any one may see in his pet dog's attitude to life. Think it out for a moment in the light of a mere "dog's day"—his energy, delight in repetition, his development, down to his raptures of delight in your sudden, unexpected returns home. From this standpoint we get ready to approach two completely new attributes, and to perceive their very great significance. These may be called Balance and Integrity, or, more dynamically, Balancing and Integrating. These seem to be uniquely constructive. They are essentially creative attributes. Thus, a babe or a dog loves repetition for fun; a man or a monkey requires repetition for practice; but only the creative turn of mind both loves *and* requires repetition for *Balance*. Again—the most creaturely creature may desire completeness in the satisfaction of its own desires; but only creative energy seeks to integrate forms for Integrity's sake, and this over an ever-widening and all-embracing range. Indeed, the greater the range of integrating, the greater the achievement. If Milton's *Paradise Lost* were a complete unity from the first to the last line, we should rightly think of it as a "greater" work than such a complete unit as his "Sonnet on reaching his 23rd Year," though the integrating of both may be perfect. This attribute of integrity is discovered in smallest things—*e.g.* in every dewdrop; it is there without effort, and naturally.

It is important in the pursuit of music to realize that listeners as well as composers must rejoice to balance and to integrate. Our musical response is, as has been said, a creative response. Nothing is more devastating than to be required to listen for forty minutes to a Symphony, when our own powers of balancing and integrating seem to run out in five minutes!

What, then, do we mean when we conceive a complex Symphony, or a simple tune, or even a perfected single *pianissimo* tone of instrument or voice (comparable to our dewdrop!) as being Beauty made audible? We shall probably still have frankly to agree that we simply do not know! But what we *do* now know is that, when a tune of many notes makes the impression on our mind of being as integrated and well-rounded as the simple dewdrop, we find it "beautiful." And if a whole movement, or still more, a Symphony in four movements, makes the same impression of being integrated, we marvel at the inspiration of it and exclaim, "This must be genius!" by which we mean it must have made itself whole in the composer's mind; it must have been mysteriously loved into wholeness by him with splendid tenacity—Carlyle's "infinite capacity for taking pains."

It may be suggested that Wholeness *is* Beauty, and that this power to make whole is what is called genius or inspiration—as when Mozart has completed a Symphony of which every note seems inevitably "right." Many readers may, however, feel inclined to retort, fairly enough, that when they try to think the mere prosaic thought "Wholeness," they get nowhere near the thought "Beauty." It is only possible, in reply, to suggest that we must at least put this comprehensive attribute in the chiefest and last place whatever name we may give it, because by nature it seems the all-containing attribute. I myself find more help in thinking of the other attributes—often and tenaciously—not only as being lovely and necessary, but as lying within this great seventh attribute. We say to our music, (1) "Be lively, give us a full cup of life! (2) Satisfy our delight in all fine form, every form being wholly to our mind! (3) whether by timely Repetition, or (4) whether by Gradual Change, or (5) whether by sudden and Surprising arrival of a missing part of the whole, or (6) whether by unfailing Balance of parts: (7) at all times, in all Music, let there be Wholeness!" And there will be Wholeness.

It may be that the reader, in some such deliberately sevenfold thinking, may get gradually a little nearer to the desired comprehension of our musical experience of Beauty. It is astonishing, by the way, what a vivid picture of every order of creative joy lies in the age-old story in the first chapter of Genesis. In three of the many terse sentences there, we hear Chaos yield to creative Glory thus:

> "Let there be . . ."
> "And there was . . ."
> "And, behold, it was very good . . ."

Music re-enacts these three joys perpetually. "Let there be!" cries the will-full composer. "And there it is," says the active performer. "And, behold, it was very good," says the responsive listener. But we should carefully note that it was the Creator Himself who saw, and lo! "It was very good." The composer is the contemplator. The hearer best responds with contemplative *creative* listening. The needed degree of *creaturely* listening will take only too good care of itself. To attend much to it is often likely to cheat us of the best altogether. (Because I have found that this has continually happened in my own case, I cannot but venture, like a slightly provocative older brother, to warn my reader about it!)

Before we leave this chapter's attempted analysis, of things so wonderful that they seem for ever to defy analysis, let us now strive to discover, with detailed care, the workings of our seven attributes in some homeliest, simplest example—say our own National Anthem.

To take the seven attributes in their order, first try

to think the tune into lifelessness, in order to realize what life there is in it. Reduce all signs of animation to a minimum. The liveliest thing about our tune is the way it rises in its whole course from [music] to [music] and back. Very good; for the moment forbid it to raise its head:

Even this maltreatment leaves it life enough to maintain a rhythmic pattern; so we must iron out that

And even now a patriot could say, "Very well; you deny me the liveliest part of my delight, so I will sing the poor drooping notes that are left me all the more heartily and emphatically, [music] and I'll hold on 'King' as long as I choose." So it is necessary to take away both volume and speed! Indeed, every feature and vestige of interest in the tune must go before we can take away its life.

All this is fairly obvious, and compels us to link up our second attribute, Form, with the Energy which fashioned it. Realizing this, and taking Energy once more for granted, we may adopt the opposite and positive method of analysis, and watch Form emerging in the first line of the poem as a musical unit of impression, recognizable if heard again in two ways; in rhythmic measure: [music] (apart from its tuniness), and in melodic rise and fall [music]

In this line we start fair melodically and rhythmically:

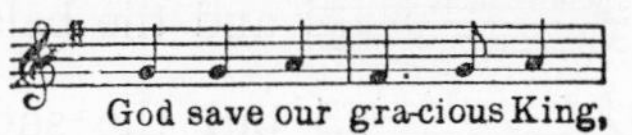

If this phrase duly "registers" in our mind, and if we

have the very small skill needed to memorize it instantly, so that we know it again, then we are ready to enjoy our third attribute of Repetition *plus* our fourth of Gradualness (or development of design) in the very next line; for the rhythm is designedly repeated :

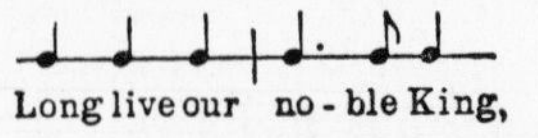

while the melodic bend is ingeniously developed :

Notice that the bend of the phrase is now contrasted, so that attribute (5) is actually beginning to assert itself as early as the fourth bar. This is often the case in alert tunes, and is correspondingly enjoyed by alert responders. A glance at the way in which the rest of the phrases take up this contrasted phrasing (and in surprising ways) will well repay the reader ; had it not been for the two "downwards" and in the fourth and fifth lines, the "upward" in the sixth: could never have had its own clinching effect, as it thrusts the patriotic Englishman for one moment to the summit of both poem and tune : God save the King. It is easy to trace the repeating, gradating, and contrasting processes. It is far more important to note from the first the all-pervading sixth and seventh attributes of *Balancing* and *Integrating* at work. The first line is balanced by the second, and the third is a rounding or integrating line. Notice specially one subtle symptom of this : the first line rose to the second and the balancing line sank to the third but the short third or integrating line took both principles of the rise and fall, and riveted up each impulse in turn to the key-note G :

We are now at half-way house, as it were ; and the second part of the tune, as a whole, both balances and fulfils the first half. There is ampler life in it ; an extra line and increased range show this. The basic rhythm is twice repeated ; it is developed into something far more interesting in the sixth and seventh lines, still recognizable as the two-bar rhythm of the very first line and the summing-up short measure of line four, but showing more movement, more adventure, and more immediate contrast between the rising and falling movement :

becoming almost triumphant in its sweep to the summit-notes of the whole tune, and quite decisive in its straight fall to the " final " or keynote. The following disposition shows the various balancing parts, the brackets indicating the larger and smaller balancings :—

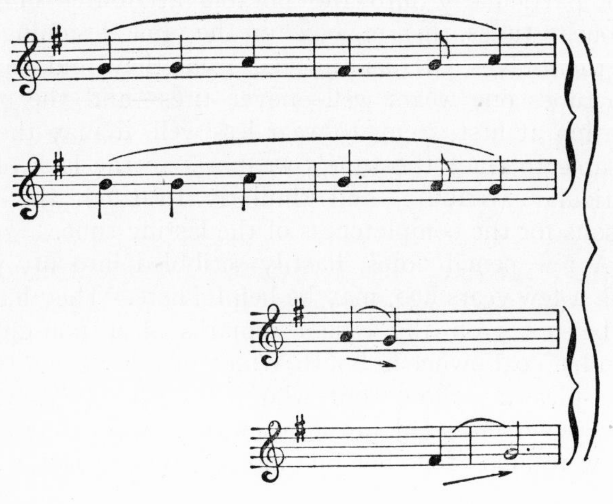

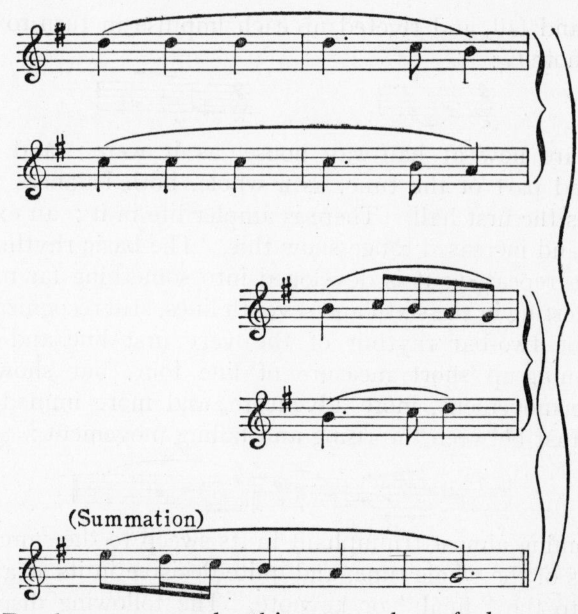

Readers may apply this same plan of close analysis to any well-known tune, and with profitable curiosity peer particularly into the notable attributes of their favourite tunes, then melodize in the same designing way for themselves. If, as time goes on, they find that of two tunes one wears well—never tires—and the other, pleasing at first, seems to wear less well, it may then be possible to trace the tune's weakness to the lack of one particular attribute, and similarly to track the total reasons for the completeness of the lasting tune.

A few pencil notes, hastily scribbled into my note-book a few years ago, may be helpful here. They happen to be notes on the casual remarks of a non-musical friend, a coal-owner in South Wales, who loved a "tune" or a pleasant chord, but who professed no knowledge whatsoever either of music, or why it appealed to him. We were alone together one morning just before he left for business. A fragment of "The Rising of the Lark" was played, to which he listened with intense delight, and then remarked meditatively, "We never tire of a good melody; never weary of it." Looking out on the tree-tops in his steeply-sloping garden, he added, with a comprehensive sweep of the hand, "Melody is everywhere." And, indicating the early morning sunlight on the trees, "This is melody." We went on to speak of fine form in general; and his last fugitive word noted seems to suggest that a new appraisement of music dawned in his friendly, open mind there and then. He knew for the first time, at the age of seventy-five or so, that Form might become to him *audible*, as it had all along been visible; he now consciously found both manifestations to be one beauty. "Love of fine form? Exactly so," adding, as if in soliloquy, "*form in music*." May this concept of music, as of something beautiful to be contemplated quite outside ourselves, become, at no distant date, a blessed commonplace among all busy people.

Chapter 4

A NATURAL AND UNIVERSAL LANGUAGE

"Every natural feature—sea, sky, rainbow, flowers, musical tone—has in it somewhat which is not private, but universal."
Emerson.

GUSTAV HOLST, once addressing the British Music Society in London, began with these words, spoken very quietly: "Music is a natural and universal language." (Pausing and stepping to the front of the platform, he added:) "That is so important, I'll say it again: Music is a natural and universal language." Let us spend a short chapter over this quickening statement, believing it, as we do, to be true.

In the last chapter we considered music as an audible showing of Beauty—something outside ourselves, like a beautiful landscape or a thrilling waterfall or sunset—which awakened inside us a responsive delight. If Holst's statement is true, this chapter will compel us to think of music exactly the other way round, as something inside man, something *subjective* which, coming out of us, expresses our mind to any who can hear and make out our meaning. Our last chapter assumed music to have for its master-aim the impression of Beauty. This chapter will inquire: Can it be the expression—that is, the language—of humanity as well?

Perhaps the first thing to note about impressive and expressive attributes is that there is no necessary contradiction between them; but there *is* need of a qualification—namely, that anything purporting to set forth Beauty cannot set forth more Beauty than resides in the mind that brings it to being.

But let us speak of music for the moment, not *as* a language, but as resembling a language. Let us use the adjective " linguistic." It seems wiser. The beauty of nature round us is clearly *not* linguistic. True, one might not too fancifully say it is a word in the language of God Himself, who created it ; but it says nothing *from man to man*. The beauty of music written by Beethoven, however (or by any man), does speak from a man to men. If we ourselves actually made trees, trees would be equally linguistic. A work of art necessarily communicates the taste, the bent, the longing or leaning of the mind of the man who wrought it. In this sense everything we do or make, as well as everything we say, is linguistic. Everything? No; we must qualify it by saying that, in art, only what we do, say, or make for love is linguistic ; for anything done on compulsion only expresses the mind of some one else, the compeller. It is worth noting here that a bird lays an egg of a certain colour, size, or pattern, because it must. The result may be Beauty made visible. But the bird has no choice, so the egg is not linguistic of bird-nature. But suppose that a blackbird was born with the weird power of choosing and varying the colour and pattern of its eggs, that exceptional bird would become a responsible artist-bird, and its patterns would speak its bird-mind, its nature, choice, taste, or love. Its eggs, whatever their visible beauty, would become " linguistic."

Here we must go a step or two farther. Holst did not mean that music was a mere language between individual composers, communicating taste in general ways. He viewed it as a natural and universal means of communication, from those who made the sound to those who listened ; assuming that a natural and universal meaning, if meant by one, must be recognized by all precisely because it is natural; and that both partners, speaker and listener, being human, thus hold the key to it *by nature*. This seems true, and we can understand why it should be so. For instance, if we actually could and did create trees and flowers in our gardens for love as we do sonatas and songs in our drawing-rooms, both would be equally expressive of our personal taste, and in this vaguer way both, as we have seen, would be linguistic. But trees and flowers would still not lend themselves to become a human-natural and universal language as music does; because while we naturally convey our wishes, inclinations, and intentions by making all sorts of sounds, high-pitched and low, loud and less loud, speedy and slow; or by repeat-sounds louder and louder, faster and faster, slower and slower, and so on, we do not communicate our thoughts in correspondingly *visible* ways. (True, we blush or turn pale, and that can certainly be an eloquent, though very limited, human colour-language. More than that, all gesticulation is linguistic; indeed, gesture is, in its more limited way than sound, another and universal *eye*-language.) But essentially all languages, as their very name implies, are *tongues*. They are based on sounds uttered, and so is all music. And the very changes of tones which make music variously interesting and expressive, are similar to those naturally used to make language variously meaningful. Let us enumerate them.

When, in a melody, one tone is felt to be more important or interesting than its fellow-tones in a phrase, there are five familiar ways of giving it prominence:

(*a*) By greater volume.
(*b*) By raised pitch.
(*c*) By length.
(*d*) By insistent emphasis or repetition.
(*e*) By sudden contrast.

These five are also the very familiar ways in which one word can be given vital importance or interest above its fellows in a mere remark. Quality of voice, too, must be included here, its betrayal of character and intention being highly linguistic.

But the reader may well say at this point : "Yes, all that is true, but words tell me about particular things, like cabbages or cooks. Music is not a natural way of saying any such informing thing as, 'The man cooked the cabbage.' How, then, can it be called a language ?" The answer to this puzzle belongs mainly to the next chapter, where we shall try to make out how chords, like words, can and do come to have quite particular meanings associated with them.

We should here notice just two things about ordinary language and music respectively. (1) It is obviously true that music is not a language that communicates *facts which are subjects of thought*. (2) It is equally obvious that languages (Latin, English, and the rest) do name, in exact words, the *facts which a thinker is thinking about, as well as the thinker's own thought about the facts*. The way this is done is interesting. If I confine myself to ejaculations like Oh ! Ah ! Oh ! ! Oh ! ! Ah ! ! these sounds are even less able than music to communicate any fact at all. But Latin peoples, for example, gradually came to agree that if one man murmured a sound like *mensa*, he expected those to whom he spoke instantly to see an object called a table with their mind's eye ; if he very slightly raised the final vowel and murmured *mensæ*, he expected them to see two or more tables ; and if again he changed the shape of his mouth a little, and kept his tongue away from touching the roof thereof, murmuring *musa* or *musæ*, the whole subject of his thought and of theirs would, by long-agreed association of ideas and the common faculty of memory, suddenly change thoughts of tables to thoughts of songs ! No verbal language, therefore, will be universal until all minds in the universe have arbitrarily agreed that certain facts or subjects shall be associated with certain sights, sounds, or ideas. As I hope to show in the next chapter, music can indeed make itself a local language like Latin or English, in its own special ways; and the accepted meanings of music have become so many and so interesting, as used by the classics from the so-called Golden Age onwards, that there seems nothing for it but to try humbly to learn them, without allowing our joy in music to become restricted by them. But more urgent still, let us not fail to remember that the nature of music gives it power to become something immeasurably more than a local language for part of the earth's inhabitants; something, indeed, that it was before the world began, and would be to-morrow, even if to-night a cosmic accident suddenly scattered our sun and its planets and all of us into space. This must sound a wild claim, but it serves to remind us of the real nature of music as being concerned with unearthly attributes like Energy, Form, Repetition, Progress (gradual and sudden), Unity or Centrality, and Balance. Music is a record of these lovable things. It only exists because they prove thrilling to this pigmy creator, man, on this speck of a planet, here and now. As well imagine that these attributes, and all loving records of these attributes, would disappear with our planet, as imagine that Beethoven's Sonatas would disappear from earth with the death of one single pianist in one locality, and with the destruction of his one piano! What Holst summed up in his memorable seven words, was the fact that music recorded man's innermost mind. Being as natural to him as his outer man, it must inevitably record his real interests *naturally*; and when we come to look further, we find it is itself compact of, and concerned with, such superhuman and *universal* things as Energy and the rest; things universal, and seeming to our minds beautiful, good, and to be pursued.

If we wished to find out the manners and customs of remote cave-men, we could do it through written records, if these existed, and *if the key to their language existed.* But note carefully that we need no key except the unaided human mind, to show us their minds and wills through the things they scrawled upon the walls of their caves ; that is, through their primitive eye-music. If a schoolboy is continually drawing pictures of engines, we are able to gather that his mind and interest run on them ; if our mind does the like, we are in natural communication, and his mere hieroglyphics are a *natural* language to us both. And if he is continually drawing symmetrical forms, we gather that he is interested in something *universally* present, called symmetry ; and we, too, being interested, his drawing becomes a natural *and universal* language between us, because of its symptoms of contemplation of a vast quality too great to be called anything less than universal. In this way we may begin to see music as Holst seemed to see it. It may be Beauty made audible, or any one quality of Beauty—Energy, Persistence, Variety, Balance—made audible. It is far more. It is even more than a man's taste for these things made audible. It is communication about these wonderful realities and timeless interests, from one man who naturally dwells with love and wonder upon them, to any other men within hearing who care enough about them to listen. Let a euphony such as a perfect fourth be once uttered by one man for pure love of its euphony, and for love of dwelling upon it, and be purposely repeated by another for the same delight ; and a natural and universal language of music has begun among men ; from which moment its development is a matter for unending discovery and mutual endorsement, as between man and man, initiator and initiant, composer and listener.

Perhaps it is reasonable for a moment to allow ourselves to wonder how on earth music is to become at once a universal and an *individual* language. As to this, we shall be bewildered only if we allow ourselves to imagine that a universal understanding of music can interfere with individual freedom to compose it. If every one in the world understood English, and enjoyed Shakespeare, English would become a world-language (not a universal one, which is different). Would that fact lessen the possibility of and the stimulus to individual genius to transcend Shakespeare? Obviously it would not; it might do exactly the reverse. Nor must we fall into an opposite bewilderment, that of wondering whether the perfect freedom of millions of individuals to compose each one as he wills, makes the idea of music as a universally understood language quite absurd. Of course not! Does the fact that the word "mother" means a million different mothers to a million different individuals, interfere with the universal idea, use, and understanding of the word? When Chaucer (as he himself describes) went on his knees on the grass to watch the opening of a daisy—"the day's eye," as he called it—he took a highly individual course. It is doubtful whether more than two persons among two hundred million may ever have followed suit. But he heightened for ever, for all men, the value of the entirely comprehensible and very common daisy by his extreme measure of reverence for so tiny and negligible an example of creation's glory. The meek inherit the whole earth.

We should note here a remarkable fact which seems to belong to this chapter, leading us aptly from thoughts of music as a universal to music as a local, or, at least, temporarily localized, language; which, in our Western experience of the last three or four hundred years, it has quite definitely become.

It is impressive to find, in all parts of the world and

in all stages of civilization, as well as in all periods of history known to us, persistent and perpetual copies of the scale of five notes already mentioned—sometimes called the gapped scale, sometimes the pentatonic—dominating the melodic efforts of men everywhere. This was pointed out by Cecil Sharp, after he had collected over a thousand tunes in the Appalachian Forest alone, and after he had collated numberless folk-tunes. With far less knowledge, but from a striking cumulation of unsought evidence (sent from such widely different parts of the globe as Khartoum, Tibet, Siam, India, Central Australia), I have long watched with wonder, and finally quite without surprise, the signs that this universal alphabet of five tones obtains everywhere. Perhaps the two greatest personal surprises have come from India and Australia. Some years ago, Rabindranath Tagore sang strange, complicated Indian melodies to me in private, in London. When he remarked, " Those are our classical melodies," it was easy to understand how careful an education one would need to follow them at all well. When, however, he sang an Indian people's melody, it proved to be as purely pentatonic as any folk-melody of Scotland or of China! Again, when records of aboriginal music were recently brought to Adelaide University by her professors, who had taken them down from the songs of paleolithic men—houseless and unclothed—this (sung with strangely true tuning) was one of the most notable of the songs recorded (by my own brother) on a phonograph, and repeated numberless

times. Here is Wagner's most haunting fragment from the *Ring*:

Here again is one of the most entrancing passages of Vaughan Williams's "Lark Ascending":

It seems reasonable in face of evidence like this, and on all counts, to urge the music-lover—man, woman, or child—to make himself or herself thoroughly at home in this scale. Do as Robert Burns somewhere recounts that a Scotsman recommended a fellow Scot to do who wished to write a true Scots air; namely, play "on the black notes of the keyboard" in any orderly rhythm, according to any loveable plan of action or reverie; for the reward is likely to be great.

Chapter 5

A LOCAL LANGUAGE

"All speech, even the commonest speech, has something of song in it; not a parish in the world but has its parish accent; the rhythm or tune to which the people sing what they have to say! . . ."—Carlyle.

In trying to form an idea of the real nature of a great building, or let us say of an island or any tract of country, we should naturally view it many times from more points than one. We should seek to know it in as many aspects as possible. Ultimately, we should desire to comprehend the whole of it, to know it inside out; to enter every room, if it were a building, to tread every inch of it, if it were a territory. In trying to search out the real nature of music, we take up three different view-points, choosing those that enable us to see it in its chief aspects. Ultimately, we shall hope to comprehend it, to experience it with increasing delight and understanding to ourselves. In this, our third line of inquiry, we shall think of music as a localized language, acquiring associated meanings upon which composers and listeners can find themselves, by usage, tacitly agreed. We come nearer, and look more closely into, its ways and parts.

The very fact that sensitive musicians of India sing classical melodies of the East which sensitive musicians of the West are unable to understand (and vice versa) leaves no doubt that music can be a very local as well as a universal language even while manifesting beauty to the ear, for love beyond all language.

There seem two distinct ways in which it can become

a local language. We speak of a local " brogue." For example, we know when a man comes from Yorkshire, because he inflects all his sentences in the local Yorkshire fashion. There is a Yorkshire " curl " which is unmistakable. In exactly the same way music can betray its locality and its period by certain turns of melody or harmonic mannerisms, or perhaps by rhythmic custom rigidly followed. But there is a second and larger way.

Men of a whole country may be unanimously agreed that a certain sound shall be associated with a certain fact, act, feeling, thought, or intention, so that if you make, for instance, the sound " Yah " anywhere in that same country, they will all know that you mean " Yes " ; or if you make the sound " Gootentahg " they will know you are wishing them a friendly " Good-morning." Yet, in another country, no one would get your mind. So, if you " say " the following carefully on any piano in Europe or the West: and especially if you say it three or four times, emphasizing the last chord :

everybody in the West will understand you to be meaning a kind of musical conclusion, finishing whatever you had come to say ; but Easterners would have to learn such a meaning by education or accumulated experience and association. Musicians of every grade in the West, for more than a hundred years, have agreed to use these chords with this meaning, so that this formula has " passed into the language," as we say. There are still an immense variety of individual ways of making this particularly well-known, well-worn musical " remark," just as there are of saying good-bye ; from the style of the pompous old gentleman who takes the trouble to extend it into, " I wish you a very good evening," to the boon companion who will not even frame the essential syllables, but playfully substitutes, " By-bye," which his appreciative friend varies in response with, " Cheerio." So, in the locally linguistic sense, any one who has often enough heard Mozart, Beethoven, and John Smith the hack pianist say this:

will *immediately* understand all three variants to mean exactly the same thing in differing moods, as *e.g.*:

In Part 4 of this book we shall explore in detail the workings of music as a " local language " of Western Europe. One can imagine how entrancingly interesting it must be to philologists to make a parallel pursuit of the sounds we call words, and to track out the ways in which a mere aboriginal grunt may gradually develop into a sort of word, destined to harden or stabilize at last into a recognized, well-defined shape, becoming fashioned like a coin of a certain metal, shape, and value, struck as it were, in the mint of man's mind, and put into general currency throughout a whole country or continent. Think how absorbing it must be to trace the likeness and differences between such a word as the numeral " one " in all its variants, all the world over: *one, un, an, ein, unus, mono,* and many others, linking up whole epochs and civilizations from east to west. The like interest is possible in music. Doubtless there will arise in time musical philologists, whose job it will be systematically to track rhythms and melodic bends, and, later on, chords of every known kind in every variety across whole continents, showing us what significance they have all acquired down the musical ages. But it is, alas, early days for this; nor must we in our lifetime expect such good fortune as to get much light thrown upon so deep a matter, spread over so vast an area. All we can do, as we proceed, is to guard ourselves from rushing into confusion in our desire to arrive at some of the many alluring conclusions possible.

Let us recognize here, once for all, that there are certain kinds of words needed in all ordinary languages which are all-important for men to know, but which are of no importance whatever in music. To many persons these words are the specially significant ones of ordinary speech —the kind of word which conveys *definite* concepts of facts and meanings, as *brush, nailbrush, toothbrush*; or *triangle, square, octagon*; or *shilling, penny, farthing, button, bone button, brass button.* But it is no concern of music ever to insist that certain chords or intervals must mean that we are thinking of certain definite facts or things. (A dinner-gong does, it is true, mean by agreement, "Come and eat," but that does not make it musical, though it may thrill the hungry boarder into exclaiming, "That gong is music to my ears!") It will perhaps save us much trouble and make our analogy of language much more secure—saving it from ever becoming mere foolishness—if we fully recognize that, though music *could* be most amusingly used in this small-minded way, it is not. Thousands of words with definite meanings have no need of any counterpart in music. There is a huge department of language which never had, and probably never will have, the smallest connection with music or the linguistic side of music. Song writers know this to their cost. You cannot set a word like *cauliflower* or *corkscrew* to music, except for some derisive or comic purpose. Musicians and poets, however, turn instinctively to the kind of word which, from the wideness of its meaning, may be called *non-definite*, in contrast to the *definite* words we have instanced. These so-called indefinite words are their vital vocabulary. Such words as *life*, *love*, *stillness*, *will*, *energy*, *repose*, though actually far from being indefinite, all defy definition. Farmer Smith's field is *defined* by a hedge. You can peg out and *define* 658 acres of ground and sell them as a square mile. But take away all hedges from the whole world, take away the idea of all limits whatsoever, and the land is still there. Hundreds of common words have no "hedges" to them. They have meanings, certainly, but these are far from definite. Many have not quite the vast *in*definite meanings of great words like Love and Life, and of all the "chord-words" in the language of music that this book is pursuing. Nor dare we call them *in*finite meanings, though we would love to do so. We must simply say that they are meanings *with no known finition*, and so avoid a whole set of mental pitfalls. By the way, if the reader is interested in relating his favourite poet and his favourite composer, he should notice here that there are also numberless between-kinds of words, of particular importance to poets, with definite or bounded meanings to the brain, but boundless suggestions to the mind. Even scrubby little words like *farthing*, *button* (such as we enumerated above) may to a poet or any imaginative mind be expansively suggestive of collections at church, the infinite generosity of some churchmen, and the horrid meanness of others, the heaven and the hell that awaits them all; and other memories of men singing the famous lines,

> "Were the whole realm of nature mine,
> That were an offering far too small,"

their contribution being the vulgarity called a threepenny bit. There is no end to the process of imaginative thought resulting from small words quickening expansive associations ; and it is well to notice that even paltry words, as also casual chords (with a very definite place in the musical language), work in just this way upon the mind, its far-reaching fancy being quickened associatively into endless interests, all arising from one or two common words or chords that on the face of things seem extremely limited units of utterance. Verbs, for example, like *push, pull, stroke, kick, kiss,* have quite clear, limited meanings in common parlance. Yet what man ever utters them without giving them an imponderable significance of his own, quite beyond their bare definition ? This, again, is exactly the linguistic way of music. Strike a familiar chord and in both its context and delivery you mobilize its meaning. In fact, music is a dynamically associative language. For that reason, all words, big and little, with any " go " in them, as we say, come nearer to music than do static words like *mantelpiece* or *floor*.

Two more vital points must be thought of here. (1) Men have a happy way of making words *while spoken* increase their own meaning by the manner in which they are uttered. Thus a man will not say of a chapter like this, for instance, that it went: on and on! He will do much better than that, and in speaking of it to a friend, he will say it went :

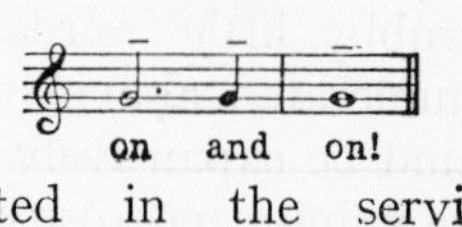

One continually hears even the unimportant word *and* elongated in the service of the word *on* to express the essential meaning of continuity :

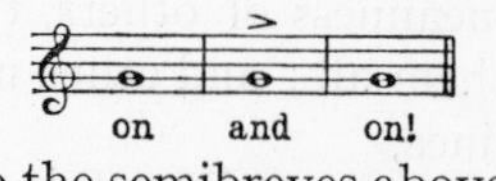

In like manner, the words, " Quick ! Get up ! " would never be uttered to the semibreves above. This would be nearer the utterance of the man who meant it :

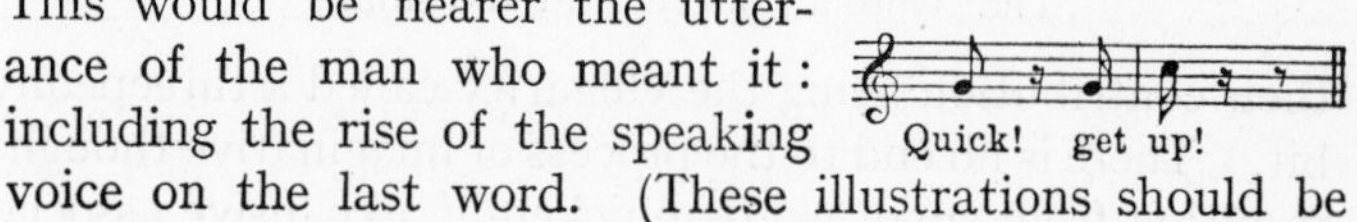

including the rise of the speaking voice on the last word. (These illustrations should be carefully sounded.) Inner intention, mood, inclination, taste, can in such a way all pass into and through the word as it is uttered. This supplies, perhaps, the closest and safest analogy that may be drawn between local speech-language and local music-language. If a composer sounds an exquisitely smooth concord softly and long, it has become linguistic in an unmistakable way. But it is also true that if he sounds a discord that merges lingeringly into a concord (in just the way that Handel, Mozart, Beethoven did), he is asking us, more unmistakably still, to share the accepted meaning with him, in some context, perhaps, which has renewed it.

(2) Our concluding point must stand in the form of a lingering and recurrent question mark (not to be answered, perhaps, even in three-score years and ten). If we want to know another man's mind, is it perhaps true that we get more of it through the form into which his words, when linked together and presented to us, happen to fall, than through the words themselves? Do we know still more of it through the actual way in which his voice relates the sounds in uttering them? This seems likely, for in no other way can we so instantly detect his values behind the words themselves, and, through the sum of his values, discern his motive in ordering them into his service. Without feeling at all certain about it, we may surmise that here lies the link between the accustomed languages of associated words and the great language of associated chords which Western Europe seems to have been slowly forging since Palestrina wrote this:

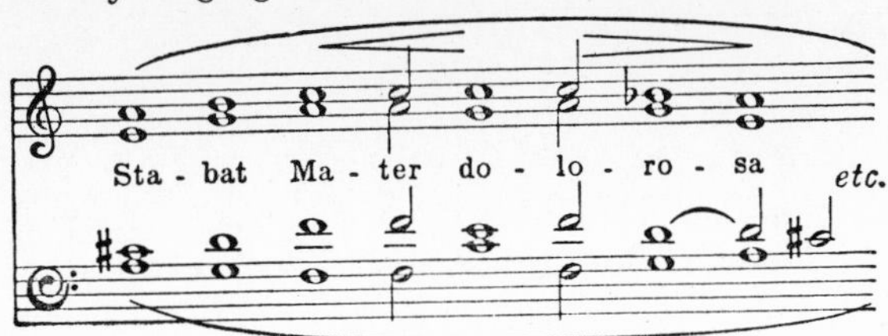

and since (about the same time) Byrd wrote this :

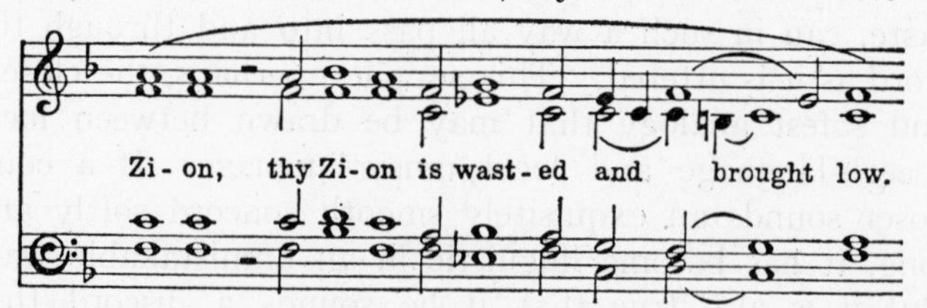

For the above musical sentences, though uttered in an inexpressive whisper, remain eloquently communicative of the inmost mind by the very ordering of the chords themselves.

Into all this we are to look in Part 4.

Chapter 6

CONVERGENCE

OUR three main lines of inquiry into the nature of music here converge, bringing us to a point from which we may the better set out to explore, in Part 2, the actual material in which music always works, the stuff of which this intangible invisible thing is woven.

Hitherto, we have surveyed music as it were from afar. We have moved round it, and examined its nature from different view-points, as the merest preliminary. To have considered it in these separate ways will prove dangerous if separate interests or expectations should be induced. Should any two such interests seem to run on parallel lines, and not to merge, they would, it is true, not confuse our expectations; but they would divide our interests. Should we on the other hand find ourselves in possession of two distinct interests in music; and should we further find that each interest, pursued separately, tended to diverge—*i.e.* quite refused to run parallel—we might be tempted to think of music as of necessity destined to hold merely one or other of the two attractions for us; either as Beauty made audible or as a human language. Like a man afloat in two boats, with a leg in each, we might be compelled painfully to jump for our musical lives, deciding which of two musical joys should be our dearest choice.

If a reader of Chapter 3 says to himself, " Yes, it is as Beauty made audible that music appeals to me," he will resemble a man absorbed in taking only a front view of the building he wishes to possess. Obviously his æsthetic joys are such that he loves both the look of a landscape and the sound of a Sonata, solely because of their common presentment of his idea of Beauty. Another reader, dwelling on Chapter 4, may feel an opposite trend, and say, " For my part, it is as a universal language that music appeals to me, and not as audible beauty ; indeed, for all I care it may be downright ugly one moment and lovely the next, provided it gives me a true account of the human mind." This reader may well liken himself to a man who, looking inside the rooms of music, discovers with pleasure that human nature and human needs have given them their shape and furnishings. Or a third reader may exclaim of Chapter 5, " Yes, tell me about Sonatas and *why* I like them," (somewhat resembling in this, the schoolboy who said, " I feel I could have written Shakespeare if I had known how"). This third reader's glance at music in its " local language " aspect has specially whetted his appetite for finding out why he has so often felt quite ready to understand everything Beethoven is saying, as though he personally were addressed, even though he never " learnt " music. Now it is much to be hoped that most readers will already have come to feel some first-hand musical delight through all three of these main ways, (and also by many other helpful byways possibly discovered individually—short cuts, who knows ?).

But the need of summation, and the recollection that music is essentially and always concerned with wholeness, guides us here. Let us try then to summarize our present position. Whether specially concerned with this or that aspect of music, this is the moment at which to attempt as comprehensive a view as we can of the whole promising land of music before setting out.

It is good to realize that lines which prove divergent in one direction must meet at some point if pursued in the opposite direction. It may be possible to find and halt at such a meeting-point, still aware of music's diverse tendencies. I fully believe (without possessing any real knowledge as to this) that music is in itself, *inter alia*, a very dynamo for inducing convergence, not only for drawing together lines of thought, but uniting streams of joyous interest into one whole joy. I set this suggestion down here in rash ignorance, but in the hope that it may provoke many more serviceable guesses in more knowing minds.

Let us then, turning our backs on divergences of interest, imagine we stand at their most convergent point for a moment together, making it both view- and starting-point. There, before our very ears, stretches the whole imaginable territory of music, into which we love to penetrate. How does it appear to us? It is an invisible land, yet full of a beauty much like the natural, visible beauty seen around us; but it is beauty that cannot exist until the mind of man conceives and brings it into being—a process which is going on unceasingly. Being thus created, it is bound to hold and to render not only a record of objective Beauty, but also of the subjective choosing and workings of the human mind. Now, so far as man is known to be god-like, we could boldly affirm that Composer means Creator. But, knowing his creaturely nature, we say rather that in composing a Sonata, the mind of man makes a Creative Response; and also that his Sonata is, ultimately, not a soliloquy but an announcement of a discovery, a contemplative cry to another man, to you and to me, inviting us to contemplate with him. This creative response is manifest in all men, especially in children, being the very breath of the spirit.

As men contemplate and compose, as they critically discern in order to recontemplate, man after man, age after age, helps to discover and to open up more of our vast musical territory; and the cumulative musical records of the workings of the human mind tend to crystallize, in chord and phrase when these are apt, to perish when they are inapt. If a musical phrase felicitously expresses the minds of most of those who listen to it in any given way and time, it is welcomed by them as an inspiration, and accepted for joyous sharing until it be superseded by a yet happier utterance, yet more happily shareable. It is in this way, and because of this natural, almost automatic process, that music can, and often does, narrow into localized and learnable languages, fitted to their particular time, place, and civilization; to widen in due course, and then perhaps to narrow again, if need be, into quite a different form. In this unfailing quality of adaptability it may be compared to a limitless spring of water, which narrows and widens as it flows, taking its features of beauty from this very power of adapting itself to bless the most constricted valleys or the vastest plains impartially; in doing which it shows endless variety of form, in accordance with the simplest laws, apt to meet vital needs.

So we now come a stage nearer music itself, having its delightfully composite nature well in mind, in order the better to examine and measure its natural materials and divisions. After that we shall the more keenly watch the mind and mood of man in musical action. As we pass on, our inevitable natural handicaps as observers must be remembered, though not too complacently endured—the two handicaps of ear and mind already mentioned. As, in gazing at a drama, eye and mind are fully engaged—the eye with alert pleasure, the mind with responsive delight; so, in listening to a Sonata, our task is the very same: this time the ear and mind must learn to hear and respond in instant and perpetual liaison, to the ear's pleasure and the mind's delight.

PART 2

MUSICAL MATERIAL

" Music . . . is limited in its material to tones and their formal relations, which have no other intrinsic meaning. For this reason it is that the other arts have been said to tend towards music when they are at their best."

S. ALEXANDER
(*Beauty and Other Forms of Value*).

PART 2

MUSICAL MATERIAL

Music [illegible] is limited in its material to tones and their form of relations, which have no other intrinsic meaning. For this reason it is that the other arts have been said to tend towards music when they are at their best.

S. ALEXANDER
Beauty and Other Forms of Value

CHAPTER 7

TONAL MEASUREMENTS AND QUALITY

WHAT is the material of which all music is made? As architects work in stones, so musicians work in tones. But tone is an invisible and intangible material; yet it is as really a thing existent in space as is a stone. On the face of it, to talk of the measurements of things both invisible and intangible seems less reasonable than to talk of the measurements of stones, or wood, or other seen and felt materials. Yet we can measure our musical material much as a builder can, and note how it varies, just as surely as stones vary in size, shape, and quality. And the size, shape, and quality of the actual tones used in a Sonata matter as much as those of stones used in a cathedral. As the one matters to architect and builder, so the other matters everything to composer, performer, and listener, if music is to be heard properly.

Lying on your piano is a piece of music. Is it *music*? It is merely an exact description of, or *prescription* for, music. Like any other thing, music has to be realized. And that is why performance, though secondary, is such responsible work, since a crotchet too long or too bulky, or too high when in erection, might mar the primal beauty of the Sonata itself, as disastrously as a stone of the wrong shape and size might mar the beauty of a cathedral when erected. (The reader will find that the use of the word *bulky* for *loud* helps him to fix the mental comparison between *seen* measurements of things called Buildings and *heard* measurements of things called Sonatas.)

But it will be well to go carefully to work in this matter, lest familiar words should play pranks with our efforts to think clearly. Take a sheet of ordinary writing-paper and a pair of scissors. The sheet probably measures about 7 inches long, $4\frac{1}{2}$ inches broad perhaps, and $\frac{1}{120}$ of an inch thick. Now cut a strip, only a small fraction of an inch broad, off the *long* side of the sheet of paper. Now look at it. Would it not rightly be described as a *long* strip? In fact it is chiefly length (7 inches) with scarcely any breadth or depth. Now, while looking at the strip of paper, just hum the softest (thinnest) note you possibly can, holding it on quite a long while—say for seven seconds—and meanwhile let your eye travel along 7 inches of the strip. The tone you sing is rightly described as a *long* note, with scarcely any loudness (thickness).

Notice specially two things about the strip of paper and your strip of tone:

1. It is only when the measurement of length is *noticeably* greater than the other measurements (whatever they are) that we speak of a long strip of paper or a long note at all; that is, one would not exclaim "what a *long* strip of paper!" looking at the ordinary uncut sheet, whose breadth was not far short of its length; nor would the listener exclaim about the *length* of your seven seconds of tone if it had any other interesting dimensions about it.

2. Both your strip of paper and your musical note still, and always will, require *all three of their so-called dimensions* if they are to exist at all. They cannot possibly be all length. There is obviously no such thing as a slip of paper so thin as to have no depth, or so narrow as to have no width. It may be distinguished by being a million miles long and too thin for words; but, even if it be a spider's thread thinned out to sub-microscopic width or depth, it still must have *some* width and *some* depth, or it has ceased to exist,

length and all! And the same with a tone. It cannot possibly be all length. What are the measurements essential to its existence?

seven seconds

Men speak of a long note:

or a short one:

They also speak of a loud or soft one: ff pp

Tonal *volume* corresponds to *thickness* of a thing in the tangible, visible world; and as you may have noticed, thickness is the word used, not for one but for two or more dimensions simultaneously. Your paper had plenty of breadth, but it could not be called thick, because of its paltry depth; and if you had made it, say, 4 inches deep, but at the same time taken away most of its breadth, it still could not be called *thick*. So, just as a thing that has length and thickness exists (having at least three dimensions), can we say of a note also that, however small it is, provided it has a little length and a little loudness (or thickness) it will exist, and the ear will sense it? The answer is No! of course. But why? Because music itself is not merely three-dimensional but concerns us in motion, and it is nearly everything to us to be able to measure its *movement*. We know every note has to have what we call pitch, or vibration-frequency, to be heard at all. 8va That is where we speak of a note being high: or low: (as well as long and loud). Of course 8va this last tonal dimension matters most of all to music. "Is this note too high or too low?" we say; "is its pitch exactly right?" All harmony depends upon accuracy in this measurement.

The significant fact here is that music is not static nor stockish. Music is all movement, like wind or fire. So do not let us think of its three measurements as if they corresponded exactly with the three measurements of a static thing. A high note is not like a high pole. We mean by a *high* note much what we mean by a *high* wind. In fact, a high wind that subsides to a low wind *is* music in the rough, for it registers a high note (as it whistles through the keyhole), falling as it dies to a low one, in this manner: Thinking along this line, the reader will perhaps find himself anxious (as is the writer) to know more precisely how seen measurements and heard measurements may resemble each other, and how they differ. Let us summarize, and probe for this knowledge a little further in three ways:

8va ppp

1. Tones in music, as we have seen, are *things in space* just as surely as stones in a building are, and can therefore be measured. But they are things that are audibly *always on the move*, coming and fading continuously, and we always distinguish one tone from another by its movements. So to measure tones is to measure *movements* of vibrating things. We do not measure the mere material that vibrates, but the moving waves themselves in the air. These are what the ear observes.

2. But we must now beware of saying to ourselves "Ah yes, I see; a stone is a *thing* in space and a tone is a *movement* in time!" This is only a rough truth; both are things in space and both are really on the move in time. For we now know that even a solid stone is really a mass of electronic movement, possessed of energy in essence not unlike the vibrational energy which (within its narrow range) registers to us as sound. But, while the stone obligingly stands still to be measured at leisure in space, and so interests us spatially, a musical note does not. If it could stand still for a tick to be measured, it would simply vanish! All its interest for us is

in time. Yet it remains true that men choose and measure tones to relate them into Sonatas as exactly as masons choose and measure stones to relate them into a Town Hall.

3. As visible stones are fitly chosen by a builder for their *length, breadth, and depth in space,* as well as for their *quality* and its effect upon the eye, so audible tones are chosen by builders of Sonatas or Fugues for their *length* (*in time*), their *loudness* or *amplitude* (*in space-time*) as well as for their *quality* and its effect or " shape " to the ear.

The use of the word *space-time* may bring a shade of mistiness and momentary discomfort to the mind which may have become too much used to thinking of time and space, those two inseparables, as apart from each other. We do indeed incline to take time for granted when examining things like pictures in space-ways ; similarly we take space for granted in looking at things like music in time-ways. And it is specially remarkable how readily we forget that music exists in space at all, because all our interests in it are in time ; and how completely we forget that a cathedral (still more, a mountain) exists in time, and may vanish, because all our interests in it are in space. The space-time truth about both generally needs pondering a little.

Let us take a stroll together for a moment. We will turn away both from stones that are still and from music that moves. Let us look at your garden. (What a fine chrysanthemum you have there !) Let our thoughts be of nothing but a flower. What attracts our eye ? Not its *behaviour* or *movement in time* but its *form* or *appearance in space.* But the truth about it may, before long, be shown us by artists or scientists in both ways. For we know well that its behaviour would be fascinating to every one to watch, if only it were not growing so very gradually as to cheat us of that joy. The cinematograph accelerated film has already begun to show us more of the truth about a host of such things. It may some day show us the eye-music of the flowers, indeed of the whole garden, and of the seasons themselves. Think how thrilling it will be when colour-photography has been perfected, and accelerated films of spring, summer, autumn, and winter show men, trees and flowers, forests and gardens, budding, opening, blooming, fading as they really do—but all within moments, instead of months! The cinematograph will then teach the eye to observe natural beauty *in time* as the ear habitually does.

Here the complementary truth dawns, that in spite of appearances to the contrary, music, *like material things, occurs in a given space at a given time.* The tiniest tone cannot possibly exist to be heard without occupying a point in space and an instant in time. I have heard a scientist compare an electron to a musical note. It *is* and it *happens,* in *space-time.* In this way we get at last a truer idea of musical material. We may think of music itself as of a series of events taking place in a series of instants; not a mere series of points, but located, like a building, at one point. Given the central point (perhaps from a violin in a studio in the B.B.C.) from which our Sonata emanates, our whole concern is placed and centred upon the sizes, shapes, and measurements of its *movements.** We never shall measure music with the ear as we size a flower in a garden, and say: "There is a beautiful phrase or chord, with five notes like petals 3 inches by 4." But we may, some day, reverse the process and actually observe a flower growing (in an accelerated film), moving, like music, from bud to bloom, from the start to the fading finish of its tiny life.

We are now able to perceive that music's essential

* The invention of broadcasting has enabled the player, placed in London, to find innumerable re-placings wherever a mechanism exists to return etheric waves into air-waves.

measurements can be accurately summarized for practical purposes as three, though the second of them does duty for all three spatial dimensions. They are :

1. *Length.*
2. *Volume.*
3. *Vibration-frequency.*

So we select tones for use according as they are :

1. Long or short.
2. Loud or soft.
3. High or low.

If a note loses all its first measurement, it grows short, shorter, shortest, till it ceases to exist in time. If it gradually loses all its second measurement, it gradually grows soft, softer, softest, till it ceases to exist in space. But if it gradually loses or gradually gains in its third measurement, *it cannot be said to pass away or cease* ; we can only say it becomes inaudible to man. Above a certain height, as well as below a certain depth of tone, we hear it no more. Animals, apparently, hear vibrations imperceptible to man. This would seem a great pity, if man were the highest order of being in the Universe ! But as no one can ever be quite so arrogant or silly as to believe this, we may keep open minds as to music inaudible to human ears. May not Beings higher than man hear far more than he does, even of his lowly music ?

The reader may not have the fortune to be able to test the exact vibrational-points at which his own ear ceases to register very high or very low sounds. But you may, in the organ-loft of a cathedral, come very near it. Ask the player to sound the highest note on the piccolo and the very lowest on the pedal. Even if both are still easily heard by your ear * you may well imagine how short a step it is, either way, to the point at which silence *would* ensue for you ; better still, you will realize that sound may continue long after the music

* The writer loses hearing altogether among the piccolo's top notes.

ceases. For very high or very low notes (like the notes of a slate-pencil or the throb of a 32-ft. bourdon) have neither practical interest for the musical mind nor pleasure for the physical ear. The extreme notes, even of a grand piano, verge on the unmusical.

So turn thinkingly to your keyboards, music-lovers all, and with the constant help of the sustaining pedal you will be able quietly and quite effectually to measure out tonal material for yourselves over and over again till your thought is clear—tones of just the length you want, just the strength, and just the height. And should you not be an expert reader of notation, it may help to know that when you glance at a page of music for the first time, notes that look white on a page (roughly speaking) mean long notes:  very black-looking passages mean very short notes:  Leger lines above a treble stave are pictures of high notes:  and the same below a bass stave show low notes:  As to volume, modern composers indicate variety plentifully and extravagantly with *fff* and *ppp*. Bach generally left volume to the gumption of mankind. "All will know," he seemed to assume, "what size they wish their building to be." Indeed, any one who can focus a telescope to his own eye must surely realize that turning the knob of his wireless set, to find the volume that suits the music to his ears, is very much the same kind of process, and likewise his own job as much as any one's! There is, alas, no tonal measurement more left to chance, or more abused; and many of our dear singers to-day insist on screaming at the tops of their beautiful voices, as if their lives depended on the volume they emit, little dreaming that they may be throwing the music quite out of gear for every one within earshot. Tonal adjustment of measurements is not only intensely interesting, but it matters more and more as music progresses.

We now turn to the entrancing question of tonal quality.* Touch this note on your keyboard:  When you have the chance, try to get an organist friend to show you all the different qualities of tone on that same note on the various stops of his organ. Or, better still, go to an orchestral practice, and ask the various players to play this single note on a violin:  viola :  cello :  horn in F :  trumpet in C, and flute and oboe :  clarinet in B♭ :  and any others; obtain all. They will amaze you with the variety of quality; and yet the actual tone, in all its other measurements, can remain precisely the same.

You can read all about quality in any good book on acoustics dated since the famous writings of the chief discoverer in this very field, Helmholtz.† All we can do here (perhaps all we need to do) is to note that tonal quality always means to the ear a blend of two or more tonal ingredients, and that if we could hear an elementary tone with no ingredients, it would simply have no quality. A tuning-fork note struck softly is, we are told, the nearest thing to a tone without quality or mixture of ingredients. Strike it often and softly, on a tuning-fork if possible, but, failing that, *pianissimo* in the upper middle register of a piano. We can conceive of such a soft pure tone as resembling an atom of hydrogen, the first and simplest of elements in the

* The reader may defer this matter till he reaches Chapter 10.

† Helmholtz's *Ton-Empfindungen*, as translated by Ellis, can be found in libraries.

universe. And similarly we can think of the series of our players' different qualities of C: as they hold this tone for us, as resembling a series of natural *spectra* with different proportions of the component series of colours in each. If, for example, there were more "purple" and less "green" in one, less "purple" and more "orange" in another, and so on, we should say, "Those are different qualities." Yet the series of colours in every musical *spectrum* remains constant. It is the degree or emphasis of this tint or that which makes all the difference to the quality of: or of any other tone in the universe.

A rough experiment may help. Go to the keyboard and put down the ivory of this note: *without letting it make a sound.* Hold it down (but, of course, do not touch the sustaining pedal) and now strike this note very sharply and shortly: The result will be as follows: Repeat the process with this note: and this: and lastly with one much nearer "home": The results may be depicted thus:

Having carefully observed the sound of these three preliminary experiments, actually strike the following selections of four tones, very carefully listening to the effect of each upon your ear:

After a time strike the upper notes in different combinations an octave higher, till the original note begins to sound bell-like in quality. What you have been doing in every case is exploring the upper harmonics (as they are called) or *tonal ingredients* of your original note:  Strike it now *without touching the upper notes which are its natural components or ingredients*, strike hard, hold it, and listen to it very closely and analytically, and you will gradually persuade your ear to hear its " upper partials " without any help. They are there in varying strengths ; some too faint to hear, others quite prominently. And when, a moment ago, you struck two or three of the upper notes and actually played, not a single tone but a chord of four notes, if you played them exactly together, the probability is that any one listening with their eyes shut would not hear a chord at all but merely a slight change of timbre in what still sounds to them like a single note, your original C, always the lowest of the series, the qualitative *generator* of the others.

Mere *quality* of course plays a prodigious part, both in life and in music. When, listening to voices outside a room, you suddenly exclaim : " There's old so-and-so ; I know his voice among a hundred ! " you really are saying, " There's old so-and-so ; I'd know him anywhere by his tonal spectrum ! " In the same way we recognize various instruments in the orchestra, such as clarinet or flute, each by its own tonal spectrum ; and if one harmonic is missing and another sounding in full force, we shall the more readily know it (at an aural glance) by the presence or absence of these naturally characteristic tonal ingredients.

CHAPTER 8

THE TIME-AREA, OR THE "MUSICIAN'S CANVAS"

AFTER thinking over the actual measurements of musical material, and the infinite variety of qualities available in it all ; and after pondering on the facts suggested in the previous chapter, it will be fairly easy to conceive all musical magnitudes as existent on a musical field or *Area of Time.*

If you peg out a space-field you do it visibly in feet, yards, acres, and miles. If you peg out a time-field, you are reduced to doing it in seconds, minutes, and hours, remembering always that Time, even to us humans, has more measurements than mere length. It is no mere fancy that speaks of having a "*thin* time of it," or a "*high* old time," as well as a long time. When music is distinguished chiefly for its length, the Germans have a neat word for it—*longwhilish* (langweilig).

The musician, then, actually works on a Time-area measurable in minutes. The canvas of a piece of music may be a three-minute, or a five-minute, or a half-hour canvas. The larger the canvas the more, it seems, will it need "pegging out," or the listener may lose his way in tracts of unrelated time, as an admiring eye might lose its way in vast unrelated spaces. So it comes about that as artist and architect have space-plans for relating picture or building into perfection, so musical design in a time-area brings with it as imperative a need for time-plans. We shall see how this works when we come to a later chapter (on the Rule of Four).

It is dangerously easy to fancy that Sonatas are still pegged out (as they habitually are) in their time-area, in bars perhaps of three beats, and sections probably of eight bars, and so on, simply because they were in some way long ago derived from the dance. But it seems rather like suggesting that your manner of walking was derived from your brother's habit of swinging his arms. It will be found, as it happened, that the classical European miracle of Sonatas and Symphonies actually did owe a very big debt in its early stages to the time-habits and time-schemes of the feet of dancers (and also, by the way, to *their* need for music to keep *them* to the point). But we have to look deeper than that. Any race of super-men, not given to dancing, listening-in to the reaches of time, would still need time-measures of due proportions —bars and double bars. For all musical *Order*, and all musical *Design* (that is: all the works of a musical mind at liberty in endless orderly ways), take place on a defined Time-area, every bit as much as inspired order and design in painting, sculpture, drama, or dress take place within a given spatial area.

CHAPTER 9

THE OCTAVE AND RELATED TONES

IT may now be more clearly seen how the essentially musical joys of music lie in loveable *Relating* of tones. The Artist in Tone, working always in tonal material on a canvas of time, orders his notes of all sorts and sizes into delightful relation in the three ways that accord with their natural measurements already noted in Chapter 7. In the famous theme of the slow movement of his *Seventh Symphony*: *pp* etc. as in the third movement of the *Fifth Symphony*: *f* etc. Beethoven centres us upon relating *longs with shorts* into a rhythmic figure before he allows any other interest to capture the ear. In Haydn's *Surprise Symphony* (as its name implies) the chief point of the slow movement's appeal is the mischievously violent relating of *loud with soft*, of an orchestral *pp* with an abrupt, bursting orchestral *ff*. But in every so-called *melodic interval*:  or in a phrase:  or in any so-called harmonic interval:  or in a *chord*:  the vital interest all lies in one and the same dimension—*i.e.* in the relating of *high with low*.

This, the commanding and unique interest of all music, is not always paramount above the more physically clamorous interests of *volume* and *rhythm*. But it is the master-interest of musicians; and to it the other two kinds of relatings, both delightful in themselves, are by him subjected. The more indeed they are subjected to it, the more music tends to become musical and to appeal to the mind. For this reason we must concentrate in this and the following chapters upon the possible relating of tones in the regions of high and low *vibration-frequencies.* And foremost of all tonal relation stands that known throughout music by the name of *Octave.*

Strike the two extreme notes of your keyboard. Listen critically to see if you detect any relation at all between them. Now strike any note lying *near* the two ends, both haphazard. Again listen closely, as you hold your two chance tones, to try to detect definite relation between them. It is hardly likely that you will, though keen minds may. Now strike this note: *p* and follow it by this: *p* Next strike them softly together: *pp* Ped. * and listen closely and as *relishingly* as you can. To heighten value of this experience, play a trick upon yourself, and pretend hard that you are never going to be allowed to taste another tonal relating or scrap of music in your whole life. Say a lingering farewell to all music thus: *pp* Ped. * You are now keenly tasting with your ear, and dwelling with your imaginative mind upon *as perfect a relating of two different tones* as can be humanly conceived. They are as definitely different, two individual tones in the universe, as your two extremes were a moment ago. But (if the piano-tuner has done his work) they fit thus perfectly (the one note merging completely into the other) because every vibration of the lower will coincide with every alternate vibration of the upper note.*

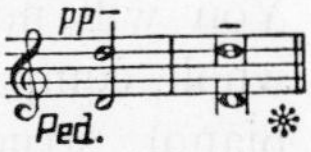

* On most pianos nowadays there are 522 vibrations per second to this note:

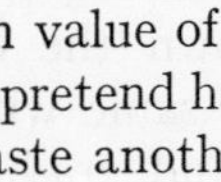

The importance of this experience of the octave to the mind lies not, of course, in the actual numbers of vibrations there are in a given period for this note or that. That may be important to the ear that keeps the register; the mind's interest lies entirely above such details, in the realm of *relating* two or more detectible energies. The actual vibration-numbers * have no more interest to us than the actual numbers of leaves on two related trees in a landscape. Our interest is a far more vital one.

It is noteworthy that, all the world over, men have made this standing relation of two tones in the perfect ratio of 1 : 2 the basis of musical design. In order to realize this fully before going further, sit at your keyboard, and notice all the notes called D (lying between each isolated pair of black notes). Each is, of course, in the octave relation to the D nearest it on either side higher (to the right) or lower (to the left) in pitch. With the sustaining pedal down, sound them all, up and down the whole compass, starting with: *f*> Do the same with all the C notes, all the B♭ notes, and gradually with all the remaining nine notes. You will now have struck every note throughout the whole compass. You have, in so doing (on a full grand piano), struck eighty-four different tones—different for ever to the musical ear; but you have only made twelve appeals in all to your musical *mind*, if it is true that all the D notes have gone (as it were) into one mental receiver, all the C notes into another, and so on.

That men *do* pop every C into one mental pigeon-hole, and every B into a B pigeon-hole, and so on, is borne out by many proofs, some of them amusing. Sir Hubert Parry used to tell how, when at sea one Sunday, he appealed to an old servant on board to play a Sunday

* In this particular case 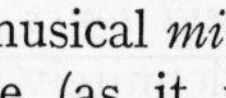 they are about 291 : 582.

tune. There was only an instrument of the penny whistle order on board. So the old fellow chanted Mornington's chant on his whistle somewhat as follows:

The thought B, the leading note, was B to him wherever it fell or was available. Lower B did not exist on his whistle, but the thought had to be thought, whatever happened, resulting in the above deliciously playful variant of the dignified original. I myself have heard an old farmer friend in Hampshire sing this phrase,

physically altered (though mentally constant) to suit his compass:

Within the whole tonal field—that is, within the total range of vibration-frequencies audible to man—there lies an infinite series of different tones, and therefore a terrifyingly vast array of possible tonal relationships. No book would hold them. But our musical concepts are immensely simplified the moment we think all Cs as one C, all Bs as one B, etc., etc. Our farmer friend, as will be seen, *completely changed* the actual melodic contour. So did the penny whistler. As melody, the shape and impulse of the tune are profoundly changed in both cases, because another record of another energy (though fortuitously) has, as it were, blown across it and brought with it a new leap of seven degrees of the scale upwards, and so made it melodically a new thing. But both men stuck to their mental guns and proved, as Rameau and others long ago discovered, that a musical concept or thought (like, for example, the chord-thought C, E, G) can persist *in any pitch, in any order.* Play, for example, this common chord in its three typical and well-known close positions: Play them in any octave; and though these three variants have, in fact, acquired many other implications in many other contexts, yet you will probably find that playing them in succession will give you no new harmonic thought or experience at all. But now we are dangerously anticipating our chapter on chords, and must return to the consideration of this all-important octave matter more inquiringly, more tenaciously; from which we may the more knowingly proceed to a catalogue of the simpler tonal relations (all known by the unhelpful name of *intervals*) lying within it.

First, if it be true that musical thought shows signs of being everywhere both dominated and clarified by this one single relation out of an infinite series of possible relations, why does such a thing happen? And can we reconcile our free minds wholly to it? Is it arbitrary? Is it a fashion? Can we find any permanent within-and-without reasons for it? Well, it seems fairly easy and worth while to guess at two such reasons—one to be found in music itself, and one in our minds. These, if correct and if clearly grasped, may combine into a sort of "fixing solution," for ever fixing our own "mental imprint" of this musical relation called the *octave,* confirming its permanent and unique function in our minds. Let us consider them.

> 1. We find that the octave above every audible tone in Nature is heard as the strongest and first *component* of that tone.

This was apparent in our small experiment a few

moments back. But to discern a tone-within-a-tone is not at first easy to every ear. Let us try to make it more certain. Strike a single note: *f* strongly, with the sustaining pedal down, and listen analytically to its tones until you hear this: *pp* reposing, as it were, inside the root-note, but still clearly, entirely itself. Then do the same *without* the sustaining pedal, holding the note down without sounding it, and listening for the other. Try it again and again till you succeed in training your ear to discern it with ease.* Try it with many different notes (at odd moments of the day) till your ear becomes a quick, efficient, tonal observer—in fact, till it becomes, through use, a properly equipped servant of the mind, not only for this experiment, but quickened for good and all.

When, in some such way, we have realized that this *octave-relation* is the most intimate, most simple, and most discernible natural way of relating two tones any time, anywhere in the world, we shall half realize why it has taken so supreme a place in musical minds—as paramount a place, in fact, as the figures 1 and 2 have taken in arithmetical minds.

2. We find that when any second sound heard makes *nearly* an octave (with a note already sounding) but not quite: or and if then it passes, or merges, very gradually into that perfect relation: the ordinary mind attains more complete consciousness of harmony between two tones in this than in any other interval. It is able, possibly, to say the simplest "Yes" to which music can lead it.

Now it is not at all easy to put either into thoughts or

* It is a directional help to the inexperienced ear if the secondary tone be first softly sounded, so that it is definitely expectable when the time comes to listen for it *within* the generating note.

words the responsive process of the mind when experiencing something outside itself to which something inside is able to say "yes." When you are on tenterhooks about anything in the world, and suddenly experience solution and relaxation of suspense (you find yourself, perhaps involuntarily, nodding your head slightly, or smiling—indeed, if it is very sudden, you may burst out laughing, and then you call "it" humorous), your experience is due to some inward endorsement of outward happenings. You exclaim "Bravo!" or "Fine!" or "Of course!" One old musician, whenever he heard inspired music convincingly played, was in the habit of saying "IT'S IT!" But it is obvious that the *it* outside must fit the *it* inside, if the two *its* are to make IT.* Is it not this very primal experience of the mind that the relating of two or more tones in music brings about at the commanding behest of genius on both sides? Initiating genius, in composing, bears the pains; responding genius, in listening, may attain the reward.

But many readers may exclaim that their responsive delight in this universally basic tonal experience, called the octave, is very nearly as slight as their response to a single tone! That surely is a good sign. By complete mastery or assimilation of the octave we are ready at once to move into a larger tonal heritage. Nevertheless, the octave resembles *all* other intervals (some of which we may find very difficult to recognize) in *one* most informing way: it is, as they all are and will remain, not the record of a single tonal energy, but of *two energies as one*. And at the happy recognition of two tones in one, all harmonically-minded people begin their delight and training. It is hardly too much to say that the man who relates two or more tones into one joy, and only he, has begun to be musical at all. Obviously all the world

* A friend has suggested as a working formula:
"It multiplied by it = Infinity."

must begin with, and retain, this simple power of relating with that joyous recognition which alone is the sign that the relating has really come to pass. To lose so primal a power would be fatal. To keep and cultivate it is all gain.

Indeed, let us be reckless for a moment and go much further in our guessing. Let us suppose that our delight in music is at root not merely musical, but is nothing less than a profoundly creative delight in being able to enjoy, and even control, the interplay of two forces; or, to put it more fully, the joyous exercise of integrating two or more movements into a new experience of movement. When we integrate what may be nick-named here *Two-or-moreness*, we master it, and we enjoy that mastery. Moreover—as is obvious—we enjoy moving on from mastery to mastery in all kinds of vital ways, and in nothing more than in the art of music. To master any two-or-moreness is to reduce it to a one-ness ready for further adventures in integrating. Let us here for convenience think of any single experience (completely mastered) as pictured or graphed in a simple straight line. By way of illustration outside the realm of music, look at a single directional line drawn on a piece of white paper; look steadily and hard at it for ten endless seconds, thinking of it as a mere record of movement, let us say the imaginary route of an aeroplane. Its interest is real, but slender, and

⟶

very quickly over. The imaginative mind wants to get on instantly and "do something about it," as we say. Take another straight record—this time of a vertical motion, say the route of a balloon: ↑ The result, if nothing happens, is merely boring; indeed, all records of single directional forces are bound to pall quickly. But now think for a moment of any two such straight natural forces, first observed singly and then observed integrated. To get a rough graph of this, imagine a pith-ball dropped vertically from the car of a balloon, no breeze blowing. The record of the force of gravity would give us a straight downward line: ↓ Now picture the pith-ball blown transversely by a breeze. Again we get a straight record: ⟶ But integrate these two natural forces; and our pith-ball will delineate the integrated event, with the wholly new interest of a curve in it:

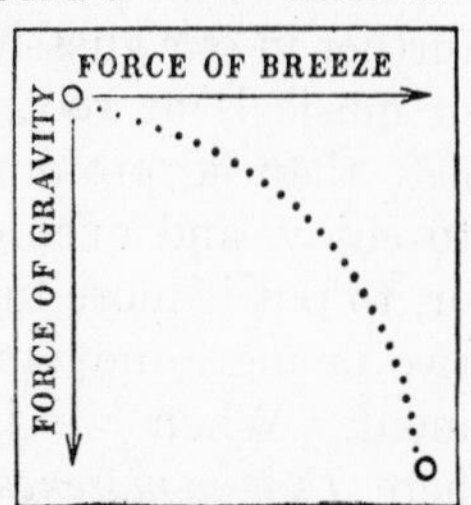

Is it indeed possible that our root delight in a simple curve, as well as our root delight in a musical *interval,* are but two showings of one interest, and are thus both half explained? It may be that we all find delight habitually, without knowing it, in things or experiences of things which record two or more motions superposed into one. This may possibly be the mind's perpetual master-interest in such widely differing things as a novel, a quarrel, a crossword puzzle, a football match, a Fugue. Certainly such a guess agrees well with our actual experiences of so-called *intervals* in music—*i.e.* the relationship of tone with tone. Or think of another rather beautiful and very familiar example of two natural forces seen to be interacting and integrating, in which one force is fixed or constant in nature while the other is variable. Picture a cornfield in stillness, the corn-stalks standing upright in evening sunlight, and think of it as of a single note of exquisite tone: A transverse breeze blows across the field: and the straight stalks yield to the new force, and in any graceful bend give a fine picture of two forces more thrilling than either could be singly. Perhaps it is in such simple relatings of sights or sounds that Art (audible and visible) begins to exist in our minds; and our busy bee, the brain (knowing well that its 1 + 1 = 2 must, in Art, always take a back seat), pays baffled homage to the creative mind which discovers with distracting delight that, in action and art, 1 + 1 make some new, third thing—compared with which a mathematical 2 is simply negligible.

So it can happen that tonal ratios, read on a page, are the dullest thing in the world. Look at a few of the simpler musical ratios, with their exact tunings represented in notes related by name:

1 : 2 = D : D′ = an octave.
2 : 3 = D : A = a fifth.
3 : 4 = D : G = a fourth.
4 : 5 = D : F♯ = a major third.
5 : 6 = D : F = a minor third.

An experienced musician will, of course, like an experienced chemist reading a prescription, taste them with his inward ear as he reads, as the chemist might seem to taste the very blend of drugs on his experienced mental palate while reading the prescription. But perhaps you and I do no such thing. We do not know musical formulæ well enough to "taste" what they indicate. But now take those dull-looking tonal ratios, lying there on the written page. Go to the keyboard, and (as a music-lover who is determined to be a rational learner as well) do the sensible thing—taste them with your ear for yourself, one at a time, over and over again, in every kind of way that occurs to you, until, like a chemist determined to know the relation of the simplest components of all prescriptions he is ever likely to be called upon to deal with, or like a good *littérateur* who is determined to master the simple concepts most favoured by poets, you not only become able to recognize these five simple *intervals* in all music on hearing them again; but you are also able to give them each specific and relative values of *their* own and of *your* own:

The repetitions here shown are mere indications of the numberless ways (which readers may devise for themselves) of fixing the *sound* of the intervals for the ear's sake, and the *significance* of them for the mind's sake. For preliminary purposes, of course, the first of these two "sakes" is the more important. No music can be enjoyed and taken in thoroughly till the ear can deliver correct messages to the mind. As well try to grasp a Shakespeare play of which the ear cannot distinguish the chief words, or the eye the chief characters, as tackle a Beethoven Sonata, all intervals of which sound "much the same." For ideal purposes, however, readers must hasten (slowly, perhaps, but with as heavenly a speed as is possible) *to give a value* to each and every interval. I have been told that Mr. Gladstone (knowing the value of giving values, and also the insidious dangers of vague sentimental religiosity) once said: "Have an intellectual equivalent for your faith." This may be paraphrased for present purposes into: "Have imaginative equivalents for your musical experiences." You may either lean back in a concert room and let a swirl of pleasing and skilled music wash past you, occasionally seeming to envelop you as a summer sea may pleasurably envelop even a mentally deficient bather, or your whole being may, so to speak, sit up to it all; no, you may positively leap with your mind to meet it. Invest music for yourself, so far as you can, with more and more of its primal significance. If it is too placid and calm for your taste and enterprise, then dive deeper; if it is too multiform and tumultuous for your present powers, you may still manage to keep your musical head above water, and marvel at its significance. Musical material is so vast, yet so much in the making (or rather, in the discovering) that, at best, we may only acquaint ourselves with it by degrees. Yet sounds that baffle us to-day may, by patient attention, be made familiar in an amazingly short time.

We should now tabulate and think over the tonal relatings which are at our disposal, sounding them again and again at the keyboard, till familiarity makes examples so vivid in the mind that the ear needs no material reminders of them.

If the octave is the simplest and most easily "*yessed*" * relating of two tones, which are the most complex and bewildering that we may learn to conquer, and so *yes* them all?

Take an inch of elastic and stretch it and relax it alternately. Through how many points does it pass? Obviously an infinite number. In like manner relax a violin E string to sound, say:  and, while sounding it, tighten it up exactly one octave:  If you play the whole time from note to note you will have covered an infinite series of tones between them. Now look at your keyboard, and also at a footrule.

* It is necessary to ask the reader's consent to the use of the listener's verb *to yes*, because it not only seems to come nearest to the meaning required, but it may save the use of many words, like "recognition-of-euphonious-relationships-in-process and mental-acceptance-and-affirmation-of-same; all of which means merely "yes." Is there not good musical use for the German word *Bejahung*?

You will find from C to C twelve tonal stations, or stopping-places, and no more—like the inch stations on your footrule. In both they are a matter of practical convenience and expediency; but in the modern keyboard there lies hidden an interesting romance, as well as a make-the-best-of-it mechanism. For man can conceive of and delight in many more tonal relations than lie there in black and white within the little tonal chamber of the octave. Go to Kensington Museum and ask to see the many experimental keyboards that ingenious men have, at various times, devised to meet with more exactitude the exacting demands of the mind of music. You will be bewildered by their very appearance; even Paderewski or Schnabel would have to refuse to try to play on them, and would probably refer you to the story of Bach's "Well-tempered Keyboard," which you must read elsewhere. But if, starting with the sound of our beloved octave: we move forward as far as we need, or dare, along the endless line of tonal relations waiting to be discovered and used by man, we may shut no door on delight, and yet avoid the danger of opening too many. Our first list of five simplified ratios (on page 79) has given us, in fact, not five *intervals*, but a ready access to endless riches; for we are free to follow our mental custom already suggested, and to combine one interval with one in ways that may reveal new joys at every turn. Here let us remember that physical limitations of the human ear place natural limits to the number of stations we can usefully set up within the octave. Let us also remember (what Bach knew well when he invented his "escalator" of twelve equal steps) that limitless material has never proved a friend to limitless ingenuity. On the contrary, it is a willingness to make use of simple and limited material which seems to enable limitless genius to reach lowly and limited men, to their astonished happiness. Mathematics could, in fact, enable us in five minutes to draw up a table of tonal relations here, quite out of touch with reality though most imposingly thorough to the eye! We must tread a simpler and more practicable way.

To our five simplest intervals:

the next simple and most natural addition would bring us a new kind of smaller *minor third,* that of the tonal ratio 6 : 7; this has so far played no recognizable integral part in our music. If ever used (as by Vaughan Williams in his Pastoral Symphony) it is as a visitant and not as an enrolled member of our scale. But we have many other intervals, some obviously more simple than 6:7 (such as 3:5:), some looking much more complex (such as 15 : 16 :), and, by the way, uncompromisingly hard to listen to, if concussingly stated: How have *these* come? Yes, by our natural ways of putting one and one together and making a new thing. Three thoughts will help to explain:

1. The tonal relations used in our most involved music, so far as we have gone, *never involve any prime number higher than 5.*

2. If two simple tonal ratios be sounded at close quarters, the mind is soon able (as usual) to merge its two old and known sounds into one new and hitherto unknown sound. As soon as this resultant sound passes into the safe catalogue of known sounds, it may combine with others to produce more new sounds, and so on *ad infinitum.*

3. Though the musical mind can both conceive and enjoy the concepts of what have been christened

enharmonic intervals, and which are smaller than a semitone, such as: yet it is notable that no tonal relating smaller than a so-called chromatic semitone (24:25:) is given physical counterpart and sounded to the ear in Western, or harmonic music, though smaller melodic steps are systematically incorporated in classical Indian music and unsystematically recognized in Western melodizing, by voices, strings, and all instruments that lend themselves to melodic subtleties.

From the three above considerations we more readily see how natural limits which might seem hampering prove, on the contrary, helpful, setting no conscious tonal fetters to the unfettered tonal imagination. Two ways of evolving numerous new relations out of our first five will soon be obvious. They rather resemble simple addition of two intervals to create a new interval, thus:

and something vaguely like simple subtraction, thus:

These processes are alike in one significant way: they bring one new relationship to mind, because two were there already. To see this indubitably, let us think in relations of persons instead of notes:

All have power of intimate friendships, each with each. At first Tom befriended Dick: Dick also befriended Harry: There is no idea of Tom and Harry being friends till Dick one day introduced them :  Result, a new friendly relationship:  In the other case, however, Tom befriended Dick as before:  but he had a more intimate friend, Sam:  He introduces Sam to Dick; result:  a new relationship—not so friendly quite, and only at its best when Tom is in the room:  on good terms with both.* Let us now, with this domestic analogy well held in mind, relate (as systematically as we may) all resultant tonal relations that seem to follow on our first five, choosing :  (Tom) for convenience of cataloguing, as President of the Society of Tonal Friends (see page 86).

In these tables we have but indicated the ways in which two knowns bring us the hitherto unknown, two *olds* bring us *news*. Music is on the move daily; along the lines we have exemplified here, all known intervals (and many still unexplored) can easily be found by any thoughtful music lover. A few years ago, for example, I searched in vain through treatises on Harmony for the beautiful interval of the augmented third:  and its companion the diminished sixth:  Though the augmented sixth and diminished third:  and, still more frequently, the augmented second and diminished seventh:  were plentifully used and tabulated, their obvious companions had not been made known.

Let us now sum up our results in practical and condensed form; here is a catalogue of intervals, being the basic tonal relation called octave, together with all

* In the mediatorial quality of *Tom's* presence lies a delicious parable.

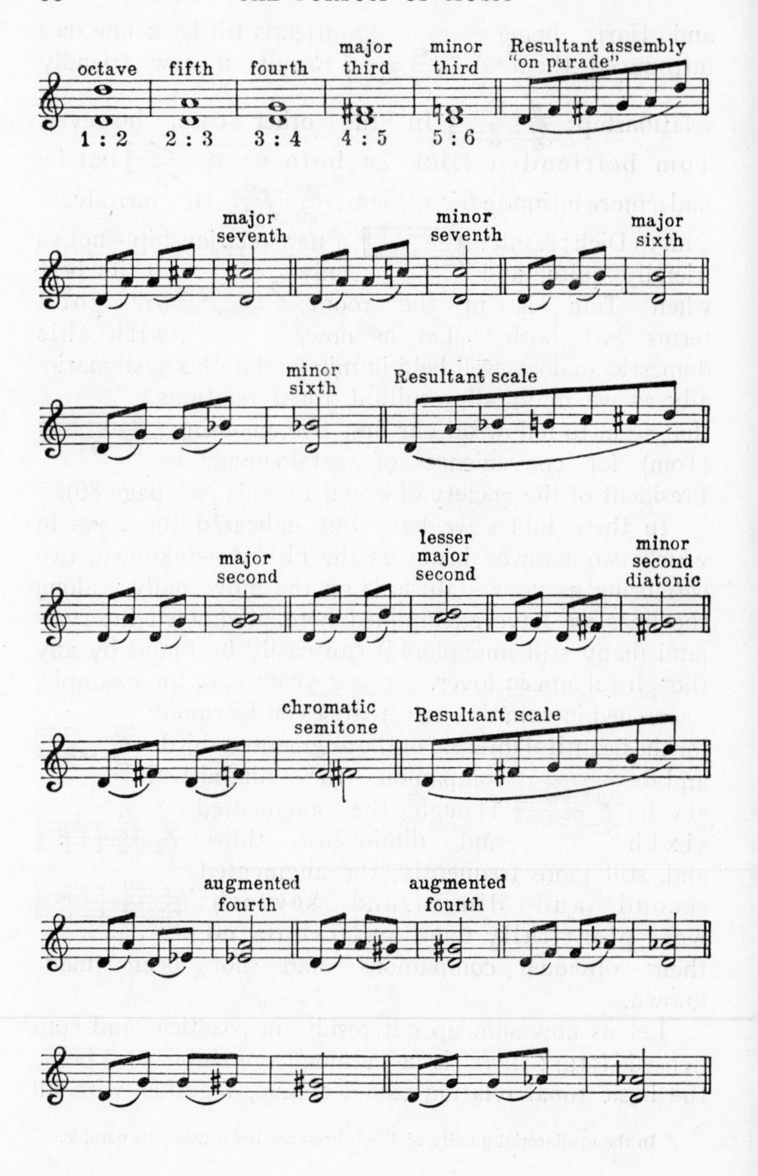
octave
fifth
fourth
major third
minor third
Resultant assembly "on parade"
1 : 2
2 : 3
3 : 4
4 : 5
5 : 6
major seventh
minor seventh
major sixth
minor sixth
Resultant scale
major second
lesser major second
minor second diatonic
chromatic semitone
Resultant scale
augmented fourth
augmented fourth

less simple tonal relations lying within its euphonious walls :

1. Octave.
2. Fifth.
3. Fourth.
4. Major third.
5. Minor third.
6. Major sixth.
7. Minor sixth.
8. Minor seventh.
9. Major second (greater form).
9a. Major second (lesser form).
10. Major seventh.
11. Minor second.
12. Chromatic semitone.
13. Augmented fourth.
14. Diminished fifth.
15. Diminished seventh.
16. Augmented second.
17. Augmented sixth
18. Diminished third.
19. Augmented third.
20. Diminished sixth.

It is well to recall Mozart's warning (to his contemporaries) never to dream of an augmented octave ! No, said he ; if you ever see this : (as, by the way, you may in his *Don Giovanni* Overture) it is an *augmented unison*, heard in an upper octave. And with this thought it seems wise to couple another. If you should ever see and hear this passage : you will guess, I think rightly, that the composer meant B ♯, not C ♮, in his upper melody, and this thought and meaning is not to be flinched at, even though it compel your mind to include henceforth the concept of the resultant augmented seventh : and its inversion, a diminished second : among possible tonal delights. The keyboard gives you but an approximation to ALL your tonal concepts except the octaves themselves ! Are you surprised ? Are you shocked that musicians can think so subtly while they hear so grossly as all that? That the same sound has to serve for G♭ and F♯ and E♯♯? That a perfect thought can be communicated through a defective physical experience? Bach gave his deliberate life-vote for the tempered semitones, which shock sensitive ears to this day. Yet when Schubert (at a heavenly moment referred to later) makes everything turn upon G♯ passing to an A♭ context and back again, he requires no different sound to be made. Indeed one suspects him of trading on the fact that an enharmonic thought has no differentiation of sound in it. It is like a pun in poetry. Like true word-play in literature or poetry, the possibilities of subtle chord-play are endless. Perhaps when you write this and play it sympathetically, (for choice on a 'cello):

you have made the very identical joke which the inimitable Tom Hood made when he said:

> "They went and told the sexton,
> And the sexton toll'd the bell."

Many readers may find it hard (as I do) to rest in a position which seems to require from us either a vote for physical in-tuneness at the cost of restricting the musical field, or (with Bach) for unrestricted imaginative freedom of mind, working within a tonal field which at every point but one offers us only an approximation to our thinking, and something less comfortable than our ears desire. It is strange. I should be grateful for any light from any reader.

Chapter 10

THE MUSICAL "SPECTRUM" AND TONAL "ROOTS"

THE last chapter seemed "hard going," and ended on a note of puzzlement; so it is a relief to turn and set before the reader anything so easy to enjoy, so obvious, and yet so important to our intelligent pursuit, as the first six tones of the musical "spectrum." Their beauty, when sounded together, makes one think of them as of a rainbow made audible. Analyse a white ray of light and you get the colours of the rainbow. Analyse any musical tone and you get (in however faint hues or degrees) its tonal "*spectrum*":

The seventh and higher harmonics are practically inaudible in all but exceptionally favourable circumstances to exceptionally sensitive ears, and to most of us resemble colours fading out at the edge of the rainbow.* In studying the audible "spectrum," it is convenient and wise to add Nos. 6 and 8 to their more powerful elders and secondary generators Nos. 3 and 4:

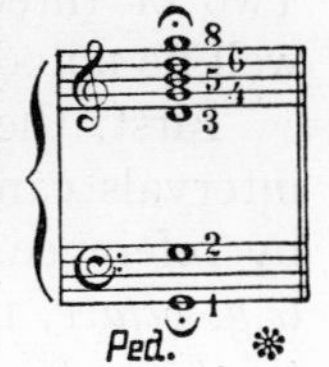

* This is Sir James Jeans's delightful simile.

Transpose it into more sonorous octaves, spread it out in *arpeggio* (as it is "harpily" named), and dwell upon it many times, as, for example, thus :

This series exemplifies and combines, in a way both natural and attractive, not only the five simplest ratios named in the preceding chapter and their corollaries, the minor and major sixth, but also seven other variants which may conveniently be seen at a glance in notation, if catalogued fully as follows :

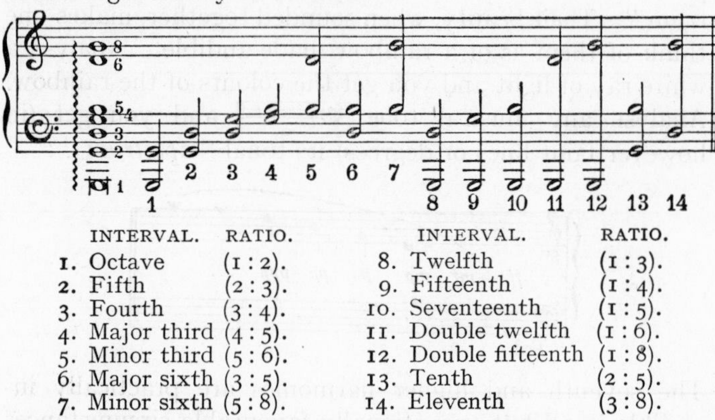

	INTERVAL.	RATIO.		INTERVAL.	RATIO.
1.	Octave	(1 : 2).	8.	Twelfth	(1 : 3).
2.	Fifth	(2 : 3).	9.	Fifteenth	(1 : 4).
3.	Fourth	(3 : 4).	10.	Seventeenth	(1 : 5).
4.	Major third	(4 : 5).	11.	Double twelfth	(1 : 6).
5.	Minor third	(5 : 6).	12.	Double fifteenth	(1 : 8).
6.	Major sixth	(3 : 5).	13.	Tenth	(2 : 5).
7.	Minor sixth	(5 : 8).	14.	Eleventh	(3 : 8).

Two or three points made clear by this catalogue may well be noted.

First, the exact ratio of every one of these familiar intervals can most conveniently be found in a moment by reference to the numbers on the tonal *spectrum* itself (*e.g. octave*, 1 : 2, is seen between the first two ; *minor third*, 5 : 6, is seen between the fifth and sixth of the series, and so on) ; and this gives us the hint to think all other tonal ratios, obvious or abstruse, into their appropriate places, later on, on the rungs of this unending natural ladder of *harmonics* (as they are called) in order the better to measure their degree of complexity.

Next, it may be noted that the ratios of the second seven derived intervals are, looked at as a whole, simpler than those of the first seven. This has great importance in scoring or piano-writing. For example, Chopin will be heard to get far more beauty of tone out of a chord disposed thus:

than Beethoven does out of the identical chord written so:

It is the actual notes of both chords that are the same—D♭, F, A♭. The six ratios involved by Beethoven, however, are 4 : 5, 2 : 3, 1 : 2, 5 : 6, 5 : 8, 3 : 4. Compared with Chopin's: 1 : 3, 1 : 4, 1 : 5, 3 : 4, 3 : 8, 4 : 5, they are found to be less simple. Moreover Beethoven's notes are grouped in so low a tone register that the *two lowest* give off certain upper partials strong enough to be audibly quarrelsome * as between their respective members as follows:

Speaking generally, the harmonic series proves a splendid guide for musicians who desire to dispose tonal relations in chords euphoniously. It is as if the same chord or musical thought could at any time be put (*a*) either extremely harshly, or (*b*) extremely acceptably, to repel or to please the ear, or (*c*) be graded anywhere between these extremes of beauty and harshness at discretion. And such guidance derived from the *spectrum* by no means ends with the first six of the series. For though harmonics, like Nos. 7, 11, 13, 14, 17, 19, and more remote primes, have no present place in our musical thoughts or system, their places in the *spectrum* give us still *a good approximating standard* by which we may find

* Even a simple minor third on certain instruments and organ stops can sound horribly dissonant.

and test the best dispositions of many-toned chords or combinations of tonal relatings with which we are familiar. Though we may never use, for example, the ratios 6 : 7 or 7 : 8, we are continually using something very near them in our familiar chord-concept of a minor third below a given note, plus a small major second above it (5 : 6 and 9 : 10) thus: 5 : 6 9 : 10 3 : 4 and the middle tone F (a true minor third above D, and a true lesser major second below G) lies so near in sound to the natural harmonic seventh: 8 7 6 4 that nature's rule bestows upon it approximate smoothness, fortifies our chosen arrangement of the tones of our own chords, and helps us to find a euphonious way of putting our chord-thoughts so that they shall strike the listener's ear kindly. Yes, kindly, by the way, but not *too* kindly; for it does indeed soon become possible to carry this so very far, making an intended discord so pleasingly consonant in actual effect that few listeners will perceive that it has any urge at all towards *resolution* (the name given in music to the relief of consonance logically following dissonance).

Study of many examples will make clear these points as to euphonious disposition of tones approximating Nature's way; the reader has only to dispose the chord of C major, duplicated or triplicated (C E G, C E G, C E G) into all sorts of different parts of the keyboard and orders of distances, to hear how harsh (when in close positions and in low registers), and how lovely (when openly placed) the very same concept may be made. (This is particularly valuable and eloquent when music consorts with other arts; it would enable a composer, for example, to depict twin brothers in an opera with one and the same harmony—the one all harshness and ungainliness, the other all grace and gallantry.)

The perfection and comprehensiveness of the natural harmonic series may prove fatally alluring to the theorizing side of our minds, drawn to try and explain all music by its means. Theorists have long " derived " the so-called dominant seventh : from the ratio 4 : 7. They have gone further, and derived the so-called dominant eleventh : sometimes from the ratio 4 : 11, and sometimes from 8 : 21! But every one should know that the seventh we use in the above example lies a natural and thoughtful semitone (15 : 16) above A, and a natural and thoughtful minor third (5 : 6) above G; unquestionably we have no experience or thought of its lying a natural seventh (4 : 7) above C. In like manner, the F that is thought of as a so-called dominant eleventh in the second example obviously lies a most natural and thoughtful semitone above E (15 : 16), and not an unknown harmonic above C (4 : 11 or 8 : 21).

A severer natural warning against pursuing too far our " musical rainbow " arises from our actual use and experience of the minor chord, since the minor third from the generating tone is excluded from the *spectrum, ad infinitum.* As ·9 takes an eternity to merge into 1, so long (for a different reason) would the minor third take to be, as it were, squeezed into the *spectrum* ! Some theorists have found it tempting to supplement the natural harmonic series by working in the opposite direction, and so deriving a minor triad " from nature." It is done in this way:

Take a pipe 1 foot long and blow through it. This column of air vibrating will produce this note: Now take a series of pipes, 1, 2, 3, 4, 5, and 6 feet long respectively. These will give you the following result :

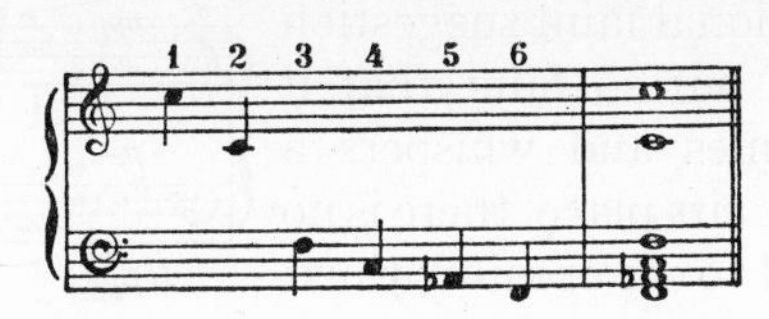

It is astonishingly tempting to say : " As your spectrum gives you a glorified confirmation of your use of the major chord, so this natural series of organ pipes gives you a corresponding confirmation of the minor chord. Take them in conjunction, and nature herself is explanatory of the prevailing human taste in music ! " But further thought upon what actually goes on in the world of sound, tells us that this organ-pipe series has no practical bearing whatever upon our experience and use of the minor triad, or of any other chord. To hear it is to realize that its effect is thick and unenlightening, in glaring distinction to the smoothness and beauty of the harmonic series. What is the reason for this ? Once more a small experiment at the keyboard may help. Sound these three notes successively:

and listen very eagerly for the " spectrum " of each :

The notes must be struck very loudly, and held a very long time at first, till the ear becomes skilled in tonal *peering*. A good trick to play upon oneself is to look hard at the ivory of the very note which one wants to hear ; it induces a closer listening *focus* upon each note in turn. I generally find (and sensitive readers will probably also find) that, when once the ear's reluctance to hear delicate components of a conglomerate tone has been surmounted, it is left with the first four of the series and an occasional faint suggestion of the fifth, but so faint that if any one comes and whispers a *minor* third in its place, there is no trouble at all to ear or mind, thus:

result, a comfortable *minor* chord. The above experiment should be transposed into many different positions on the keyboard. It will be found gradually that in experience *the first three* of the spectral series count mightily. To hear the truth of this, strike any low note, C, *fortissimo*, and follow it with any *pianissimo* upper E flat. The complete chord of C minor:  will rest in the mind. Now strike the very low C again, adding and repeating as often as you choose an upper F *pianissimo*:

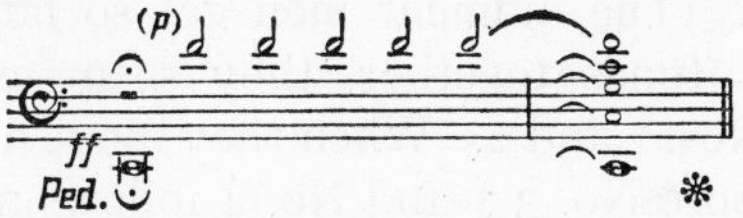

(p) ff Ped. *

The result will not be a chord-thought of F, of which C and F are suggestive (in the abstract) to any musician. But the principal harmonics overheard:  will play their habitual part, and, however many times the visitant, F, may be reiterated, the aggregate *thought* will be this:  and the generator C will prevail, undisturbed by our quiet F. It should be remembered here that if C threw off no G, C and F would sound as a perfect fourth, and stand on more equal terms, to be interpreted according to their mental context in every case.

This and all like experiments seem to prove that simple tonal ratios (*i.e.* intervals) do stand on their own ground, when overtones are unnoticeable; that, in actual experience, the lowest sound is apt to dominate the situation because it throws off harmonics of more natural strength than its upper companions, and that the first three of these are apt persistently to be heard. So it comes about that the interval of the perfect fifth, and, still more, of the twelfth from the lowest tone heard, has tended to become a dominating factor in all music, whether noticeably present or only heard among the faintly audible harmonics.

To sum up: we have in our musical "spectrum" (or nature's harmonic series):

1. A foundation of harmonic music audible in single tones of quality all the world over.

2. This is foundational precisely because it is audible, and only *so far as it is audible*.

3. The audibility and thinkability of the first three "spectral" tones are so universal that they tend everywhere to affect and command all musical thought. The moment men get so far as to sound different tones together, they seem everywhere to choose Nos. 1 and 2. When they move a stage further they choose No. 3; and No. 4 follows naturally.*

4. No. 5 of the series, though it has caused men to love and rest upon the major third in preference to the perfect fourth or minor third (or any interval other than the octave and fifth), has, in experience, been so faintly present as a harmonic to the ear that it has left room for the minor common chord also to become a foundational chord only second in importance to its major companion. The *octave and fifth are equally present and equally favourable to both thirds.*

5. The spectrum is for ever useful to the practical musician as a guide to the euphonious disposition of his harmonies.

6. The time has not come, but yet may come, when the seventh of the series will enter integrally into men's thoughts and enrich music without confusing it. When that time comes, it must bring at least eleven † entirely new ratios with it, and later many more would be involved. The fact that, without it, the natural octave is full to overflowing

* Of this Hucbald's Diaphony is perhaps the strongest example known.

† Those may easily be worked out at the keyboard from the "spectrum," thus: 2 : 7, 3 : 7, 4 : 7, 5 : 7, 6 : 7, 7 : 8, 7 : 9, 7 : 10, 7 : 12, 7 : 15, 7 : 16.

of related tones seems against even this addition to man's intelligent delight in tonal design, at least on this planet.*

7. The fact that only the first six components of the spectra and their upper multiples have so far been drawn upon, does not prevent approximation of our *available* assembly of tones to nature's unavailable subtleties of attunement (including approximation to Nos. 7, 11, 13, 17, and 19 of the series).

The reader is recommended to explore these latter tuneful approximations as Chopin did. In the following specimen design an attempt is made at approximation of the first sixteen natural harmonics, though only Nos. 1, 2, 4, 8, 16 are in perfect tune, Nos. 3, 5, 6, 9, 10, 12, 15 being tempered, and Nos. 7, 11, 13, 14 still less near nature. Yet the resultant thoughts are clear, and the sound of the thoughts all the pleasanter for lying so near those of nature herself. (See next page.)

* The eye's well-known physical disability to distinguish two or more points of light if very near each other may perhaps be matched by a like disability of the physical ear to distinguish very near-lying tonal "points."

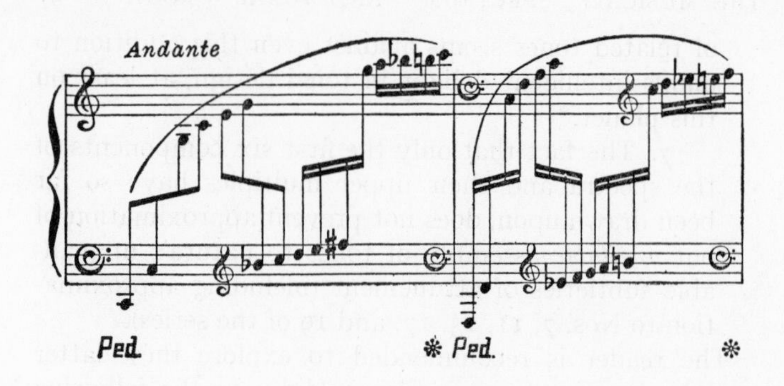
Andante
Ped.
✻ Ped.
✻

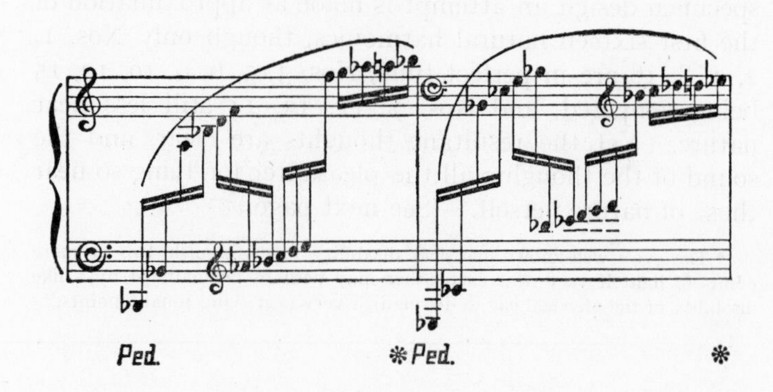
Ped.
✻ Ped.
✻

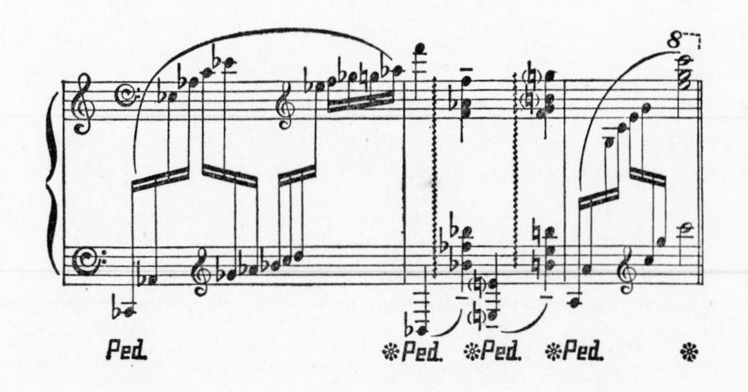
8
Ped.
✻ Ped.
✻ Ped.
✻ Ped.
✻

CHAPTER 11

SCALES AND A MELODIC SPIRAL

MUSICAL thinking is simplified by means of scales, especially to singers and all players of single-track instruments, such as flutes, oboes, trumpets, and the rest. As melodists we not only rely on scales, and linger naturally with our voices upon them, but may find as great an interest in them as an officer may find in parading the forces at his command. For a scale may well be defined as all the tonal relatings we conceive and wish to mobilize, standing on aural parade.

Many things conspire to suggest that all our scales must be, for practical purposes, paraded within the octave. This is not merely because, moving within a natural vocal compass, we find our voices normally in possession of about an octave's worth of good tones. Neither is it only because the octave is, to our minds, the most perfect and precise tonal coincidence in the universe. It is because of both these facts together, *plus* a third; for all natural melody moves from high to low *graduatedly*; and even if we were merely able to parade three tonal units, that is, if our mind had only the three most primitive relatings within its grasp (and therefore at its disposal), our natural use and thought would require them to lie *as near as possible in pitch.* Thus, for at least three good reasons in one, we take an octave for our mental parade ground:

Think now for a moment of a factory

hooter, whose full-power hoot is the uppermost of these two notes. Would it sing you a scale? No. But it would cover the whole tonal ground in a natural scoop from its vague deep beginnings to its normal note thus: Moving, as it were, infinitely scale-wise, it would pass at a given point into and through our parade ground. Only when it reaches its fixed note has it certitude. Before that point only your mind can give it any certitude or sense. It makes a singer's *portamento* with a vague vengeance; and you need a firm, musical mind made up, if you are to detect the octave below its upper D as it enters our mental parade ground. In passing you will realize that when singers behave physically like steam sirens, they also defy musical thought (I heard one do so, very disconcertingly, on the wireless, at the time of writing this).

Scales supply us not only with a paraded assembly of our tonal concepts (dealt with in Chapters 9 and 10), but with a melodist's catalogue of definite steps or natural stations in all his melodic journeys from the highly intense tones to the lowly restful ones of voice or instrument.

There are many methods of parading related tones—that is, of scale-making; all are interesting, and all lead us at last to something very like our present chromatic scale and stop there, *in a physical sense only* (for a natural reason that may appear later).

As specimens of conveniently useful scale-making, let us first imagine three beginners all entirely at home with the first three natural (so-called perfect) euphonies or intervals: and in possession of the resultant skeleton scheme:  One of them, we will suppose, has a special love for the sound of a major triad, and is always picking it out at various points on the key-

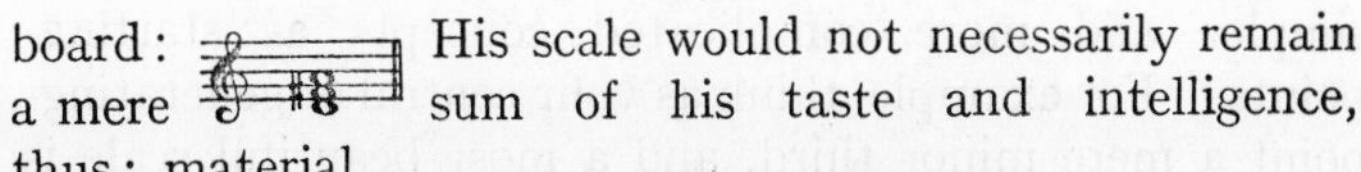

board: His scale would not necessarily remain a mere sum of his taste and intelligence, thus: material

resultant " parade " He would soon find his perfect bearings (fourth, fifth, and octave) from his favourite major third, F♯:

and a richer scale would arrive : Now imagine that our other two beginners had alighted with equal relish upon two other chords, and were respectively experimenting with and this last being the most adventurous. It is easy now to see that any such beginners as these three can use the following prescription or formula for scale-assembling :

> Strike any chord that you like to hear and wish to contemplate ; take your three perfect bearings from each of the notes of your chord in turn, and assemble the result within your octave.

Here are the two resultant scales which our second and third beginners would necessarily discover for themselves, according to prescription :

Resultant scales can be usefully evolved both from

simpler and more complicated concepts as starting-points. For example, think as your central or generating-point a mere minor third, and a most beautiful scale is yours :

Think, on the other hand, of a complex generator :

This last involves enharmonic thinking at one point, but is full of character and of fascinating melodic possibilities.

These are all vital scales though arbitrarily reached by wilful choice of chord-thoughts and logical evolution of consequent scales.

But, setting aside these specimen personal tastes, as we needs must in attempting to assess the material at music's disposal, let us try to derive scales quite impersonally in what seems the obvious order of nature. As from a single tonal concept : is derived a rudimentary or skeleton scale :

so, from the derivatives themselves, in turn, there may gradually be derived, and by precisely the same means, a fuller scale :

If, from the new derivatives, their own further derivatives be traced and added on parade, and if this be done systematically and consecutively, a natural seven-note scale first results, and then equally natural nine-note, eleven-note, and thirteen-note results will follow, thus:

Of this order of natural scale evolution there need, of course, be no end, except when our aural and mental use for them ceases. Scale material in music, like chord material, as we shall see later, is easily and plentifully available, far beyond our musical needs or aural comfort and convenience. The musical mind has limits beyond which it is practically futile for tonal or mathematical ingenuity to busy itself. And the physical ear has still more narrowing limits. For example, the mind quite outstrips the ear in its reception of the thirteen-note scale we have just reached. Experience shows the mind ready to revel in differentiating between A♭ and G♯, conceiving them in actual use as poles asunder; while the poor physical ear can only reply, "The difference * in sound is a teasing difference to me." Indeed, the mind, exacting the utmost service and deference from the ear, is by no means willing to rest at a thirteen-note scale. G♯ leads to D♯, which is again "poles asunder" from the existent E♭! In fact, it may truly be said that a seventeen-note scale is to-day a working reality to the musical mind, and a nineteen or even a twenty-one-note concept is not remote. Yet the present Bach twelve-note octave serves for them all! One does not need to be a musical pundit to find oneself, while in the key of C, in imperative need of an E♯:

It is impossible to imagine that the third note of the above melody is an F♮ by nature! Similarly B♮ will, on occasion, have to be spelt as C♭ for the truth's sake, even in a mind anchored to C the whole time. So it happens that, as the musical mind grows gradually harmonically rich, even the most serviceable physical ear must remain a comparative pauper. But let us return

* Any student of this important gateway of enharmonics would find it helpful to seek access to a piano or organ factory and persuade a tuner to let him study these two chords with the chromatic and diatonic semitone below A and above G carefully differentiated:

for a moment or two to consideration of the material scales as they actually exist on the keyboard and in general use.

As wonderful luck would have it (we can view it as nothing else), this scale-deriving process has physically worked all in favour of the ear, the voice, the melodist—up to the eleven-note position. Our universal octave gaped wide, and was filled gradually, logically, and most luckily. For, as it happened, every thought of euphonious delight to the mind, point by point, brought convenient melodic stations into the octave system. As the stations appeared they were not only welcome as well-related points of call, but melodically and vocally welcome too, as recognizable and conveniently equable division-points. Of course, the distances between the notes grew smaller as the number of thought-stations increased. But from the five-note stage to the eleven-note stage (see page 103) the course was pegged out fairly equally, in each case (as it happens) in but *two* sizes of intervals, first in tones and minor thirds, and then in tones and semitones. No wonder that the five-note scale proved melodically acceptable for beauty, simplicity, and practicability all the world over, and little wonder that it looms so large in modern music. The next two natural derivatives to arrive merely filled the minor third gaps; and this meant that a mingling of tones and semitones appeared. By the same logical and euphonious method of deriving additional thought-stations, nine notes came; then eleven notes—and still no clash, the stations becoming more equidistant everywhere, right up to the momentous arrival of the twelfth and thirteenth derivatives. Now, had these last proved to be an exact quarter of a tone apart, it is easy to imagine how different the future of our music might, indeed must, have been, especially if there were good prospect of training the normal human ear to discern two sounds lying only a quarter of a tone apart with tolerable ease. But that was not to be ; and it seems amazingly fortunate that the mind's natural way of increasing its tonal resources and delights within the octave along this unforced and almost unconscious line of seeking and enjoying the perfect ratios, should lead it ultimately by its twelfth and thirteenth step to a tonal spot in the octave which not only just filled the only remaining gap of a tone between stations, but did it so nearly coincidentally that a sound lying somewhere between the two could pass for either, even to a sensitive genius like Bach!

The following fancy may, at this point, help the reader. Let him imagine that the whimsically-minded Mayor of a certain city is asked by inhabitants, dissatisfied with having to light themselves along a certain unlighted causeway, to erect lamps at fixed points. Desiring a row of detached villas along this avenue, as near to each other as was practicable, it happened that eleven equi-distant houses were put up. There were two traditional light-points at the extreme ends.* But an avenue of lights at fixed points is desired by all. The Mayor decides to erect two to begin with. The citizens living at villas Nos. 4 and 8 hear this with joy, and fully expect the first two lamps to be fixed opposite their front-doors. The dots in the following diagram correspond with the front-doors of the villas :

But the Mayor has a mystical measuring-rod capable of measuring two fixed distances,† for the use of which he declares he has beautiful reasons. The inhabitants never could conceive why he placed the first two lamps nearly but not quite opposite the front-doors of Nos. 5 and 7 :

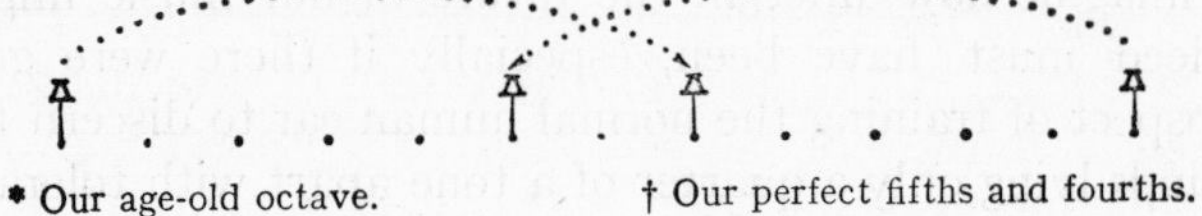

* Our age-old octave. † Our perfect fifths and fourths.

Villas 2 and 3, 9 and 10, however, now hoped that they would all share the benefit of the next two lamps. But the Mayor used his measuring-rod again, this time from the two centre lamps outwards, with the result that the new lamps fell almost exactly opposite the front-doors of Nos. 2 and 10:

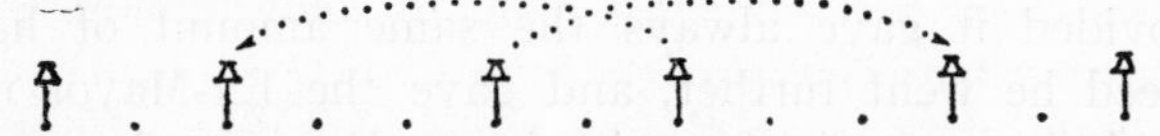

"Never," said the Mayor, "can I abandon my unerring measuring-rod, but I'll continue to do my best for you all." So the gaps along the avenue became gradually filled in thus—never quite opposite any of the front-doors:

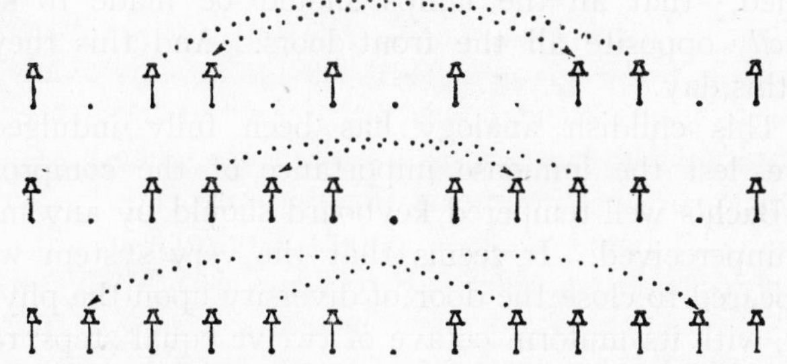

Adhering stedfastly to his refusal to put up a centre lamp, the mystical Mayor finally draws upon himself much ridicule by placing two, one immediately on either side of the central front-door, as closely together as possible:

The irritated citizens now exclaim with Browning, "Our Mayor's a noddy!" They argue, reasonably, "If we are to have fourteen lamps, at least let him place the last two *suitably*. They make a confusing blur of light; and even if they were better spaced, the symmetry of the avenue is still marred, and the arrangement silly!"

But here arises a new authority, whose wise comprehension overpowers the Mayor. His name is Johann Sebastian Bach. He decrees that one central lamp must do duty for the two. But in strange deference to the ex-Mayor's measuring-rod, he conceded that this centre-lamp should have a hidden twin-burner arrangement (provided it gave always the same amount of light). Indeed he went further, and gave the Ex-Mayor more twin-burners, beginning with lamps Nos. 1 and 11. For mystical reasons, lamps Nos. 5 and 7 were the last to be given twin-burners. "And," said Bach to the knowing citizens, "you can imagine them *single* or *twin*, exactly as you are minded." His momentous order was then issued,—that all the lamps should be made to stand *exactly* opposite all the front-doors. And this they do to this day.

This childish analogy has been fully indulged in here, lest the immense importance of the compromise of Bach's well-tempered keyboard should by any means go unperceived. It seems that the very system which appeared to close the door of diversity upon the physical ear, with its uniform octave of twelve equal steps, really opened it for ever to the musical mind. An infinite variety of resultant scales awaits us, capable of vastly greater use in some enhanced civilization down the ages, by reason of two things: 1. The endlessness of enharmonic thought, now made open to all; 2. The fortunate equidistance of representative semitonic stations as they have assembled themselves on the present tonal map.

Thousands of years hence, some little child, catching sight of a rainbow, will still exclaim to its mother, in whatever is the language of that day: "Look, Mummy, at the pretty rainbow!" And is it credible that in that age, the same child, chancing to hear a perfect chord of the harmonic series, perhaps over some super-wireless set, will not similarly derive and express tonal delight? This chord: in every pitch, at every point of the tonal compass, stands immutable; and that being so, the series of derived scales here summarized, gives full play to the melodist, at all stages of gift and attainment.

Having gained a position from which we may view Bach's twelve-note chromatic scale, or ladder of semitones, as the permanent boon it seems to be, as well as the basis of to-day's music, it will be helpful to picture it as a spiral of steps curving up some tonal tower of the mind (see next page). This gives us a good illustration, for the idea of rising sound is naturally and inherently akin to the idea of rising ground. We speak of a high wind, not because it is high in the heavens, but because it is high in the scale of velocity; thus, a high note suggests rise of energy and vibrational velocity (see page 60).

In conclusion it is suggested, especially to beginners, that it is good practice to construct for oneself smaller working scales within the compass of the fifth or fourth. Any one may share to-day with the Greeks of old the advantage of working in *tetrachords*, as, *e.g.*:

Again, working within the perfect fifth, a useful first scale-making step may be to measure the perfect fourth (upwards or downwards) from the outside tones, thus:

This can then be filled in at pleasure with minor or major thirds from the lowest or highest note, either or both:

Such a scale may be extended thus:

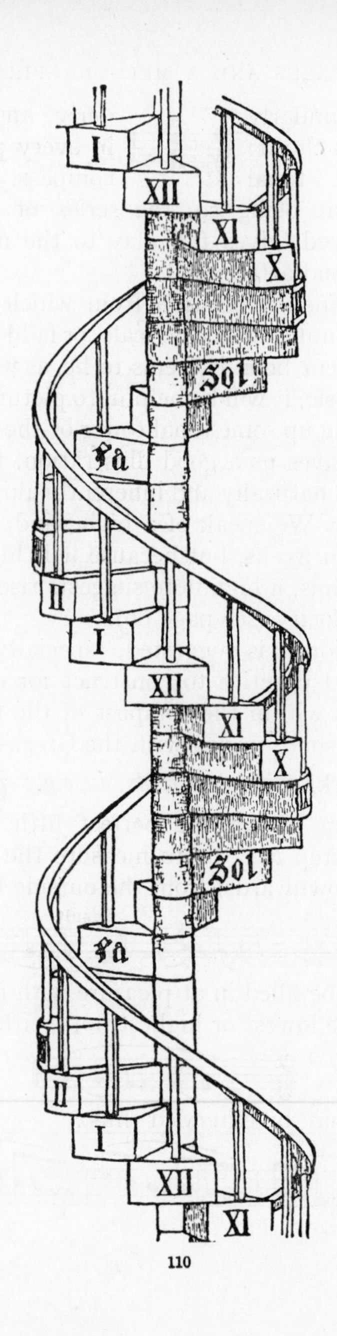

I
XII
XI
X
Sol
Fa
II
I
XII
XI
X
Sol
Fa
II
I
XII
XI

CHAPTER 12

CHORDS

WE pass now from the stock material of *notes in succession* to that of *notes in combination*, known as *chords*. Chords may first impress the ear pleasantly as mere hues, varied tints, colours, or tone-qualities. But a chord is not significant to the musical mind till it becomes a distinguishable unit of thought, differing from other chords or units of thought as a word differs from other words. Let us look closely into this.

If you play any note, D:  and then, perhaps a quarter of an hour later in the street, you chance to hear any note, G:  it does not follow that you will relate the two tones sensibly and reasonably in your mind as a *melodic interval*. It is far from likely. But if between-whiles all was silent, and you possessed a highly sensitized and retentive memory, you might do so. Two such notes sounded within a second or two of each other:  though disjointed, might not only make sense in your mind, but even suggest some recollected thought of other music heard. If they came closer:  and if you gave the second note a stronger tone than the first:  it can well be imagined that they would quicken association and expectation as syllables or words might, and some one listening might exclaim, "I thought you

were going to play 'Rule, Britannia!'" But now, sound the two tones nearer and nearer together, so that they are actually overlapping: 
(*i.e.* in ever more rapid arpeggios :

there comes at last a point where they are conceived, not as a mere interval any longer, but as a two-note chord : there happens the tiny mental miracle which was depicted in Chapter 10. To a musical mind, in the thing called a chord, two experiences are not merely related, but *merged into a new experience.* In diagrammatic form we may thus distinguish the mere *interval,* two notes juxtaposited and beginning simultaneously : from the actual musical experience of a chord—*i.e.* the vital experience of two forces as one :

In this chapter, then, we turn from all thoughts of melodic intervals, scales, and the melodic spiral to think only *chords*—*i.e.* emergent, harmonic forms ; and in them to anticipate a different and a novel joy.

Our crude analogues of straight lines and curves are merely used to suggest how vital is the difference to the mind between a first *melody-concept* and a succeeding *harmony-concept* ; it would seem deeper far than the mere difference between two lines at a pleasing angle, and a curve. At this point we can only each try to realize for ourselves the profundity and uniqueness of chord-thoughts as an experience of the listening mind, and concentrate upon them.

1. Two-note Chords

Now a two-note chord is the more dynamic name for any *harmonic* interval—*i.e.* when any two notes are struck simultaneously and perceived as two-in-one in the mind of the listener. (The unhappy word *interval* should only be used to imply the reckonable distance between two tones conceived separately though heard connectedly. It is as inadequate a name for a two-note chord, as it would be inadequate to estimate the inmost relationship of father to son by the difference in their height!)

Two-note chords are the first and greatest help to harmonic thinking, and should be sounded and studied often, by all readers, till the ear becomes familiar with their distinctive significances.*

The acutest and most momentous distinctions (or differences in harmonic significance) in all music up to the present, seem traceable to the differences between three specific two-note chords that are in perpetual use. Go to the keyboard and sound these three two-note chords † in succession, several times; before reading further, carefully note the impressions (if any) which they severally make upon your mind:

Ped. ❋ Ped. ❋ Ped. ❋

Now set in catalogue order *all* the two-note chords found in Bach's tempered scale, only using the one enharmonicism (F♯ and G♭) which arose naturally in the thirteen-note chromatic scale:

We now may hear that our three chords first singled out are the central three of eleven possibles. They are also, incidentally, those in which the component tones are in every

* Harmonic listeners can hardly forbear to think two-note chords when intervals are heard prominently, and ultimately to hear all melody, not only, as we say, melodiously, but harmoniously.

† To marshal our chords it is well to sound and spell all of them standing in close position within an octave, as we did in the case of scales.

case nearly *equidistant.* Indeed, if we speak only of physical measurements, the middle one now divides the octave into two equal intervals, measuring six tempered semitones; but the mind's ear (so far as the writer can judge from experience and conversation with others) always finds this interval when conceived as an augmented fourth (C to F♯) a thought less than the same distance conceived as a diminished fifth (C to G♭); though in fact, physically speaking, one and the same note on the keyboard does duty for two thoughts that, in mental effect, are (as already suggested) poles asunder.

In pondering over these, our three chief two-note chords, it may help us to reflect that, when smartly struck, their actual sound to the ear will be something like this:

But it is not enough for the reader to accept this statement without question, nor without personal verification. Listeners need, by experiment, personally to experience their sounds. And it is often extraordinarily difficult to persuade one's ear to hear sounds one is not predisposed to hear. Some will find it quite amusingly hard at first, and will listen for spectral or phantom notes, believing as little in them as in tonal ghosts! Also some sensitive listeners may be handicapped by hearing the weird, buzzing, resultant tones *below* all the notes, and so missing the faint tones of the "spectrum." For this reason it is necessary to play such tricks as the following upon oneself, in order to focus the ear upon the faint harmonics: having struck the generators hard, (*a*) lean to the right of your keyboard; (*b*) look up at the ceiling, first having glanced at the ivory of the note you expect to hear; (*c*) pretend to listen as it were in mid-air for some fairy Peter Pan pipe, *pianissimo.* In time, some such homely trick will bring your ear into position, and you will be astonished to find, for instance, how clearly this note sounds (played by Peter!): when your notes: are smartly rapped out and your listening is, at last, directed with skill. Try it many, many times.

A word as to the resultant or combinational tones referred to a moment back; for these have a strong bearing on our general pursuit of chords. This time, sound your previous three chords again, and play another triple trick upon yourself: (*a*) listen on the *left* of your keyboard; (*b*) look under the piano; (*c*) expect to hear some phantom old man humming a note in an uncertain buzzing manner to himself. You may then get a good aural focus, and, with luck, hear something like this:

There may be other vague suggestions of actual sounds to be heard by very sensitive ears. But it is likely that, with diligent practice of this tricky ear-directing kind, and after close and repeated listening, most readers will have the reward of detecting both Peter's Pipe and the ghostly humming notes, and thus of realizing for themselves some of the natural forces which give chords their distinctive significances—to ear first, and mind after, in all harmonic art. How these significances tell upon us in real music will concern us in Parts 3 and 4 of this book. Here we have carefully to amass and catalogue our mere material; we are to look our list of chords in the face, as it were, scanning every one at leisure, till our ears either pass them into our vocabulary of available chords, or till we have to turn away from them as at present beyond us, momentarily meaningless, perhaps indistinguishable from each other, and even ugly. There will still be abundance of beautiful music awaiting us, even with the most limited vocabulary of chords.

PRELIMINARY CHORD LIST.—Here, for practical purposes, may be given a selected list of five out of the eleven possible two-note chords, as being of special practical use :

There are two reasons for which these five only are chosen to head our present working list of twenty-nine chords all told. These reasons will become apparent as we proceed.

There seems one thing to be remembered here, before passing on. It is dangerously useless to move forward to three- or four-note chords before the two-note chords have yielded their full significance and treasure ; for the arrival of but one more note (as when a third person enters a room) means the advent of *two* more relationships ; similarly, the arrival of two more notes means *five* more relationships ! The ear of the music lover to-day is so accustomed to four-part hearing that it is the more urgent to get back to these primal two-part significances. For our familiar four-note chords were coined in a splendid mint long ago ; they have been current ever since, and seem, alas ! to have become much defaced in casual public currency.

2. THREE-NOTE CHORDS

A little calculation will show that as there lie within the Bach equally-divided octave eleven two-note chords, the total number of three-note chords is fifty-five. All are possible; but I do not propose to give the full table here, partly because it will trouble the reader's eye with a needlessly dazzling array, but still more because, when two or more of the three component tones lie within a semitone of each other, as, *e.g.*, here:  they scarcely ever qualify for practical use as tonal clusters or chords. They are too ear-defying. Even chords whose notes lie clustered at least whole tones from each other:  have only quite recently passed into currency; for music is still in the making every day.* It is proposed therefore, for practical purposes, to tabulate of the fifty-five possibles, only those three-note chords *of which no component stands closer than a major second to any other*, and those only in one spelling.† Here they are:

CHORD LIST A.—All possible three-note chords, of which no two lie nearer than a major second.

* With a little trouble any reader will be able to make an exhaustive list of all the soundings there are from two-note to eleven-note chords (spread as arpeggios, or clean-cut as deliberate scales if the ear becomes too baffled). In experimenting, let all examples lie within the octave. Remember Mozart's scathing reproof, already quoted, of those who spoke of an "augmented octave." (See page 87.) Here, for checking purposes, are the exact numbers of all possible soundings, including all inversions of all chords from the simple two-note chord to the whole chromatic scale:

Two-note possibilities 11, three-note 55, four-note 165, five-note 330, six-note 462, seven-note 462, eight-note 330, nine-note 165, ten-note 55, eleven-note 11, twelve-note 1. The following is a more useful list to the musician. It is the list of all possible chords *without* their inversions. Thus, in this shorter list, the dominant seventh counts as 1 (for all positions of its component tones) and not as 4 (for its root-position and three inversions):

Two-note chords 6, three-note chords 19, four-note 43, five-note 66, six-note 80, seven-note 66, eight-note 43, nine-note 19, ten-note 6, eleven- and twelve-note, 1 each. Thus the total of all soundings in every inversion is 2,047; total of all chords and cluster-concepts, 350.

† By this is meant that though:  is a different thought from  they are the same sound in a tempered scale, and only one version of that same sound is given.

But a much more practical list to the musician is the following selection of 10 of the above total of 28, since the remaining 18 are but inversions of these to be used at pleasure:

CHORD LIST B.—Selection of the three-note chords which, with their inversions, afford examples of all the above soundings.

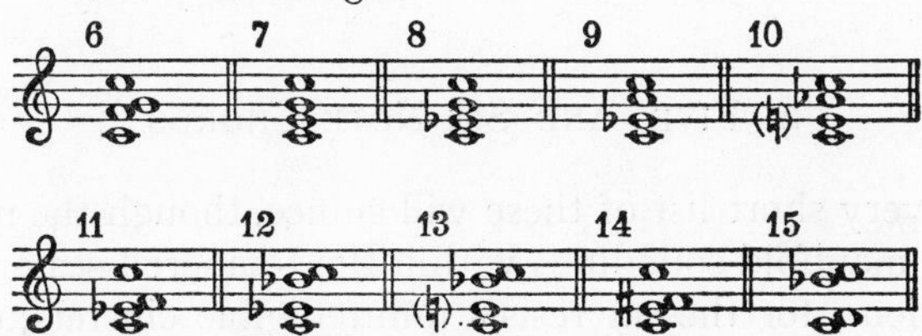

3. FOUR-NOTE CHORDS

Of the whole list of 165 possible four-note clusters, the majority would confuse the acutest ear in its most trained state. Of the 43 possible chord-concepts (mentioned in the footnote to page 117), there are again 10 which concern us intimately for the same practical reasons which made the 10 three-note chords important:

CHORD LIST C.—Selection of *ten* four-note chords which, with their inversions, afford examples of all four-note soundings, in which no notes lie nearer than a major second.

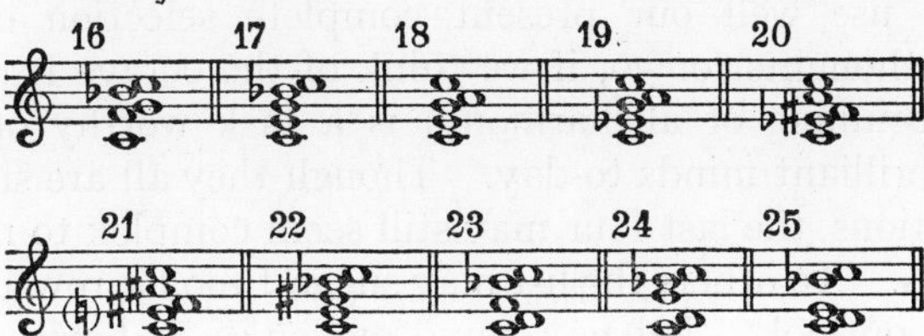

It will be seen that all the classical favourites are here, and that there remain several distinctive chords which have, so far, scarcely been explored by any of the classical thinkers in chords. It should again be noted that no attempt has been made to indicate enharmonic variants of the very same soundings; for example, chord 22 (was it not a favourite of César Franck ?) can be a totally different concept if enharmonically changed to :

4. Five- and Six-Note Chords

A very short list of these will suffice, though the name of the manifold soundings within the tempered scale may be legion ; for the ear resists unintelligible clusters, even of intelligible tones. Indeed, there is but one six-note sounding (out of the possible 80, or, with all permutations, 462) which actually eludes the clash of semitones within itself.

Chord List D.—Selection of three five-note chords which, with their inversions, afford examples of all five-note soundings in which no two notes lie nearer than a major second, together with the only six-note chord fulfilling the same condition.

To use well our present complete selection of 29 chord-thoughts (or 30, if we think of the octave itself as the beginning of all harmony) is a task worthy of the most brilliant minds to-day. Though they all are simple formations, the last four may still seem complex to many readers. To others the list may suggest too narrow a harmonic outlook. Let us remind ourselves that with care (and standing in open order) chord-cluster can be added to chord-cluster. till all the notes of the chromatic scale (yes, even with enharmonic duplications thrown in !) may be heard in one compound chord simultaneously.

Certainly, the material here summarized affords men an inexhaustible supply for future Sonata music. Nothing, perhaps, will exemplify this more vividly than to think what transmutations of thought await us in enharmonic changes of any or of all our 30 chord-thoughts ! Even the simple octave itself (as we have already seen), at a touch of the musical mind, may transmute, thus:  And our latest chord (the whole-tone chord) has more implications enharmonically than we can easily think or convey. Try this very quietly :

To sum up. In our four chief scale formations—pentatonic, diatonic, tempered chromatic, enharmonic ; and in our 30 chord-thoughts, from  to  we have material far beyond Bach's usage, yet all lying implicitly within his well-tempered scale, awaiting ever new and joyous use by all music lovers who desire to follow up his great labours, and who do not incline to blame Schumann for too extravagant homage when he said that music owes as great a debt to that one devout and indefatigable mind, as Christianity itself owes to its Founder.

CHAPTER 13

METRICAL UNITS

"There is a harmony in all matter as well as in all spirit. Matter becomes, as it were, the medium of an artist, in which his spirit is perfectly expressed. The whole universe is like . . . the notes of a musician. . . ."

CLUTTON BROCK.

WHAT is the natural metrical material upon which music-makers work? In addition to the more uniquely musical material of tonal *ratios*, *scales*, *chords*, etc. (dealt with in Chapters 9 to 12), may there be found, ready to hand, metres as varied, as universally intelligible and acceptably logical in their own way, to serve the constructive requirements of the musical mind on that which we have called our Canvas of Time?

We know that the disposal of musical fantasy of every kind is inevitably made upon our Time-area. But to suggest metrical units, or measured patterns in time, for the flights of the free-born musician, seems rather like suggesting mathematical restrictions to a bird in flight in the heavens. But let us here inquire together into possibilities.

We have already realized that, free as the composer may be, he must be *intelligibly* so to his confrères, performers and listeners alike, if they are to collaborate in creatively responsive fashion—as indeed they must. We also know that, just as inspired poets—Dante, Milton, Bridges—manifest their most intelligible freedom within agreed metres of childlike simplicity, reaching the vast number of their listeners the more surely by this very means, so composers, performers, and listeners stand to gain unitedly by knowledgeable use of the time-field in their own world of music. If this be so, we need but mention the rudimentary "first order" of metres, or measures—that in which various laps, or lengths, of equal pulses are balanced with each other into couplets or double couplets to serve as agreed framework for a melody. For example:

To hum the tune called "Stuttgart" to this metrical pattern is to realize that such metres can be cut to any size for any purpose. We add one specimen of a nursery rhyme to show the adaptation of the *length* of lap to the baby mind:

A child of five will delight to make up its little tunes to such a metrical pattern. This parvanimity is unfit for grown-up use. Metres more magnanimous and spacious, with far longer laps, are desirable.

The work of the inquirer into metrical material for musical purposes starts in earnest in the region where shorts and longs combine in obedience to happy ingenuity. It is not enough to beat out for ever equal time-throbs in a measured scheme of equal lengths and speeds. We require more scope, more thought than that, more design—interesting metrical schemes and patterns for musical purposes. And, in truth, an unlimited possible array lies once more at hand. All we want, however, is a *limited* array; for music is not metre; and even if it were, music and metre are not mathematics: all three can, however, be mutually serviceable to each other.

Let us examine a few of the possible metrical units of shorts and longs with two or more note-values.

There exist only two ways of making two-note units of two-note values. Expressed arbitrarily in crotchets and quavers, they are:

3/8 | ♩ ♪ | ♩ ♪ | ♩ ♪ | *etc.*
3/8 | ♪ ♩ | ♪ ♩ | ♪ ♩ | *etc.*

But, of course, even at this threshold of calculated possibilities, the relative value of the two lengths of notes may be infinitely varied. Into that we need not enter further than to give one practical example:

2/4 | ♪ ♩. | ♪ ♩. | *etc.*
2/4 | ♩. ♪ | ♩. ♪ | *etc.*

The reader can follow up all practical varieties of the same units at pleasure.

There are six *three-note* metrical units with two-note values. Again given in mere crotchets and quavers, these are:

4/4 | ♩ ♩ 𝅗𝅥 | ♩ ♩ 𝅗𝅥 ‖ *etc.*
4/4 | ♩ 𝅗𝅥 ♩ | ♩ 𝅗𝅥 ♩ ‖ *etc.*
4/4 | 𝅗𝅥 ♩ ♩ | 𝅗𝅥 ♩ ♩ ‖ *etc.*

5/4 | 𝅗𝅥 𝅗𝅥 ♩ | 𝅗𝅥 𝅗𝅥 ♩ | 𝅗𝅥 𝅗𝅥 ♩ ‖ *etc.*
5/4 | 𝅗𝅥 ♩ 𝅗𝅥 | 𝅗𝅥 ♩ 𝅗𝅥 | 𝅗𝅥 ♩ 𝅗𝅥 ‖ *etc.*
5/4 | ♩ 𝅗𝅥 𝅗𝅥 | ♩ 𝅗𝅥 𝅗𝅥 | ♩ 𝅗𝅥 𝅗𝅥 ‖ *etc.*

These, in their turn, can, of course, vary the relative note-values at will, without essentially changing the nature of the metrical units. But three-note units might also have three different note-values ! This would give us just six more kinds of metrical units, of which these are worthy specimens :

Beethoven made a four-note rhythmic unit resound through the world in the Fifth Symphony :

We dare not stay here to catalogue all the 74 possible *four-note* units, with two-, three-, or four-note values successively. Still less must we try to set down the 270 five-note units, of which the following are haphazard specimens :

It would be well if the reader were to take the above, and a few others of his own devisal, and straightway melodize upon them in order to grasp the vast metrical range available, thus :

and in any number of other ways and moods.

We dare not, however, stop short here in this brief summary of metrical units available for musical purposes. A composer, working upon his Time-canvas, may be as joyously concerned in his metrical as in his melodic or harmonic experiences. He is not one kind of creature melodically and another metrically. Can it be that the fundamental delight (see Chapter 9) in the manifestation of two or more familiar movements applies here also? Can we at least begin here to explore the musician's metrical material from this, the dynamic, rather than the measured or arithmetical standpoint? Could Beethoven have been in all else free, and in this one (metrical) regard a mere calculator at, for example, such a moment as the opening bars of the *Allegretto* of the Seventh Symphony already quoted on page 70?

This leads us to a different, more lively, and fascinating line of inquiry which the reader may well prefer, and along which we may possibly find ourselves nearer the musical truth. For wonderful *metrical units*—we must almost certainly seek the greater adjective here, and name them *rhythmical units heard in time*—may emerge in the following way.

First imagine a hundred different sized clocks set ticking in the same room: result, amusing confusion, defying disentanglement, and suggesting no intelligible rhythmic design. But now set three related clock-times ticking in this order:

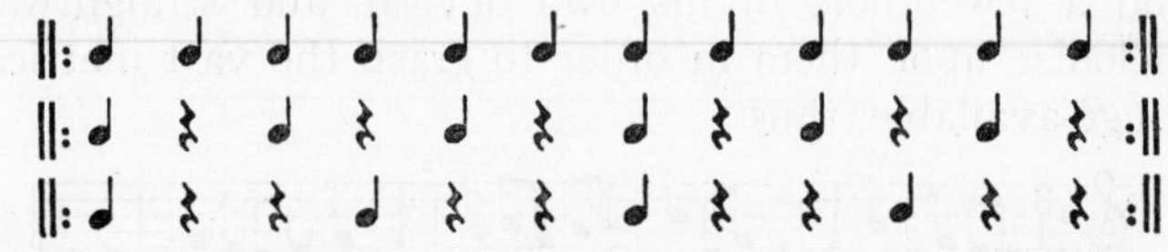

Do not expect your mind to have an interest in any of

these three units of speed, more than the momentary interest you felt in the straight-line record of a single motion in Chapter 9, page 77. For here, obviously, is another kind of record of a single kind of motion. But now conceive them as unified. Add them together, not on the page, but in creative experience. You will find the result of adding Nos. 2 and 3 together will sound thus:

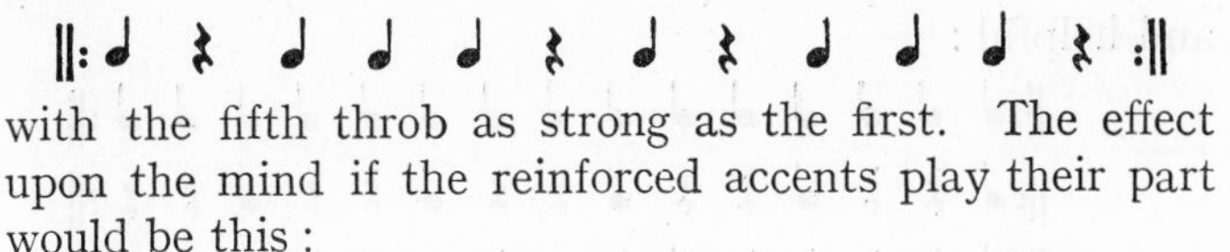

with the fifth throb as strong as the first. The effect upon the mind if the reinforced accents play their part would be this:

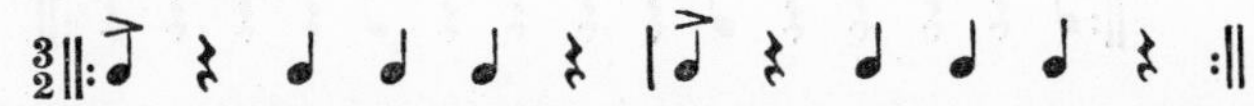

or, if the reinforced beats had not only accents but the power of a bell to sustain its note, the result would sound:

And if the chief notes be suffused into *sostenuto* instead of *strength,* the total result would sound:

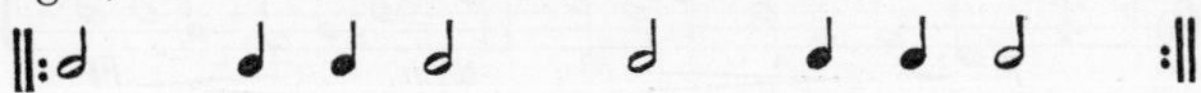

Let us translate this at pleasure into a metrical thought, and give it a tag of words to sing to ourselves:

Look now at Beethoven's metrical unit named above:

Is it possible that along this second line of inquiry we shall alight upon something nearer the unconscious, unaccountable glory of such music when the whole mind is given to it—on both sides of the equation, composer's and listener's, Beethoven's and ours ?

In conclusion of this general review of material, and as a mere specimen of the results of recording two or more energies in the metrical world, we hope the reader may find the following less obvious example, combining the less usual primes (of threes and fives), stimulating and helpful :

of which a musical application might well be :

Of such there is no end. The metrical material on our musical Time-canvas is possibly as inexhaustible as all our other materials discussed in this our Part 2, of which we now together take farewell for more lively fields of inquiry.

PART 3

THE MIND IN ACTION

"... Thoughts that voluntary move
Harmonious numbers. . . ."

MILTON.

CHAPTER 14

PHRASING

MUSIC begins its appeal to the ear, one may suppose, when any tone is heard and contemplated for pleasure. "Listen," says a nurse even to a tiny child, "to the pretty music!" To the mind, however, music, as we have seen, begins its appeal when two or more such tones are impelled into relation. The ear hears tones for pleasure; the mind is quickened to relate them for love. If only two tones are thus purposely related, the mind is in action; and the result is a musical Phrase. That composer who leads us to set the highest value upon the simplest of such phrases, is he to whom clearly we are the most indebted.

It will readily be seen that the musical mind in action is not concerned with such thoughts as those treated in Parts 1 and 2 of our inquiries. Watching a finely played game of tennis at Wimbledon, and hearing a finely composed Symphony in Queen's Hall are thus far alike, that in both we are absorbed in the *deed*—in master-strokes, whether of composer or player. Neither they nor we reflect, while in action, upon the nature of the action, or the nature of our interest in it, still less upon the material at our service. Art is made manifest in Act, whether to actor or observer, musician or music lover, player or spectator. "I deliver this my act and deed," unconsciously says Art. So music, as we know it, consists of a series of tonal strokes finely related; and such musical deeds of the mind, once achieved, may be recalled to rejoice the mind again and again. But music is only a deed when wrought into tones. Even though a man becomes so skilled and experienced as to catch the thrill of a new Symphony by merely reading it in silence undisturbed by performance, it is still the series of tonal deeds heard inwardly that thrill him. Conversely, though mental response be so slow that the physical ear must be strongly stimulated and insistently reminded of all the sounds, before the music is even mentally registered, still it is the mind alone which is able at last to say, " Behold, it was very good."

Turn back for a moment to the analogy of tennis, or any highly skilled game. As we watch men play, we may appreciate a single stroke, the skill and mastery of it, its bearing on the game as a whole. In a Symphony we watch the happening phrase in the same way, admiring its skill, freedom, and aptitude, and contemplating its bearing on the Symphony as a whole.

But here note that, though it is possible to admire, in a lesser way, a single superb stroke at Wimbledon, and a single superb phrase at Queen's Hall, with little knowledge of the whole aim of either "game," our admiration is definitely enhanced by fullest awareness of the "rules" exactly as the artist's skill is enhanced by masterly observance of them. Further than this, audience and artist must ultimately know the rules so thoroughly as to be able to forget them, in the rapture of stroke after stroke, game after game, and—Set. Phrase after phrase, movement after movement, and—Symphony.

Here, however, we must beware of our analogy. For rules of Sport and rules of Art are clearly different in kind. Eight times eight make sixty-four in perpetuity; squares on chess-boards are unchangingly 8 by 8; during centuries, this rigid basis and a few simple by-laws of play in the game of chess have remained adequate. Similarly, $2 \times 2 = 4$; and four courts remain the fitting and unchanging basis for tennis, within which players of genius may show new and dazzling strokes from age to age. Yes, and to some extent we shall see (in Part 4) likenesses between these and the rules of Western music. Certain simple musical bases continue from generation to generation, with gain to listeners and no apparent detriment to the genius of the most wonderful composers. To parody Lovelace, Beethoven might truly have said :

> " Four bars do not a prison make,
> Nor double bars a cage."

For the musical master-stroke lies within the restricting line. Take away the delimiting line, and who will know the mastery ? Yet the composer's attitude to Rule is profoundly different from that of the champion tennis player. In the latter case the rules were neither made, nor are they improved upon, by players. But the rules of music in this or any age are both framed and maintained at the will of the creative musician ; and whatever rule or change of rule can give freer play and finer mastery, that he instantly takes for his own. In music, rules (as Haydn once said) are " all my very humble and obedient servants." They are therefore, of course, not less but more binding in action ; for they are things made for love, kept for love, broken for love, remade for love, and kept for love again. Art, singularly enough, seems to know no other way, even though its limitless mastery be still only made manifest through limits set and agreed. So true does this prove in music that, when rule seems most strictly to prevail (as, for example, in Bach's Fugue known as the " Saints in Glory "), it can most truly be said, this time with Lovelace unparaphrased :

> " Angels alone that soar above
> Enjoy such liberty."

And to begin to understand this liberty we shall, in the writer's belief, need to study lovingly that part of music called Phrasing.

There is, as we contemplate it, no more important thing than this in music. A musical phrase, in certain vital ways, corresponds to a verbal phrase in conversation, poetry, literature of all kinds. It is, as already suggested, the musician's stroke. It is his unit of impulse, of intention, of idea, of meaning. It is the primary unit of all music in action. Some readers may indeed feel that they get nearest to the first significance of a phrase if they think of it as a breath of the creative mind. For it is in phrasing that music lives and breathes. Phrases are symptoms of creative Being. In order to see the truth of this, let us set going the dullest, most small-minded order of tune we can think of :

What happened at the fourth phrase ? Play it a couple of times. Was it not like a small protest of the mind, induced by the " nothing doing " style of the poor little first three phrases ? Let us follow forward in imagination the tune-forming impulse, as it develops freedom in the next lap :

Play these two four-bar sections as one eight-bar section. The melodist's mind has obviously taken a rather deeper " draught of fresh air " at his fifth phrase ; but apparently he spent himself by the small extra effort, for the melodic phrases grow short and complacent, and droop. Now, one of two things could have happened. Either he could have refused to subside quite so ignominiously, and could have aspired to surpass all previous impulse,

or he could subside into faintly recollected pleasures,

suggesting a mind musically short in the wind; with the result that the tune becomes trite, peters out, and makes very poor company. The reader may, profitably, analyse a hundred or so popular melodies from this angle, watching each tune's melodic respiration as it were, and studying the phrase-forming mind in this closely human way.

It may then be well to alternate this method with another, and to take tunes to pieces in order to find their framework—their main lines of impulse. Take, for example, the first phrase of a very familiar tune:

Take the tune "down" and examine its parts. This is done by deducting rhythmic shapes and all ornamentation, leaving none but essential notes, which may generally be detected only by the prominence given them.* These, for example : are very clear framework notes in this case. But what are the essentials after that? We can at least be certain of the last note : Yet we do not feel that this, taken as a whole, is a true account of the main lines of impulse. It is not a complete framework, for the leap down to G has given that note new prominence, and it must be included in the mental frame : Moreover, the upper D remains in our minds, having been quitted by leap : So the true nature of this phrase might be depicted by a sort of X-ray process, which will show its bones somewhat as follows :

Leaving nothing but the bones, we hear two distinct lines of thought emerge :

This is a particularly useful line of analysis for the student of phrases. As we shall quickly find in experience, and in the succeeding stages of this inquiry, only baby-tunes, jingles, and rhymes coming, as it were, from the nursery of music, behave in the clean-cut way of our first illustration (see page 134), in which phrase after phrase, another and then another, succeed each other, lightly strung together to make a tune. These make rudimentary music. They are charming, childlike, melodic card-houses, delightful for the children, palpably childish

* Outlying notes—low or high—are made prominent; so are notes taken by leap on an accent; so are notes that are repeated. The reader will detect other methods of giving prominence suggested by or arising from these.

when they are displayed, as sometimes, with all the pomp of full orchestral heavily-costumed processions. The student will quickly find, in all great-range music, far maturer melody showing continuity in many-stranded phrases, of a kind which requires an altogether subtler appreciation and analysis ; and it is here that the X-ray mental photograph of phrases proves useful. Often it will reveal a bare interval or two as the very basis of a long melody, as in Handel's moving aria, "Total Eclipse," from *Samson* :

Or again, the X-ray truth about Bach's final treble entry in the "Saints in Glory" Fugue lies clearly in the prolonged "dying fall" :

Here it is by the three eloquent interruptions in the ordained fall that it is made unforgettably real, and, as we find it, true to experience. Or once more, let any lover of the *Siegfried Idyll*, by way of diversion, first play these notes as phantoms in his mind :

Next, let him imagine himself enraptured with them

and with their phantom relations lying around them in the domestic diatonic scale. When he has done that for quite a long time, perhaps musing at the keyboard upon them and around them, let him take his X-ray impression of the exquisitely happy opening of the Idyll :

He will find Wagner's mind lingering and musing upon these few elemental euphonies:

pleasantly inflecting them, in unbroken creative contentment.

It would seem well all through this part, to think of the phrase as not only a creative musician's stroke, but as an unfailing register both of vitality (staying power), and personal taste. Considered thus it is seen to be full of variety, full of delicate matters of choice, full of subtleties that can never be measured in crotchets and quavers. Measured notes, crotchets and quavers are indeed needed to approximate the musician's real phrasing values, but they are the merest approximation. Play, for example, this subtle and wonderful phrase of Bach with ruthlessly strict values, as of a brass band commanded by an unfeeling but most justly accurate sergeant-major :

Then play it over and over again to yourself, very quietly, and more and more nearly as you feel it ought to be played (as it originally was played), on an imagined oboe; play it softly and flexibly, with devout old Bach's own vision of the solemn scene that inspired it, the thought of the Garden of Gethsemane. It will now become a phrase, and you will vividly realize how merely approximate it must ever be to spell such a delicate deed of the mind into mechanically or arithmetically related notational values! A man's body does not breathe to measure. How much less his mind! Did ever a soldier breathe in metronome measure to the beat of a brass band? The metronome helps him to regulate his step, but cannot regulate his breathing.

Here reflections and comparisons crowd upon our minds to aid us in our pursuit of the truth about Phrase, amongst them the following:

1. We are sure note-values are necessary helping friends of true phrasing, yet they *must* leave the phraser free, if they are not to kill the music.

2. Relentless metronomicism may also, on occasion, be a help, a thing to lean upon; more than that, players and singers in a team may even revel in it; it supports, unifies, heartens them; yet it must leave them individually free to breathe, to think and feel as they will and must.

3. This breathing or thinking business matters more to soldiers than their marching; they could breathe without marching, they could not march without breathing. It is the same with the musical phrase.

4. But regimental breathing, thinking, feeling, etc., are none of them *noticeable*, whereas the march is; and so the march is *the thing* for the moment. "There they go," say the crowd. "What a fine show!" Yes, the march is the thing (though one of the crowd, it may be, caught sight of one soldier's face and remarked, "Did you see that face? Poor fellow, he looks in pain!" And then, humanly speaking, that face was, for a moment, "the thing"; the interest was suddenly transmuted).

5. In the case of music, however, the note-values

in the phrase (which is music's breath and life) are NOT the thing.

6. Phrasing matters more than the very note-values by which it takes place; these latter support, but they are not the very life, as is the phrase itself.

7. More than that, phrasing *is*, every time and all the time, *the thing* in music; it is (like the soldier's breathing) music's life; but, unlike breathing, it never goes unnoticed. Everything in a phrase is noticeable; a man's inmost mind is heard in it, yes, and *assayed*, and often found wanting.

8. So a *march* is never *music*; though we have music on the march, they are *two* things; and each is "the thing" in two quite different ways.

Perhaps the above promiscuous throng of thoughts may help reader and writer alike neither to belittle nor exaggerate or otherwise mistake the part played by mechanical mensural arrangements as represented in every music primer thus:

With a super-micro-tonometer (if such existed) we might hope to examine the phrasing of a vital musician like Kreisler. We should expect to find that he never yet played eight semiquavers exactly to measure; and never could eight Kreisler quavers on Saturday make equal measure with one of his Sunday semibreves.

Here, then, is the perpetual paradox of true phrasing, to which our readers must find for themselves increasingly discerning reconcilement. Mensural music, in fact, is not music at all, as we understand it here. True, the measures are needed; they are there, ready prepared. But the music becomes real only when the musician is free to fill each measure instantly and at will. Expediency decides and prepares the stock size of the measuring vessels (whether *semibreve-gallon* or *semiquaver-gill*). These measuring vessels are recorded on the stave merely in order that genius, reading them, may fill each vessel recklessly to the brim, in a series of care-free, passing instants. A phrase, in short, is always a timeless stroke moving to time.

We are now to spend four chapters over four main aspects of the Phrase in music. We shall follow the phrase in its four different aspects with a single aim, that aim to be discussed in Chapters 24 and 25. We shall, throughout Part 3, take up the position (as it were) of watching the composer's brush in action on his canvas of time; and we shall try to do this in detail here in order to be the better able, later, to hear Sonata music clearly, and "hear it whole," or rather *hear it wholly into place.*

We may, in these chapters, eagerly hope and reasonably expect to detect signs of the large mind even in the little phrase, and to get ready to grasp a whole Symphony the better, when the time comes. For it does not take half an hour to get at the spirit of a Symphony. An ordinary listener may well find himself instantly in greathearted company on hearing a single master-phrase.

Our four-fold inquiry into phrasing may here be summarized thus:

1. How a single strand of inspired melody makes the *tonal phrase.*

2. How a double strand opens up the (at first bewildering) *miracle of counterpoint.*

3. How a chord-progression introduces us to *harmonic phrasing*.

4. How a *rhythm*, with no musical variation of pitch, can, in itself, give music the articulate *one-note phrase*, forming a basis for expansion into manifold rhythmic phrasing.

CHAPTER 15

MELODY AND TONAL PHRASING

"... A phrase of notes resembling stars,
Simple and spiritual notes of light...."

MEYNELL.

THERE seems no better starting-point for our four-fold journey than first to dwell briefly upon any single strain of melody, the simpler the better. Sing, play, or hum the following leisurely, giving it the highest values possible to you: (Incidentally, you are sharing a vital deed of thought with men of a thousand years ago.) The bend, or urge, of your own mind may straightway impel you to vary it: or, if the impulse is too strong to rest there:

or slightly further:

(Be sure to play or sing such phrases *into* the *tempo* that is exactly to your mind.) So the melodic impulse may work on; and, in such ways, vital and personal delight may endlessly move you into musical phrases which, returning to you, or invading the ears of others, will quicken further contemplation. These are but slender instances of a vast principle, but they will, for the moment, enable us to analyse the whole musical process as follows:

1. A bare thought or concept occurs, of two or more successive tones significantly related.

2. Pleasure in the thought follows.

3. Responsive movement results in *phrase*.

The bare thought, the pleasure in it, the consequent responsive movement, *together* produce the phrase. Let us look into these three factors carefully for a moment.

Many readers of such a book as this may, at present, incline to believe that only the second part of the above process really concerns them. They will say to themselves that a "tonal concept" is something quite beyond them. But is it? A Symphony is beyond their conceiving. But is this?

Or this? And does it really take a Schumann to write, *e.g.*, "Der Wilde Reiter"?

All that has happened in these two Schumann phrases may be put in this way. First:

1. The bare concept of the perfect fourth.

2. Pleasure in it.

3. Responsive movement.

Next:

1. A bare concept of the natural "colours" of the musical "spectrum."

2. Delight in them.

3. Responsive movement.

And if the reader persists in modestly imagining even such simple processes as still beyond his own powers, he can at least say, "When (1) occurs to some one else and is passed on to me, and (2) I take pleasure in it, I do at least (3) listen dynamically"—that is, not only composer and performer (initiator and interpreter), but the listener also may, by musical responsiveness, escape inertia. The listener phrases. And that is obviously true of alive, intelligent listeners when listening to alive, intelligible music. Turning again to our threefold definition of tonal phrasing, the reader will find that a very slight change in the wording gives it at once far wider scope. As the three sentences now read, they define a *Phrase*; but if in (1) we substitute for "*tones* related" the words "*phrases* related," they at once define a whole melody or movement. Then, for *phrases* read *movements*, and a *Sonata* may be defined; and so on, expandingly without end.

But it is No. 3 of these that concerns us most of all. To watch, and ourselves make response, is to concentrate attention upon the way in which the composer's hand is impelling his brush over the "time-canvas." As far as this chapter goes, we are restricted to watching *all that happens along the melodic line*. But moving beyond this restriction for the moment, it will save time if we try at once to define or crystallize the essential parts of *all* kinds of phrase to be discussed, or, indeed, of any larger unit of composition, even that dignified by the title *Movement*.

The essential factors in any melodic movement itself, in the act we call *phrase*, seem to be three. The first of these may momentarily be called *Initiative*, the second *Aim*, and the third *Arrest* (or *Stay*). The world of music would grow alarmingly fuller of adventure if all music lovers were equally gifted with initiative. But it would be far less full of confusion if they all possessed the second and third factors, those of sustained aim, and of knowing where to stay their hand.

These three words—Initiative, Aim, Arrest—used at a venture, may not suffice to convey the measureless importance of what they represent. Start, and Aim, and Stay seem quite a sound Saxon trio of terms. Let every one, however, make his own (insisting with Humpty Dumpty, in his memorable talk with Alice, " When I use a word it means just what I choose it to mean—neither more nor less ! "). Whatever words we may individually select, let us dwell, in some detail, upon these three vital parts of the phraser's stroke.

As to (1) the Start.—It should first be clearly remembered that it is concept, and pleasure in concept, that have together brought us to this stage at all. Realizing this, as we look both *back* and *forth* from our starting-point, we must also realize the unfailing musical principle of Continuity in its most practical bearing—perhaps amusingly obvious, but often tragically ignored. What is our true position as melodists, standing on this pin-point, so to speak, of impending initiative ?

(*a*) We want to start.

(*b*) We cannot dream of starting a musical phrase till *concept* and *joy* push us.

(*c*) We are duly pushed by these two, but then

(*d*) We cannot dream of starting till Aim and even Stay pull us forward !

It is all very curious, yet this it is that seems to distinguish the work of an artist from that of an artisan —the creative melody from the created melody reproduced, the real phrase from the apparent. And it is this inseparability of a total of now no less than five * factors in the musical transaction that makes for unity, be the concept as small as Schumann's composition for the child mind (quoted above), or as vast as the C Minor Symphony, or as instant, on a big scale, as the Jupiter.

* Concept, Delight, Start, Aim, Stay.

As to (2) *Aim.*—This, in its turn, gains its sustaining force from the concept tenaciously kept in mind ; and the joy is automatically increased and suffused both ways. But more is required. The mind that conceives, rejoices, and takes *aim* to fulfil its first conception, and then merely *stays,* will soon find itself reduced to delivering a detached series of musical hits. While it stays it must not stop. For if it should, for a moment, stop conceiving, in order that *aim* and *stay* shall both have their turn, and rest (or be arrested) till a new *start* follow, then music would find itself in the absurd position of a being that ceases to breathe in order to run !

The truth is that in melody conception and joy never really cease ; they persist concurrently ; so the word *aim* is bound to be inadequate, unless we know it as *sustained aim.* Even then, it accumulates, as it persists, into *adorned aim ;* or *modified aim ; aim in suspense ; aim meeting and transcending* circumstance ; *aim passing into aim,* with imaginary rest-points where there is no rest, but only intent inspiration for another " lap." (If this paragraph seems, at first reading, too involved, which very likely it may, the reader will do well to re-read and develop it.)

All the above points may be noted vividly in the following example from Mozart's Overture to the *Magic Flute* :

The start exemplifies the eager *push* of the joyous concept, the *pull* of the aim (upward a fifth) to a staying-point at which the melody refuses to stay. If the reader still feels any doubt as to this indivisible union of start, aim, and stay, let him try to imagine Mozart thinking his staying-points thus:

As to (3) *Stay*.—This seems quite the best word for the stopping-point of phrase. One is reminded of the old carol:

> " And there it did both *stop* and *stay*
> Right over the place where Jesu lay,"

the old Saxon monosyllables (often) serving us more thoroughly than words of later date. But we will abjure the word " stop," because it nowadays signifies too decisive an end to action. And though the word " end " itself might serve (its more dynamic sense of *motive attained* being remembered), *Stay* seems preferable to all, in that our *stay* may be the minutest point, and because *staying power* actually implies the power to go on! It is the latter connotation of this little word that gives it pre-eminence in this context, and of this no one will be in doubt who has studied the phrasing of the most inspired composers, and tried, divertingly, to decide where each phrase begins and where it ends! The stay is there; but where? As an example, take this, from the jolly Mozart Concerto in E♭ for two pianos:

Is that a case of two phrases, or three, or more? Certainly the long B♭ feels like a first point of call. But many a listener might say, this is one thought:

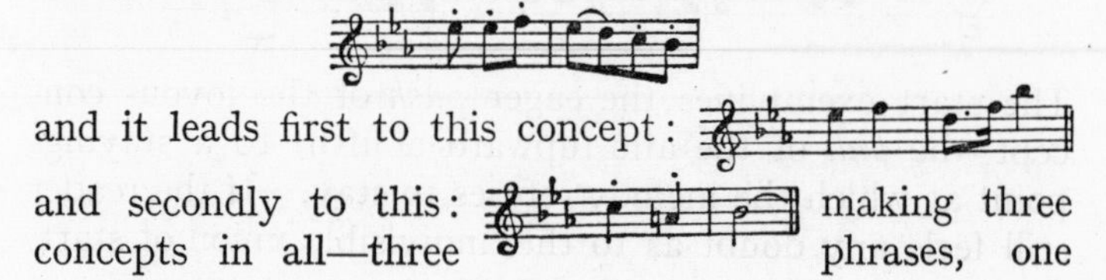

and it leads first to this concept:

and secondly to this: making three concepts in all—three phrases, one of which is traversed twice. And certain it is that on turning to Mozart's own thoughts a few bars later, and in subsequent parts of the *Rondo*, the two-bar quaver figure is used and repeated, as though he himself thought of it as a phrase—*e.g.* :

Whether this be a sign of the first unit of thought or not, the eighth note of the whole tune is clearly one of the notes frequently found in fine melodies and movements, which serve as both *stay* and *start*, and which yet pass in a flash—like the amusing stationettes called "halts" on our great railway systems, at which never a train is seen to stop. It is a note which stands at once at a starting, a during, and a staying-point ! It ends one concept :

starts another,

and is yet standing in the very midst of a hurly-burly of melodious fun :

These slender examples must serve to show the vital continuity of the phraser's art in music. All inspired processes in music prove to be concurrent ; though none are more skilful at the game of detaching a fragmentary phrase within a phrase, and then finding new inspiration in old fragments, than the Mozarts and Beethovens of the musical world, whose conceptual joy is so ceaselessly at work that the tiniest fragment is apt to crystallize into a new phrase-value. There exists a wonderful object lesson in Beethoven's sketch-books, where the following appears as an earlier form of the theme in A♭, upon which the whole of the slow movement of the C Minor Symphony is built :

If this be compared with the theme as it finally stood, analysis seems to reveal a formative mind breaking up the first concept into smaller and into seemingly still more unpromising phraselets :

and

and then transforming the former for the most part into a *chord-concept* : instead of what may, perhaps clumsily, be called a *step-concept* ; then breaking up the latter at once into two separate thoughts, and proceeding to expand the first new thought beyond recognition by giving what may be called *derivative concepts* free rein, to culminate in a trumpet fanfare, as thrilling as it is elementary :

Let the reader be once more reminded that to dwell with one's whole mind even upon two tones is to weld them into a unit of thought ; and that a thought of such a kind thus becomes a phrase. To say that every articulate phrase or concept is inherently a sum of smaller, and a part of larger concepts, is no more baffling than to remind the lover of nature that his favourite tree is but one concept, as he might well say a tiny Phrase of God ; yet it is a sum of branches, sub-branches, twigs, leaves, leaflets, each of which has its articulate veins and tributary veins ; each as beautiful, contemplated microscopically, as the whole tree, which itself is but an apt monosyllable in any sunlit forest's morning message to man. And as the power to conceive a large phrase includes power to grasp the lesser or sub-phrases within it, it is clear that the mind of every music lover must needs ceaselessly practise large and ever larger aural grip, with an ever more comprehending mind for detail on the "time-canvas"; and this, not *after*, but *during* the progress of the composer's brush upon that canvas!

Practice in this arduous and worth-while pursuit may begin simply but tenaciously with tonal phrase and melody. Much repetition is needed. But this will stale no good thing if it be always (as before hinted) the kind of repetition that is associated with *perfecting*, and never allowed to become vain, inattentive, perfunctory.

Chapter 16

THE MIRACLE OF COUNTERPOINT, OR COMPOUND PHRASING

"... 'Tis with Art wherein special beauty
Springeth of obstacles that hath been overcome
And to graces transformed ..."

Bridges.

LET us now praise unknown men; and erect an imaginary monument to two imaginary persons, paying them perpetual honour. We have in mind those unknowns who first conceived and took delight in the simultaneous sounding of two independent melodies, and so launched upon the world the little miracle now called Counterpoint.

Who has not heard a distracted mother exclaim to her spirited family, "Oh! do not *all* talk at once!" Whereas the contrapuntal composer delights in bidding all his children talk at once, if with relevance (see, for example, Mozart's art in the "Jupiter," page 153).

But how did this thing come about? How did our original two unknowns find it out? Naturally enough. For as soon as men, singing in two parts, realized the material at hand, counterpoint could not but follow. And now, some one asks, "What is counterpoint?"

We are told that the Greeks "magadized," which, being interpreted, means that they sang in octaves. Now, as long as two or more singers continued to sing at the distance apart of but one interval, counterpoint was impossible. But if and when any two melodists decided to duplicate any melody at another interval than the

Violin I
Violin II
Viola
Cello
Double Bass

octave (as, according to history, Hucbald, a monk of Flanders, apparently did a thousand or so years ago), the dawn of counterpoint was imminent. The first manifestation of the miracle could not then be long delayed.

Sound again our former scrap of melodic impulse from the last chapter :

Get a bass voice to sing it, and, with it, a tenor to "ma-gadize" an octave higher :

Suppose the tenor, having a cold, says that he cannot reach the high notes without strain, but suggests singing it in the next most pleasing harmonic ratio—*i.e.* in perfect fifths :

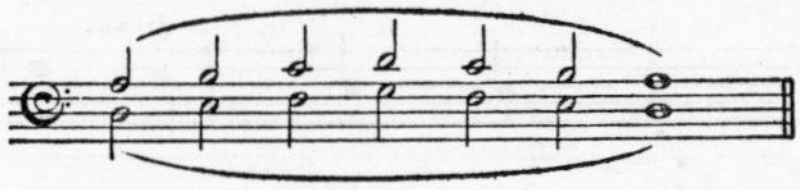

(The reader will find this very device historically and plentifully exemplified in Hucbald's *Organum or Diaphony.*) No one will deny the great beauty and interest of this variety of melodizing, least of all our contemporary, Vaughan Williams, to whose splendid work we stand for ever gratefully indebted ; (nor would Robert Louis Stevenson have done, to whom consecutive fifths were as " music of the spheres "). Let but three voices assemble to melodize together, and we can see the age-old singing in octaves amplified into the thousand-year-old singing in fourths and fifths :

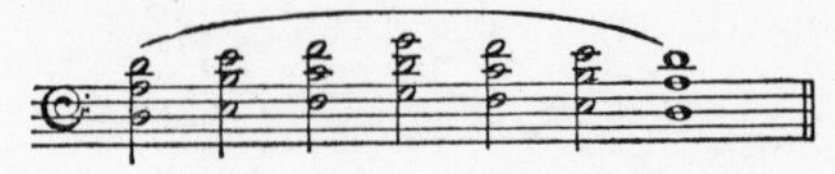

So long as no voice moves from duplicating the melody at one set interval to duplicating it at another, the *canto fermo* itself remains intact and supreme. And if a hundred voices were to sing the same melody at a hundred pleasing intervals (if it were possible), it would still be the same melody—now best called coloured melody.*

But let us imagine two monks of old, singing their evening hymn at an agreed set interval, and ending it so:

(The reader should secure a friend to sing this with him, several times.) Then imagine that, after doing this for long, in accordance with the custom of their time, the tenor monk was, one evening, moved to return suddenly for love to the original and more habitual relation of the octave at the close, thus:

What more natural? If this, in turn, be sung two or three times, and the effect compared with the original, it will be realized that, in truth, a momentous thing has happened. This melody: is for ever different in rise and fall (or contour) from the original: Two definitely different remarks (phrases) are therefore now being made (sung) by two singers simultaneously, and yet they are sensibly and reasonably and beautifully at one! This happening may be thought of as the very source or cradle of "counterpoint." Musicians, in fact, use this unattractive word Counterpoint to describe all

* Giraldus Cambrensis piquantly describes an instance of this more than seven hundred years ago.

possible concepts of two or more separate melodies sounded simultaneously, each going its own way, but regardfully and wholly relevant to the others.

At some such moment as that imagined above, and probably in some such intuitive and unconcerned way, counterpoint must have dawned upon the minds of men. All honour once again to the anonymous adventurers through whom its beauty dawned. Its effect upon the development of music has, needless to say, been incalculable.

It should be noted that there are other natural ways in which the miracle may also have been discovered, notably by the chance of a single voice having held on to a drone-note while the *canto fermo* proceeded; or more interestingly, when one voice or melody dwelt upon a note while a more enterprising voice went on, to be followed later by its companion:

This independence of mere rise and fall may have been accidentally, or even intentionally, demonstrated still earlier, if, of any two voices singing the same part, one had dropped or risen at a given moment to a more convenient octave for its particular vocal compass—as when two singers might have been chanting some such phrase as this:

and the second voice, finding the last three notes of the phrase too high, might suddenly have dropped thus:

But in such a case there would, of course, be none of

the adventure of actually singing other notes than that of the original melody.

In whatever way the simultaneous sounding of two independent melodies came about, it brought music face to face with a new and unique conception of the art of the *Phrase* ; like a new kind of drama, in which two or more characters make intelligible sense, though uttering different things simultaneously. In counterpoint, two musical voices, speaking concurrently, demand no extra ear in the hearer, and no Siamese-twin mind that can think two thoughts at the same moment. It seems indeed clear that here we acknowledge the arrival, in musical experience, of something which we may most conveniently differentiate from *simple phrasing* by some such name as *compound phrasing*.

We saw in an earlier chapter, in more rudimentary instances, that, to the mind of music, the record of two simultaneous energies or interests is not a case of 1+1=2, but rather *one* multiplied by *one* equals ONE ; or, as previously expressed, *it* multiplied by *it* equals *IT !* For this reason, we should listen expectantly (in Bach, pre-eminently) for *phrase* multiplied by *phrase* equalling PHRASE. This new deed of the mind, then, we will (at least for the moment) classify under the title Compound Phrasing.

Some composers come to wield simultaneous melodies, much as conjurers keep balls or plates simultaneously in the air. But the question is, where are we, listeners, in this kind of multiple musical transaction ? Our minds must not be left behind. How may we equip ourselves not to miss the fun ? Since the composer, unlike the conjurer, is not out to baffle and dazzle the senses, but to illumine the mind and amplify its joy in action, we shall probably best become efficient listeners to counterpoint by tracing, if we can, the means to which composers themselves resort to save both ear and mind from confusion : helping the one to hear *definitely in two strands* (or three or more), and the other definitely to phrase them into one. For this is the fundamental difference between melodic and contrapuntal listening. Turn again to the composer's hand at work.

Before looking into three of the chief contrapuntal means of presenting two melodies simultaneously, while still preserving their identity, let the reader, concentrating on the merely physical aspect of the task, straightway try a small personal experiment—that of laying this book open on a table before him, and lightly *tapping* one page with one hand, while *stroking* the other with the other. If you attempt to think the two hands simultaneously into action, your mind and hands are likely to prove momentarily baffled and impotent. But if one hand is set going for a moment (say, for the period of two, four, or eight taps), and if the other hand is then set to its different task, the thing is easily achieved. Indeed, the experiment may be carried further, and when the two differing actions are set going, then it will be found that the head can be made to shake independently, then to nod, the toes can be set to waggle—any triple or quadruple task can be gradually mastered. Bearing this simple illustration in mind, it can be realized that contrapuntal listening is subject to like laws, invisibly and intangibly obeyed. Let us look into this.

1. Get two violinists to play you the following:

They are duettists, not contrapuntists. Then try this:

They are still duettists playing "coloured melody," not contrapuntists instigating compound phrasing. Now, as we have clearly heard in the first example earlier in this chapter, we can give them independence by a change of direction (see (*a*)), or even by letting one remain on a stationary line, while the other moves up and down (see (*b*)) :

though their rhythmic identity still persists. If the rhythm is very pronounced, and the change of direction very slight, contrapuntal listening hardly comes into action at all. But should the rhythm be very delicate, the contrapuntal listening would be easily established by this kind of directional means alone :

At (*a*) in both above examples, the movement is called *contrary motion* between parts, and that at (*b*) is called *oblique motion.* If one fiddler sat still on one note, while the other did all the work, the result would be all oblique motion of parts :

A homely example of oblique motion is afforded by a bagpipe, as between the drones and the tunes.

Bach is reputed to have given his pupils a golden rule for extemporizing two independent melodies or parts : *they were to think their melodies into contrary motion.* And if the reader will recall his listening experiences, he will agree that, when the treble and bass melodies (which, for natural reasons, are those most potently heard) move in contrary motion, their independence in unity is naturally and certainly the more easily established and enjoyed.

2. The thought of oblique motion between companion

melodies leads us easily to a second main way of enabling tunes to remain *two,* while conspiring to give us but one ampler joy. Ask your duettists, trading upon contrary motion, now to play the scales thus :

and you will immediately relish their *twofold-ness.* But let them go a step further, and wait upon each other :

now the mind is much more easily intrigued, and without confusion. How is this ? Oblique motion need only take one step, and the idea of *contrasted longs and shorts* as between two friendly conspirators, vastly enriches the composer's contrapuntal resources. In old days (and in many wise ways to-day) students were given contrapuntal exercises in contrasting mere values. These may be seen described in any dictionary of music under the heading of strict Counterpoint. Think of a father and a toddling little son at his side :

and you are watching something very like what is scholastically classified as *Counterpoint in third species.* Much more spicy examples than this occur in Morley's 1597 book,* mingling metrical interest amazingly.

3. But holding one part back in long notes, while speeding another in short notes, is but one, often beauti-

* *A Plaine and Easie Introduction to Musick.*

ful and always effectual, way of differentiating the parts by varying their note-values. It would be impossible to omit mention here of a third fruitful field for composers of the contrapuntal turn of mind, that of *rhythmic differentiation* opened up by the very same means of contrasted speeds, or varied degrees of animation. The idea of a child with typical trot, and a father with equally typical stride, leads us naturally to the thought of parts harmoniously blended, yet rhythmically differentiated, not by mere stride, but by variously characteristic figures. Bach, of course, affords countless examples of this variety, of which one only need be quoted here. In his first organ Sonata (for two keyboards and pedals) this is the chief subject :

The two rhythmically vacant moments at the crotchets give Bach his instant opportunities, and a contrapuntal bass is heard taking advantage of them :

These two parts should be sounded and enjoyed, first separately, and then played together. When, almost immediately, the second keyboard part joins in, and the movement is in full swing (the three parts are continuously busy almost the whole time), Bach has charming fun in passing contrasted figures from one part to another. Here is one exemplary moment in the triple conversation :

If these congenial lines be played separately, each will be found to have a character all its own, due to the *contrasted rhythmic shapes*. The three voices intertwine and complement each other without confusion. We may add a fragmentary quotation from a delicious pair of parts (one had almost said persons) to be found conversing thus, in the second of the Forty-Eight Fugues :

It may be questioned whether Bach himself, or any performer or listener since, could be said ever to have heard this aright, if it is heard as a mere dual experience of two phrases. No ! the result is a new unity. As our two single records of force (↓ and →) were earlier seen to become in action one (as a curve ⌒), and as two clock-times ♩ ♩ ♩ ♩ ♩ ♩ *etc.* and ♩. ♩. ♩. ♩. can become one rhythm :

so, surely, two vital little " persons " conspire here, so that the dynamic listener has one contrapuntal experience, and achieves one compound *phrase*. Is it pressing the word *phrase* into too large a service to put it in this way? Yet it is the very word needed to carry the essential conception of oneness to our minds; for the moment, at least, the writer is unable to find a better; and he would beg the reader to help himself to any other words that enable him to appreciate its innermost and ever more exacting expanding possibilities.

Whither, then, does counterpoint lead the listener? To a more spacious experience of Phrase in the sense we have described earlier, five-fold but continuous—*concept, delight, start, aim, stay.* The reader should try to get a good gramophone record of Wagner's *Meistersinger* Overture, and (lifting the needle deftly) repeat to himself, over and over, the exhilarating counterpoint heard from bar 153 on the stately bass beginning:

The more he grows familiar with the various melodic motives (the musical persons in the musical transaction !), the more richly will this contrapuntal amalgam glow and burn through hearing into his mind. But Wagner's dictum should here be recalled: that all music is, and remains in essence, *melody*! Meaning, of course, that however elaborated, it cannot do other than reach us by a succession of tonal impressions in time. This seems tantamount to a warning from a wonderful man to put our whole musical hope and strength into Phrase and Phrasing; never to be the victims of a sophisticated conception, least of all a tonal or "contrapuntal squint"; not to consent to the trick-thought of being drawn two ways simultaneously, but rather seek to be drawn one way by many strands—with an ever-increasing mental mastery, and the ultimate reward of attaining to more heavenly speeds and amplitudes in our music.

To conclude: it may be well for the reader to hold on to that word "amplitude" just used, lest he feel daunted. This he need never be in face of the most complex counterpoint, if it is masterly, and if he, for his part, only looks for an amplitude of experience up to capacity, here as in all things. He may indeed, in the case of the contrapuntal phrase, well substitute amplitude for *aim*; thus changing our formula, *start, aim* (*sustained*), *stay,* into *start, amplitude* (*increasing*), *stay.* Revert, for example, to the most trifling, incipient contrapuntal joy, as it dawns in a nursery rhyme:

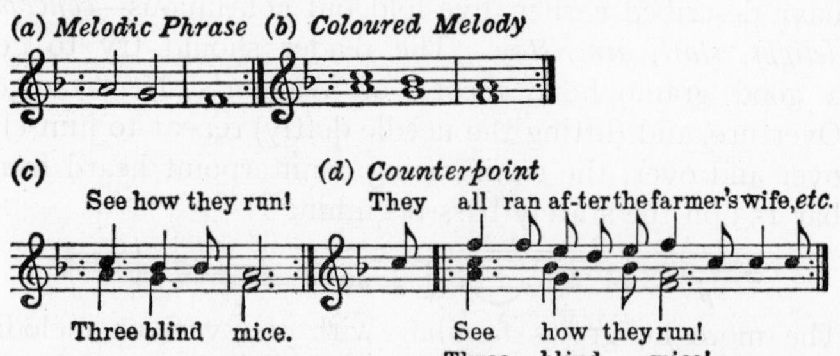

At (*c*) the first little free-will kick of speech-rhythm gives a bare tinge of rhythmic counterpoint (if such it may be called within the limits of doubling the tune in thirds). At (*d*), independence of slightly more than a rhythmic kind is asserted, and amplitude is attained up to baby-capacity. Contrary and oblique motion are both in play; and counterpoint is conceivably not too grand a word for the result. But compare this example with "Sumer is i-cumen in," of which history books make so much. Here, instead of: you will find in the so-called "PES" two old gentlemen showing their newly discovered independence by this canonic framework perpetually repeated: and instead of "all running after the farmer's wife," in one phrase, we find summer "i-cumen in" in a variety of strains or phrases, which oblige the two canonic parts by fitting their particular melodizing both to " pes " and to each other :

being followed by many another, such as :

In these ways, amplitude and high spirits attain their end.

One word more, and one more example may be welcome. Bach has this austere, not to say pessimistic, subject for Fugue No. 4 in the Forty-Eight :

If, as is obvious, the aim of a counter-subject is to amplify and fulfil, such a passive first subject invites the active mind to intensify, deepen, and generally to increase its hold and to enrich its output. The very deliberateness of the theme challenges the mind to movement, for the musical mind naturally abhors a vacuum ; and Bach, of course, is quick to respond contrapuntally :

But its very suavity also challenges clashing qualities, and here is the Bach answer to that call :

with its welcome scrunch in the third bar. These ideas gradually crystallize into triple counterpoint. In the course of the Fugue, Bach's mind may well be heard moving towards them, then growing eloquent over them when found. He revels in their attainment, much as a scientist or a responsible statesman might revel in the discovery of some formula in words at last crystal clear to all, which should convey to his fellows some new truth, or deeply-rooted policy hitherto clear to none, not even to his own scientific or patriotic mind :

In the joyous mastery of such complex problems, Counterpoint might indeed be likened to mathematics or to fine statesmanship; since all its problems are problems of balance and of reconcilement—as are those of the scientist or inspired statesman.

Chapter 17

HARMONY, OR CHORD PHRASING

"That troubling of the air which common men
Call harmony. . . ."

Dobell.

IT has sometimes been strangely said that the terms Harmony and Counterpoint are really synonymous. The reader may have been puzzled, also, by the common statement that Harmony is music read vertically, and Counterpoint music read horizontally. Music lovers unaccustomed to reading music may fail even dimly to guess what this means. It merely refers to the fact that though in Europe *all* music is read along the page horizontally from left to right; and though in studying a melody the eye travels steadily along a *quasi* "sky-line" on the stave (the rise and fall from note to note, if traced with a thin pencil line, resembling the outline of distant hills on the horizon of the mind); yet, in reading a single chord, the eye travels for the moment *vertically,* as in scanning a tower on the horizon :

In this chapter, however, we are not to consider individual chords as towers in this so-called vertical aspect ; we are rather to forget all about the appearance on the page of the mere sign which men make when they want to show that particular sound-amalgam called a chord. We have to concentrate here, as elsewhere, and tirelessly, on the master-thought of the *Phrase.*

Clearly there are chord-phrases in music. It is, again, the composer's stroke on the time-canvas that concerns us ; only this time he wields a manifold- or chord-brush, executing harmonious phrases. We are not at present at all concerned with the mere relating of tones into chords; that we already have examined, and must continue to do later. We are to deal here with the chords as our units; and we already have our chord-material at hand in Chapter 12. Nor are we concerned here with relating tones into mere melodies; this occupied us in Chapter 15.

Having chords, then, as units of material, let us take (as extreme test) two or three, entirely haphazard; for example, sound this:

pp and this: pp and this: pp

on the keyboard. We may now say to ourselves, have such as these the makings of a *chord-phrase*? Can they be woven into chord-sense?

At this stage we are somewhat like children who have drawn three chance objects out of a bran-pie at Christmas; or like a lexicographer who has chanced upon any three words of his total vocabulary, and perhaps written them down, saying, "Can I make sense of these?" Not that a harmonic phrase is a haphazard thing, as we may hope soon to see. But it should have its hap and its hazard. For example, if counterpoint were the rule of the day, and three relevant melodies were strung together, say on an operatic stage, the composer might be posed with most piquant harmonic hazards, amenable only to the very resourcefully harmonic mind.

Chords are to the ear and mind of the musician rather like metals to the chemist—distinct from each other, diverse, and of definite character, varying in complexity, rarity, and usefulness. They are, first, units of impression, becoming only by usage units of thought. If we could imagine some creative chemist or super-chemist (or should we say alchemist?) flashing metal after metal, in dazzling sequence, before our eyes, melodizing them into some elemental but logical music of their own, we shall not have pictured anything very far beyond the creative achievement already begun and perpetually to be expected of the harmonists of the future.

Realizing that the musical mind, in conceiving a succession of chords called harmony, is precisely the same adventurous and ideal phraser that willed a succession of tones into a tune, we must expect its chord-phrases to behave in like ways ; they will start, become interesting, then *attain* something—some idea, and so reach their staying-points. We shall watch the musician's hand, however, wielding this bigger, more wonderful composite- or chord-brush ; no fine, line-drawing, camel's-hair melody brush this time, but one that mingles colours and chord-notions and chord-complexities, till we ordinary mortals have humbly to ask him to " do it again," perhaps many times, that we may not be hopelessly daunted.

In truth, however, the chord-facts are not really so bewildering as all that, largely because we all have nature's tonal spectrum (see Chapter 10) in permanent possession, upon which we may all at any time practise ; it supplies us with a veritable clearing-house for chords, however complex they may seem.

And here we may properly digress, to notice the telling and entrancing fact that the history of man's harmonic advance along the centuries can be traced with singular and significant accuracy if we climb steadily upwards among the first twelve tones of the natural harmonic series. These are already familiar to readers of Chapter 10. Merely for convenience, we may set the first twelve down here in only approximate notation, numbered upwards from any low note G :

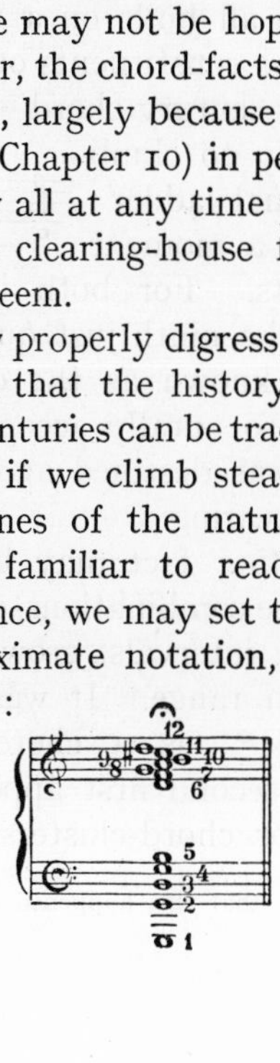

Now in Nos. 1 and 2 we trace nature's explanation of Greek magadization and all the unisonal habits of mankind:  Climb to Nos. 2, 3, and 4, and we find ground for Hucbald's diaphony of one thousand years ago:  Climb further, and Nos. 3, 4, 5, and 6 give us the ideally smooth disposition of a three-note chord:  and in it the major triad shines out. The music of the Golden Age (sixteenth century) was all built on a three-note basis. Pursuing our journey, the seventh (said to have been first coined as a chord-thought in the mint of Monteverde's daring mind, in and about the year 1600 in Florence) appears in Nos. 4, 5, 6, 7, and 8:  The seventeenth and eighteenth century musical glories were all built on a three- and four-note basis. To find all the constituents of a characteristic and favourite nineteenth-century chord—called the dominant ninth—we have only to climb one further rung on nature's tonal ladder:  But we must turn back for a moment to four-note chord concepts. For both in order of history and in popularity, the ninth just quoted yields place to the peculiar chord known as the diminished seventh:  a chord so aurally acceptable and intriguing that it was destined at one time to become hackneyed beyond bearing.

Here an interesting fact may be specially noticed, namely, that all these combinations, derived from nature's tonal series by slow intervals, grow naturally gradually closer and closer in range. It was when the seventh was actually struck * (as a chord-thought) that the clash of the major second first appeared in unprepared chord formations (or chord-clusters, as we have called

* It is easy to surmise that this happened experimentally, long before Monteverde's day.

them). And it should be noted that, as we move up the harmonic series and take any cluster within the compass of any octave in the series, the largest interval will, of course, be at the lower end of that cluster, thus: and the smallest interval will be at the upper end, thus: This obviously remains true, however high up one may explore the series. Now, this being so, it should be observed that if the outermost or containing tones of any selection whatever (standing and sounded an octave apart in every instance)—*e.g.*:

be raised by one semitone arbitrarily, the immediate and automatic result will be to reduce the largest interval (that nearest the bottom) by a semitone, and in like manner to increase the smallest interval (that lying nearest the top) by a semitone! Try it in each of the above chords. This may have a momentous effect upon the power of the listener to take in a many-toned chord with the ear, especially when the intervals between the higher notes are getting almost too acute or too small to be acceptable to the physical ear. And this seems, in part, to account for the importance and, one may believe, the popularity still to come, of a select four among chords; though (as we shall hope to see in Part 4) the major reasons for their importance and popularity are far more profound than their mere physical acceptability. Here are the above three-note, four-note, five-note, and six-note natural chords or harmonic clusters modified in the way just suggested:

Here is a catalogue of the chords now derived, placed

in climbing order, together with suggestions of the approximate period of their appearance in musical history, coupled, in some cases (it is hoped not too arbitrarily), with prominent names of that period :

Here they are again, all assembled into position between two Cs :

1. Universal. (All centuries.)
2. Tenth century. (Hucbald.)
3. From eleventh century onward to sixteenth century. (From Franco, or earlier, to Palestrina.)
4. Seventeenth century onward. (Monteverde.)

4*a*. Eighteenth century onward. (Bach.)

5. Nineteenth century. (Wagner, Chopin, Schumann, etc.)
6. Twentieth century.* (Debussy.)

The above epitome of imagined historic harmonic happenings has been given here in detail, chiefly to suggest to readers that they themselves, if they would attain the mastery of chords and chord-phrasing, may find it good for personal practice to put themselves through a course of chord-study *in exactly this order*—like musical travellers, or harmonic birds of passage, skimming the

* Curiously, Nos. 3*a* and 5*a* seem still to await their true fulfilment.

centuries in deliberate flight; from unisonal thought to diaphonic thought, through three-note concepts (upon which the contrapuntal age thrived) to four-note, five-note, and six-note practice. Such a flight may be undertaken in a few magical minutes of concentrated listening and thought. But it should be frequently repeated. Who has no leisure for the practice of such imperishable interests ?

And now we must return to the main business of this chapter—that is, to watch the composing hand of our imaginary chord-phraser at work, and perceive, if we can, some of the vital ways in which chords pass into chord-phrases.

Having guessed that all music naturally moves in every department from an effortful grasp of a two-fold concept towards a more and more effortless enjoyment of manifold concepts, we shall expect to find that the natural trend of a chord-phrase will be from simple chords to less and less simple (all within power of the ear), and that the stay will always naturally occur where chords have momentarily attained an objective, and are about to "resolve," as it is called, into relatively simpler chordal elements. This is borne out by experience, and the chord process commonly known as preparation, discord, resolution (as, for example, in the following) :

has become, alas, one of the most conventional applications and tacit acceptances of our vital phrasing principle of start-aim-and-stay. We are not concerned until Part 4 with learning music's customs, or noting its harmonic conventions. But can we here discover something basic, natural, and far-reaching in the behaviour of an inspired composer's chord-brush, something which may throw light for good and all on our study of harmony ? We shall be better equipped to follow both the Harmonic Highway of the classics, and the byways and experimental Harmonic road-making of our own day, if we can but discover a few things in men's habitual chord-ways that hold unexplored natural possibilities, and that transcend the very customs they explain. This is perhaps an ambitious suggestion. But aim at the harmonic sky, and one may hit a harmonic tree!

Let us then at once and bravely—brazenly, it may seem to some—suppose that, ten thousand years hence, in any human civilization with musically sensitive ears, chords will still be related in four inescapable ways: (*a*) disjunctly, or by tonal leap:  (*b*) conjunctly, or by tonal step:  (*c*) connectedly, by means of a pivot-note in common:  (*d*) enharmonically, by means of an unheard change of thought (this is the chord-play or musical punning already referred to):  Are there any further ways than these four to come? There may easily be far-reaching *extensions* of men's thinking-powers in store, as, for example, along enharmonic and subtle lines—double, triple, quadruple enharmonicisms, at present beyond our enjoyment or intelligence. Or the human ear may become, æons hence, so much more sensitized that it can relate outlandish distances and jump from:

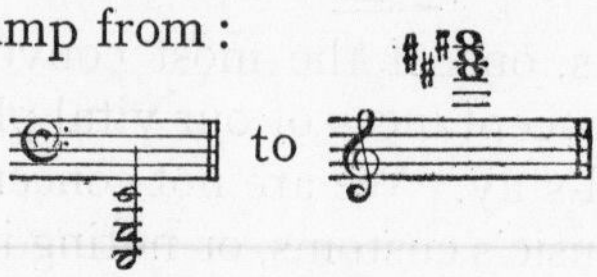

to

without being in the least baffled, but quite comfortably and complacently enjoying the leap over tonal spaces. Yet, however cultivated ear and mind may become, and with whatever imaginative celerity they may be mobilized, we dare suppose that the above four natural relatings will always prevail; and further that:

(*a*) *disjunct* relating of chords will inherently remain relatively strong compared with

(*b*) *conjunct* relating; which will remain relatively smooth, compared with (*a*), but in itself relatively strong compared with

(*c*) *pivot-progression*, which will, in its turn, remain relatively suave and gradual compared with (*a*) and (*b*); whereas

(*d*) *enharmonic* relatings will remain far subtler than either (*a*), (*b*), or (*c*), and far more dependent upon the mind's imaginative response.

In other words, the *characters* of the relating will remain permanently distinctive in their four orders in these four ways which we have found inherent. We dare not believe that they are yet apprehended by the majority of listeners. Their day is at hand rather than attained.

Let us now hark back to the three chords fortuitously proposed as samples at the beginning of this chapter. Play them as they stand there, regardless of effect,* and then use them in some such way as this following:

until the effect is neither too jerky nor too erratic for any reader's ear or taste. In such a form they afford, haphazard, an example of disjunct chord-phrasing, lettered (*a*) above. Let us now try to bring them

* It may be as well to state, in passing, that they were thrown out here in the first place without the slightest thought either of continuity, or of subsequent illustrative use here.

into such positions as may exemplify the three other ways of relating chords into a phrase. To relate them conjunctly, our next step of course will be to sound them as near in pitch to each other as possible without changing their present form :

This at once sounds more hopeful if we are in search of connected harmonic sense. As they stand, indeed, they happen to make a very easily related tonal phrase (melody) :

but they have not so good a bass : We must be clear as to what is meant here by "not so good." We simply mean that if our musical aim is conjunctly to relate three chords (which are music's *words*), this is not a good bass in respect to that aim. If our aim were to *jerk* an over-soothing harmonic thought into life, then the leap to F♯, and the tread to F♮ the moment after, might be, on the contrary, a "good" way of provoking the mind to work. Two interesting things come into view here. To get our "good" conjunct bass in this instance, it would be convenient if we could put the fifth (G) of the first chord in the bass:

We can ; and our being able to do so calls attention, in passing, to the delicious fact that, in music, a chord is what a word might be in literature if it were mysteriously capable of remaining itself (with only a slightly changed flavour), while its letters and consequent sounds were successively inverted. Imagine a comic man who was able to refer to his HAT alternatively as an ATH or a THA, quite confident that his audience would know that he was referring to different aspects of the same article of clothing! The second interesting thing about conjunctly relating chord-thoughts into chord-phrases is even more important. To see it the more clearly, we need to glance at a literary parallel. Words are linked into eloquent sentences entirely by pertinent choice of such words as will naturally relate themselves in sound and sense, and which, so related, will convey the mind that wove them into that relation. Now, in such a process, words that stand obstinately disjunct and disconnected from each other in all ordinary associations or uses, may be yet brought into relation by any imaginative mind and, *with the help of a few auxiliary words*, may make reasonable if not illuminating sense. They may, in short, be reconciled by context. This chapter is being written in an upstairs room. Downstairs are three people. It has just occurred to me (as the best means of exemplifying this particular truth) to go downstairs and suggest that these three friends write, on three scraps of paper, the first noun that comes to each of their minds haphazard (corresponding to our three fortuitous chords above), and then to try, with the fewest possible additional syllables (corresponding to passing-notes in music), to make what sense I can from them. . . . .

The nouns have been collected (contributed in all ignorance of the purpose for which they are required) and are now before me, and may be placed opposite the three original chords in the hope of working out a successful parallel. Here they are:

(Not very propitious, certainly! But they must serve.)

The first thing noticeable is that to play the chords as they stand, and then to say the words as they stand, gives any mind susceptible to impression from both, much the same experience of whimsical abruptness. As potential music and as potential literature they have, also, about the same degree of lumpiness. That, at any rate, is to the good. Perhaps they favour an inflammatory and vehement interpretation. Both chords and words seem provocative; challenging. If one's first approach to any sense the words may convey is this: the "Dog" is all a-"Flame" to slay the "Mugwump," it might be musically interpreted thus:

But this reading does not, as we had hoped, afford any serviceable example of conjunct relating. Further than ever from it! Let us therefore force ourselves to give it a more conjoinable verbal interpretation, such as: "The dog lies before the lambent flame, gently caressing the mugwump." This gives us opportunity to weigh the natural significance and usefulness of both conjunct relatings and pivot-note relatings of chords, that is of both (*b*) and (*c*) out of the four ways named, which are indeed the habitual resources of all composers. It may be put this way:

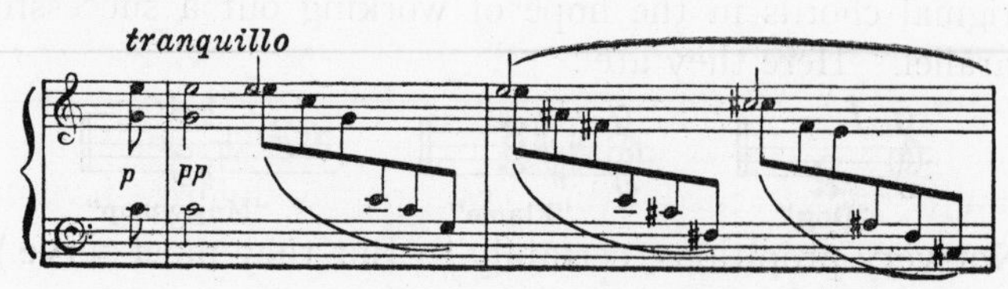

The reader will find it interesting to search for a literary counterpart to the fourth order of chord-relating, namely the enharmonic—which means that an element already in one chord is (without any change of sound) discovered to be of new and surprising significance in another. The nearest analogue, as has been suggested in Chapter 9, is the pun. But an impressive enharmonic change of mind in music is often something so delicate, so elusive—something like a waft of the most fleeting fragrance in a flower-garden, in its sudden charm and inexplicable and vanishing loveliness—that the simile "pun" seems ridiculously inadequate. Yet in essence enharmonic chord-play resembles word-play. Both depend on identity of sound to the ear, and diversity of connotation to the mind. Our trivial three-word and three-chord examples above seem to leave very little chance for us to peer through them for enharmonic instances. Yet, if a *littérateur* could lead us, in a sentence or two, to picture a surprising and deep affinity between the dog and the mugwump, he would have to do it, musically speaking, *enharmonically*. Let us recall that our chord-dog has approximately, and *inter alia*, latent harmonic attributes :

Let us pretend that this particular dog has also acquired an uncanny power of speculative philosophy, and has discovered his very distant affinity to the mugwump, and is meditating upon it, as figured in this phrase :

("The dog felt within it a kindling, kindly oneness with the mugwump.") But enough now of this chord- and word-game, which may already have wearied the reader, though it may, on the contrary, rather have quickened him to interested thought; it is a game that will be found well worth the playing by oneself, and in the effort made, it may be found more informing than any book on the true nature of chord-phrasing in music. There are no bounds to it. Bounds of course must be set in each age. They are necessary in sheer self-defence, and must be in common-sensible accord with the position, circumstances, mentalities, and, above all, the various motives of each listening age. And, once more, it is important to remind ourselves that all chords remain *experiences of ear and mind*. Chords used in any other way are aptly called "paper-music." It might well be stark, staring uselessness to gaze at a chord on paper and hope to experience it, *unless* the ear and mind had behind them as long a course of chord-reading in music as they have had of word-reading in English prose; and perhaps it is near the truth to say that not one man in a million living in our age is in that happy position musically. True, the musical practitioner may inaudibly "hear" what he sees on the silent page before him, and love his silent interpretation far better than the sound of his own clumsy fingers on the keyboard, or the insensitive performance of another person. But it is given to few to feel thus. Once more, our practical prescription must be Repetition—*i.e.* dynamic, eager repetition. Do you enjoy the sound of a certain chord? Repeat it till you know it again at an aural glance—that should be your method, so long as your mind is concerned with that chord. Cultivate a certain reverent familiarity with the inspired relatings of chords in the classical masterpieces. Repeat your good chord-experiences to *absorption*-point (not, by the way, to *saturation*-point). There is infinite leisure for infinite matters, amongst which Harmony is to be counted as one. But there is also urgent need for the attainment of heavenly speed. Speed and leisure seem together equally the essence of all harmonic comprehension and pleasure.

CHAPTER 18

RHYTHM AND PHRASE

RHYTHM is obviously inseparable from phrasing. Yet we must try to consider its attributes separately from melody, harmony, and even apart from metre. Nothing, of course, can be observed to happen at all without rhythm. Rhythm may be described as the behaviour of things, or *observed happenings*. We must, if possible, be able to think of and examine it just as though, for the moment, there were no melody, no harmony, only a mere tone-shadow left.

Such a task is rather like trying to think of the behaviour of a cloud without the cloud itself, or to think of a boy running a race, without the boy: to hold nothing in mind but the running, which is manifestly as absurd as was Alice's seeing of the famous grin without the Cheshire cat. It is not, however, as absurd as it sounds, as indeed Lewis Carroll (with all imaginative readers) realized, and least of all is it absurd in the case of music. Ask the admirers of the boy running the race, and you will find that it *is* the running they admire. Ask the expert: and it is the *rhythm of the running* that he finds of interest. It is the rhythm, in fact, that conveys to the keen observer the boy's very nature—his powers, endurance, attitude to his rivals, etc., etc.: it is the rhythm, and all that it expresses, that wins the race. The rhythm is *the total behaviour of the boy*, depicting his mind, as surely as it brings him success. The grin, in like manner, was the attribute that told the character —or at least all we care to remember of the character— of the cat.

The rhythm of a cloud better expresses the rhythm of a musical phrase. A cloud-gazer, looking at an evening sky full of *cumuli* or *cirrus*, may not too fancifully exclaim, "These record the rhythms of the Creator's brush on the sky's palette." Clouds are but an ever-varying register, in recognizable forms, of natural energies, pressures, and currents at work in the heavens. The deed of the musical mind, which throughout Part 3 we have epitomized in the one word, Phrase, is just such another record of energies; and the mind's interest in controlling and purposefully recording them is as surely depicted in the *rhythmic* attributes of phrases as in their *melodic* and *harmonic* attributes. So while carefully remembering their utter inseparability in mind and sound, let us temporarily disentangle the one from the two others, in order to contemplate rhythm tonelessly, or in a shadow-tone or thinnest monotone.

We must first unfailingly recognize, and remember, the musical reasons for all the dispositions of longs and shorts in rhythms. Thus, we may easily see that a particular rhythm fell into a particular shape (of a dotted crotchet and three quavers, let us say) because of the composer's love of a certain note. He thought it, or willed it, into greater length because it was the very crown of his melodic vision at the moment, as at the asterisk in the following fragment:

Realizing this determining factor, we can still set it aside to study the rhythmic attribute of the phrase apart from the cause, melodic or harmonic, of this or that feature in it. For example, here is a playful theme from Beethoven :

And here is another, less playful, from Mozart, of the same length, in the same key and mood ; both incidentally occupying similar positions in the Sonata scheme of movements :

In order to subtract the rhythms themselves from all other factors—to show naked, rhythmic registers—let us set these two down and sound them in faint monotone, stripped of every purely musical interest :

Such fragments seem likely to serve our present purpose of rhythmic analysis admirably. They have conspicuous differences, but their speed and rhythm convey a like measure of congenial good spirits; they also occupy identical range, and may be said to *weigh* about the same. We shall not therefore be misled by any chance differences of effect due to other than rhythmic causes—such as contrasted volume, or colour, or *tessitura*, or any outside cause. They are chiefly contrasted rhythmic phrases.

Let the reader first sound these two rhythms on the assumption that they resemble some metrical scheme of verse, or dance. The obvious way to do this is to set them down in accordance with their recurrences of metrical pattern. The first (*a*) has four "lines," or phraselets, of which the second and third scan, thus:

The second (*b*) has two equal phrases, which scan exactly:

The difference of rhythmic style is now seen to be marked: (*a*) is whimsical; (*b*) is to pattern. (*a*) Sets forth a rhythm, makes a rhythmic stroke, and at once breaks it up, making, as it were, concise and playful remarks upon it; (*b*) sets out a rhythm, and proceeds to accept it, agrees with it in short stays, or rests upon it. If we go a stage further in our inquiry and set down what happens in the next few bars, we find confirmation of these characteristic differences: (*a*) behaves still more surprisingly, thoughtfully, the mind taking the initiative at every turn; (*b*), on the other hand, becomes still more contented to "stop and stay" on its set rhythmic figure:

(a)

etc.

(b)

From these examples, two main principles of rhythmic action clearly emerge. In both cases, the mind of the composer throws out an initial rhythm, of which measurements can be taken. So far it is a spontaneous deed of the mind, as is any tonal-phrase or chord-phrase—in short it is just our old friend, *Phrase*, monotone or not, spontaneously springing into being.

The two main principles of action that may take possession of the rhythmic field after the initial utterance resemble prose and metrical verse respectively. In actual life they may alternatively be compared with *Going* (walking, hastening, loitering, turning, retracing, pausing, leaping, etc., etc.), and with *Dancing*, respectively. Both these principles of movement are completely natural to music ; they are both among the inherent interests of the listener, just as they are among those of any normal human spectator, and exactly as both prose and poetry, being human, are dear to the normal lover of good literature. It would not, perhaps, be misleading to suggest that our examples (*a*) and (*b*) respectively depict rhythm in actual *Life*, and the rhythm of that section of it known as the *Dance*. This does not, of course, imply that life is not "dancey," nor that to dance is less natural than to walk. The distinction is a far deeper one. When a man consents to think aloud, you may hear the rhythm of his mind. His rhythm gives his thought away. But if he decides to think aloud in music, setting his thoughts to a *preagreed rhythmic pattern*, it is certainly not to the set rhythm that you would then turn to learn his mind; to any other factor than that. You would study his reaction to the set rhythm; to a larger rhythm of the mind, made up of the smaller rhythms.

It is in Sonata music that the workings of these two kinds of rhythm may best be observed, though it is happily often most difficult to distinguish them, so perfect is their fusion. For in Sonata rhythms we detect a composer's values. He dwells much on a note dear to him, or he speeds lightly over a group of notes that matter little to him; in this way he communicates, unconsciously, his inmost values; and it is obviously this dwelling on and speeding over features that, taken together, create all his rhythms, all the infinite varieties of tonal lengths and strengths which, again taken together, record relentlessly and rhythmically the very purpose and trend of the choice behind the tones, the mind behind the music. So these two orders of rhythmic phrase merge in the Sonata; yet they still may remain distinctive. One tends to make all its rhythmic features as it proceeds; the other uses a pre-accepted rhythm twice, thrice, or many times. It is by this twiceness or thriceness that we distinguish it, and indeed by little else in true Sonata music. In a Suite, dance rhythms may still almost dominate a movement, and we get, in effect, picture music. But in a Sonata or Symphony, a composer may appear to lean upon the metrical unit which he first flung out rhythmically—as in the Scherzo of the *Choral Symphony* : but, actually, far from leaning, he proceeds to command it, and to wield the rhythm of the lesser order within that of the greater. So the far-famed unit : may become a mere rung of a rhythmic ladder for steep ascents :

Once more, then, we must view the *phrase*, this time a rhythmic gesture of the mind, as a stroke of the creative hand at work. This is true of every rhythmic phrase in all music. But it should not render less useful the broad distinction between the two emergent orders of rhythmic phrase. That which crystallizes into a metrical unit and rides upon it may be styled a *rhythm of action*. The rhythmic unit that is not so used, but becomes merely the mind's first rhythmic remark, one of a series of remarks, may be called the *rhythm of thought*. We may well imagine that a composer who, by watching a blacksmith's job, is stimulated to set it to music, will naturally use the rhythm of action, and the result will be active music ; the composer who is setting a reverie to music will as naturally use the rhythm of thought : result, reflective music. In both kinds we hear the record of the composer's own mind, and provided he is master of both kinds he is very good company either way. Should yet a third composer desire to depict the blacksmith both at work and meditating while at work, music gives him every opportunity to consummate the blend.

Here Part 3 of this book must end. We reach a half-way house, and leave behind us for the time all our guesses about the nature of music, about its material, and its general way of working, in order that we may now study together at closer quarters some of its customary and known ways in the Western world from 1600 to 1900, or thereabouts. We must, in Part 4, carefully note the essential elements of the local language, which was spoken with such amazing perfection during three centuries by wonderful men like Beethoven or by Bach himself (who, be it noted, died in 1750, exactly midway through the period named).

As we proceed, let us allow ourselves to ponder now and again as to whether the Harmonic highway, then constructed by consent of many musical minds, and since used to such splendid purpose, shows signs of becoming the first part of a *Permanent Way*.

In quitting our Part 3 Observation Post, from which we have for five chapters been watching the free hand of the musician at work in various ways, we shall necessarily narrow our outlook if we are to concentrate upon the Western highroad. Those who listen in bewilderment to-day to the musical experiments of contemporary adventurers, will gladly turn to scan the classical highway afresh. But we shall do well to remember that all Highways (the musical one not excepted) have to be built by men over ground which once was uncharted territory. There may be many enthusiasts who feel that they would rather leave the classical highway behind them for the present. They have enjoyed the great-hearted company of the Bachs, Mozarts, Beethovens, and Wagners who metalled that road; they would desire now rather to devote their Part 4 to exploring untrodden byways. But can the most adventurous musical enthusiast contemplate taking the classics as read? All must agree that the wise explorer and the maker of new roads is never one who, planning a journey "farthest north," neglects to examine and to tread the highroad as far as it can take him on his eager way. Road-taker first, and road-maker, perchance, later on, seems a sound order. The ardent pursuer of the old road is the reliable maker of the new. No man can so well evolve new or extended rulings, whether in a game or in life, as the man who is master of existing rules. Sibelius once told me of an interesting conversation he had with Debussy in Queen's Hall green-room, in which the latter hinted that he was composing in regions along which "others would not follow." It gave the impression of a rarely detached mind in Debussy, able to assess its own work as being a delightful and useful musical avenue, but ending in a *cul-de-sac*. Even if this were true, it would to us, Debussy's admirers, have seemed splendidly worth while. But we may be pardoned if our estimate is more hopeful than his, picturing a sure way through and round his finest imagining, to enriched musical regions. To name but one contribution he made to music in general: perhaps no single composer made more sure to posterity the sane uses of the six-toned chord named in our last chapter: pp Ped. ✻

In order to imagine a tonal bridge from this chapter and this part of our inquiry over to the next, let us sound a deliberate progression at the keyboard which moves, chord by chord, through the centuries, from Hucbald's two-note sounding to Debussy's favourite whole-tone chord:

A phrase thrives when it aspires in just such a way to growing amplitudes. The above phrase moves in agreement with nature's ways, so far as we have been able to discover up to this moment. It also moves in a way that could be approved by the most tenacious conservator of the harmonic highway now to be studied. Let us go once more to the keyboard, and take courage in the thought that even Hucbald's two-note chord can make—say, on a sonorous orchestra—a newer and more thrilling impression to-day than Debussy's :

Each in fact is timeless and glorious in its own order.

PART 4

THE HARMONIC HIGHWAY OF THE WEST

"... How deeply seated is the urgence whereto Bach and Mozart obeyed. . . ."

BRIDGES.

"... Beauty with the impetus of music and the precision of words. . . ."

CLUTTON BROCK.

Chapter 19

FORMING FOURS ON THE TIME-CANVAS

WE are now to contemplate, for six chapters, what may fairly be called the Harmonic Highway of the past three hundred years; the hard highroad of music, trodden equally by children and giant-composers—by John Smith, writer of dance or hymn tunes, and by Mozart in Sonata music; by the babe singing "Ba, ba, black sheep," and Beethoven creating his *Ninth Symphony*, or Wagner his *Ring*. It is a highway of the musical mind: your mind, their mind, and mine; and because, and in so far as it has fitted the common mind of man, it has become the common highway of unmindful custom. Minds of exceptional calibre—such as those of men like Corelli, Purcell, Handel, Bach, Mozart—possessing common sense, sympathy, insight, initiative, and a useful if unconscious taste for road-defining and road-making, helped to determine the course of this highroad, and metalled it well; generations of men have since found it an agreeable and inspiring road to tread.

We shall discuss (in Chapters 21, 22, and 24) the possible secret of the highway. It seems to lie in what is still called Key, that which ultimately must mean nothing less than the relating of all chords into a "solar-centric" system, within which system any harmonic mind that finds chords thinkable can range at will. Such a comprehensive aim need trouble no reader. If he has but ability to think a couple of common chords into first-hand relation, no less a genius than Mozart will show him what potential riches he possesses, and start him on the highway, with a consideration for harmonic beginners which is almost exasperating to any opulent harmonist who impatiently awaits new turns of harmonic events ;—a godly impatience, surely, which no one can be disposed to censure.

It is well to note that neither the history of harmonic music, nor the rules of writing correctly in the classical manner, can be expounded here. They are beyond the bounds of our book, and beyond the qualifications of the writer to offer reliable guidance. Moreover, it is hoped that what is now offered may send readers with quickened zest to the excellent histories and treatises available ; to the analytical writings of Sir Donald Tovey in particular, and in general to the three editions of our unique and genial Grove, where scholarly guidance awaits us under many an important heading.

But what *is* possible here ? A short, practical survey of the highway as it stands. Our aim is to try to discern and suggest the salient points in the actual "rules of the game," as played by the classical composers—coupled naturally, and I find almost inevitably, with the name of Beethoven—and to relate them to our experience and expectation, in order the better to understand the next Symphony to be written in this so highly developed harmonic language ; the better to enjoy it and its noble predecessors; perhaps, above all, the better to descry at what points the rules of the classical game bring about their own extension or transcendence ; to find out, in fact, which of those rules resemble unchanging creative laws, and which prove to be merely the convenient by-laws of a period.

Before we come to the consideration of Key itself, two chapters must be interposed to clear the ground for us. We are, first, in the present chapter, to examine what we have called the Rule of Four—that is, the remarkably prevalent habit in every class of Western music of "forming fours" in the time scheme.

We must here recall that our Highway is not *spatial*. Though everything heard in music *is* as truly located in space as is a game of cricket at Lord's, or on a village green, yet our musical Highway is essentially a time-highway. No wonder, then, that periods of time are pegged out upon it by tacit agreement. This pegging out must not be thought of in terms of mere musical milestones, telling us how far we have gone on the time journey. True, a musical journey of two minutes (120 seconds) at the metronomic rate of ♩ = 60, if in common time, would be duly divided into thirty bars, which would probably have a species of "quarter-milestones" at intervals, to tell the hearer (by four-bar or two-bar signs) where he is on the road. But, as is the way of metaphor, our idea of treading a highway really fails us utterly at this point, for our rule of four is not a rule of length at all, but of thought, structure, and action. It is a *mental* spacing, a tacit agreement of mind as between composer, player, and listener, to think and act in such and such a way, within such and such a time-frame. You do not paint a picture or act a play "all over the place," but within a spatial framework where the related lines and colours can be duly assembled into pictures. Music, in the same way, cannot be composed "all over the time," but within a time framework in which its related movements, melodic lines, harmonies, rhythms, are all duly assembled and finely co-ordinated into a Sonata or a song, or any other kind of musical unity.

But how comes this custom of ever-recurrent four-bar division, four bars answered by four, or four half-bars answered by four? Why do even four mere throbs or pulses create in our minds the expectancy of a corresponding four to follow?

It would be well for the reader to turn aside here (as I myself did a few moments ago) in order to confirm this impression of the prevalence of the custom, by looking up the first bar-divisions of a dozen or more classical movements in succession, by Beethoven, Mozart, and others. After searching the classics thus, and noting where this rule is observed, and where exceeded or curtailed; and after also recalling the unvarying habit of such old dance-tunes as the pleasant measure of "Sir Roger de Coverley":

the reader might well repeat to himself almost any rhymed lines (say, from Gray's "Elegy," or Keats' "Ode on a Grecian Urn"). He will then be more assured of three things: (*a*) that the acceptance of the "rule of four" is a persistent reality underlying the classical triumphs of the three-hundred-year epoch with which we are now concerned; (*b*) that it is very closely paralleled in the contemporary ways of at least two companion arts—poetry and the dance; and (*c*) most important of all, that it has fulfilled the vital function of creating a reliant expectancy at the receiving end, by supplying an acceptable and gradually accepted framework for the creative hand in Sonata music.

In this last connection it is good to realize that, whatever the tacit agreement—whether it had happened to be a rule of four, or some other measure—threes and fives (as in poetry), sixes or sevens—we have in it one more instance of a human need fulfilled, when men (in this case, generations of men) voluntarily agree upon some natural outer bounds within which they may exercise and communicate their inner boundlessness of fantasy and freedom.

If, as we incline to believe, there are in nature profound reasons for the choice of a *norm* of four out of which five will seem exhilaratingly to expand, and within which three will seem (with equally intriguing effect) to contract, these reasons may possibly, civilizations hence, make the rule of four permanently recurrent in music! If, however, they should prove to hamper freedom, they will, of course, be superseded by more amenable rules. Personally, I expect the prime five to play a far more extensive and popular part in the future, though I may be wrong. It seems a heroic, satisfying unit.

It would be a fascinating study for any historically minded reader to start, say, with research into the time-frames of old Frescobaldi's quasi extemporizations on the organ in Rome, which thrilled thousands at the time, and which to-day sound so scrappy (in the light of things that followed), so childish, in their "little-bit-of-that-and-now-a-little-bit-of-that-and-now-what-shall-we-do" style. He might then search the Fitzwilliam collection, and hear how JHON MUNDAY got lost on the virginal, and gradually found it very useful (both to himself and to his hearers) to "form fours." Then he should take a side glance at the pre-Bach effort of Toccatas and the like by seventeenth-century organists such as Johann Kaspar Kerl; then trace the effect of the godsend of dance-measures upon the first writers of suites and sonatas; finally watching the gradual but sure change over from rhythms framed upon the inexorable *rule of the feet* (in a dance) into those fashioned by the tractable, convenient, and anything but inexorable *rule of the mind* (as in a Sonata movement). Here we can only take a glance or two at some of these happenings to music itself.

First let us have one look at the earliest stage. Here is Dr. John Bull, a composer of European reputation in his own day, and of amazing contrapuntal skill, preluding. He has just been striking a few chords, ornamenting them genially and, probably to his day, astonishingly, with no rule of four to hamper him—when suddenly he finds a figure that pleases him :

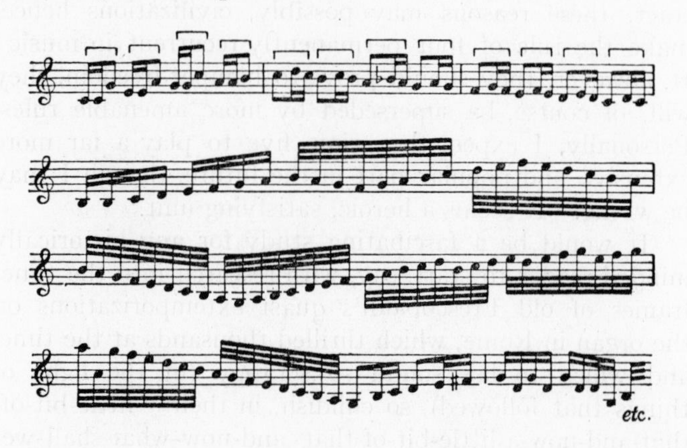

Here the natural tendency towards forming fours becomes for a moment apparent and advantageous ; but in a very few bars (as will be seen) the touch of it vanishes, and the effect is again "go as you please ; try this, try that." Dr. John Bull is quite free. Yes, but are we, the listeners ? We are deferentially quite lost, and can only await his pleasure (and his cadence) with little or no active share in the game. Turning to a piece called "Variatio," however, we find the same composer in the same collection, having accepted the help of the rule of four (already, of course, ubiquitous in dance tunes), still revelling in freedom ; but this time making his elaborate yet innocent theme conform to a scheme which enables him to enjoy, and us to admire, every free stroke of the mind :

Playing this suave and extended melody softly many times, one realizes more and more that the freedom to make this or that subtle point of melodic or imitative beauty is enhanced by the very strictness of the observance of the "rule of four" in this eight-bar conception. The delicious piece called "Dr. John Bull's Juell"* shows the same melodist, this time abandoning himself to the rule in the happiest state of mind:

Here is Mozart, more than a century later, keeping the rule of four (in Piano Sonata No. 5 in G), and enjoying a thriving melodic liberty within it:

* All three of these examples are from the Fitzwilliam Virginal Book.

In the first movement of the same Sonata his melodic vein is so strong that it overflows in the second group of four bars, thus :

Play this delightful tune several times. Then play the first four bars only, and notice that the rule of four, if we have become used to it, would suggest to an ordinary mind an ordinary four-bar reply, thus :

A very pedestrian affair by comparison ! In this way the rule itself both evokes the flash of the inspired free mind, and ensures that it shall illumine the receiving mind. These fragmentary instances are perhaps enough to call attention both to the chief gain and to the chief damage inflicted by the rule of four. The chief gain lies paradoxically in the power it gives to an inspired melody to manifest liberty. The chief damage shows in its killing effect upon all weak melodic gifts. They submit to its bounds, play a feeble game, and perish of complacency ; whereas the vitality and liberty of the inspired melodies come into their own, and are made recognizable through the very defining limits which they are held to fulfil in limitless style. The melody has an agreed framework ; the melodist has an agreed starting-point ; we, the listeners, a measure by which to go ; and all this seems good.

But our rule of four is infinitely more important to the well-being of melody than this. For is it not clear that without it, or without some still more natural and workable equivalent (if, and when, such is found and proved), genius itself might be handicapped and lack incentive ? And even if genius found itself better off without it, we, poor things, might watch the inscrutable strokes of genius much as one might watch the swing of the club of a super-champion golfer (who habitually holed in one), without any fore-knowledge either of his particular aim or of the agreed rules of the course. We have seen, in the Mozart *Presto* above, an example of the ingenuity and resourceful hilarity of the melodist in filling the customary four-bar framework without breaking bounds. This adherence to fours is more characteristic of Minuets, Rondos, and all light-hearted movements than of First Movements. But let us look for a moment at Beethoven's reaction to the customary rule in starting his early Sonatas. Here is the start of Sonata No. 5 in C Minor :

The rule of four prevails, and evokes some close melodic reasoning, expressed in a species of ejaculatory two-bar and one-bar ways, all lying within its four-times-four control. In such speaking music it is the very fact that the rule of four is safely ensconced somewhere far away in the back of Beethoven's mind, (and of ours), that gives the broken phrases a closeness and continuity of appeal which they could not otherwise possess. This is seen again in the development section, which begins as follows :

The ejaculations here lie exactly and fittingly within the third four.

But perhaps the most interesting and illuminating uses of the rule are to be seen when a melody has broken the frame, either by amplification or contraction, or by deliberate adoption of some variant rule of three, five, or seven. Here is a beautiful amplification by Brahms, four being answered by five :

By the time this is balanced by its repetition probably it has exhilarated us, much as if an artist had depicted, let us suppose, the wide pinions of an eagle suddenly outspread. Our rule of expectation, plus its momentary transcendence, gives us just such effectual delight. Now look at the reply :

It recalls the effect of Milton's sudden extension of his last line in the ode " At a Solemn Music." Though this melody subsides to calm, and that poem rises to rapture, they possess the same quality of expansive grace.

It remains for us to notice one more typical result of reactions between the melodist's freedom and the tacitly accepted law. To put it colloquially, one can imagine the former at one moment saying to the law, " I have defied you at the risk of confusion," and the law whispering back, " All will be well if you are careful to rest upon me the moment after ; you will be reassured." Here is Elgar starting the second of his orchestral variations, Op. 36 :

The vague five-bar stretch (2 + 3), at the outset of so early a variation, clearly endangered the relating of the variation to the theme itself. It is strange to see how Elgar unconsciously seems to take every conceivable precaution after this to build the variation upon an unalterable two plus two scheme, both by repetition and by obvious reply, till one almost wishes the piquant irregularity would recur, and the unexpected come to mystify us again. There is, indeed, just one later touch of a relieving three-bar measure which lightens the movement :

There is a like case in Ravel's Piano Sonata, in F♯ minor (to be analysed later), which launches its subject as a flexible three-bar (or two and a half bar) thought, and immediately spends much time in establishing a systematic two-plus-two phrasing, which has the effect of reinstating the rule :

We must not omit to call the reader's attention to one constant and vital habit of the classical writers, that of telescoping the *last* bar of a final four of any section into the *first* bar of a new section. Here is Rameau finishing his famous and utterly regular 4 + 4 Tambourin in E minor :

It is the eighth bar that does double duty here, as last of one pair of fours and first of another.

It is impressive to see how present-day composers, who are most notorious for having explored off the harmonic highroad, and from whom one might expect scant observance of what seems the most conservative, not to say childlike, of customs, still observe the rule. Accessible and clear cut, if slender, evidence of this may be found in Stravinsky's six very small piano pieces called *Les Cinq Doigts* * ; the first piece has the following outline :

* J. W. Chester, 11 Great Marlborough St., W.1. (1922.)

If the reader will play this a few times over, he will find his enjoyment of the little extensions and hesitations enhanced by the customary concept of four phrases in both of the tiny sections; and it is hard to imagine that Stravinsky has not found the rule his ally in this slender design. When we turn to the first nine bars of the final piece of the set, we find the rule very primly observed:

Schönberg seems quite the most baffling harmonist to-day. It is perhaps not too presumptuous to suggest that, through some such simple means of agreement with his hearers, he also stands to attain that mental contact which intelligent enthusiasts such as he cannot but humbly desire, and which, to a larger number of intelligent contemporaries, will make his utterances clearer. I, for one, have neither the ability nor the desire to attempt to appraise that which seems at once so manifestly sincere and (to myself) so aggressively unintelligible. But there are *Six Little Piano Pieces*,* Op. 19, which will be found very handy for studious and friendly contact with Schönberg's cryptic mind, being concise and stript of all encumbrances. Should the reader be baffled by No. 1, he is recommended to study Nos. 2, 3, 4, and 5, *using the rule of four as his special support.* Whether, or to what extent, the customary time-frame is in Schönberg's mind as he writes, one need not, though one might wish to, know. All abstract music—that is, all music standing on its own ground and making its own

* Published in Vienna and Liepzig, and also obtainable from Messrs. J. W. Chester, London.

direct and uninvolved appeal—challenges the hearer *where he stands.* It also places the responsibility upon him to meet it on its own ground, and conversely to expect a reciprocal effort on the part of the composer. Presumably Schönberg does not perversely ignore the need for mutual understanding. It is more likely that he is too often in the position of Holst, who, when a friend suggested to him that a passage in the *Planets* sounded impossible, replied, " Yes, I thought so too when I wrote it; but what are you to do if it comes like that ? " May it not be that when harmonic asperities and inscrutable melodic phrases are in the air, they stand to gain clearness through observance of the tacit rule we have been discussing, this classical habit of conceiving musical phrases in fours (or in two-twos) ?

It obviously well becomes all music to maintain continuity, not only in itself, but in and with the music from which it took its source, and beyond which it is to travel; and this is true, perhaps most of all, at moments of strikingly new departures. It would be curious, but not surprising, if the most baffling modern utterances were immediately to be found less baffling by the silent aid of so obvious and child-like a rule. Obvious? Yes; as obvious as the four walls of a room, the four quarters of the compass, the four limbs of man, the four sides of a picture frame.

There is nothing transcendent in the number *four,* as there is in the wondrous number *two.* All numbers are wonderful enough; but Two is marvellous because of the profound principle of Balance hidden within it. We defer concern with this till Chapter 25. Still we may with advantage note, in passing, that the Rule of Four could not have arisen—nor, incidentally, the necessity for a chapter such as this—were it not for the compelling fact of Balance, and that twice two (*i.e.* balance balanced) spells four !

This being so, we may end this chapter by quoting* a pleasantly informal "Reverie" by Noel Ponsonby, which leads the mind quite away from thoughts of any literal adherence to the classical rule (as laid down for us by the greater masters) and yet makes clear how sensitive harmonically-minded musicians in spirit unconsciously rely upon, and revert continually to it.

Let the reader try to ignore or defy the twice-two instinct, himself devising for his next tune a basis of three-times-three bars in three time, or five-times-five bars in five time, or some such plan. He will find that not only the companionable and natural observances as between maker and listener have their claim upon his mind, but that, were he alone on a desert island, soliloquizing for very self-defence against solitude, he himself would want to bring a balancing two or twice-two into it at long last; so, at least, it seems to the writer.

* By kind permission.

Noel Ponsonby
Espressivo e sempre legato
p
cresc.
mf
stringendo e
molto cresc.
ten.
dim.
ten.
p
rit.
dim.
ten.
una
corda
pp

Chapter 20

LEADING-NOTES, LEANING-NOTES, PIVOT-NOTES, AND CADENCE

THIS chapter needs some excuse. It is interposed both with eagerness and reluctance. As we stand together at the portals of this prodigious highway, destined as we hope to continue to tread it in wondrous company, it may be thought that we ought to seek the main entrance called Key without hesitation or delay, and then examine lesser matters such as the chapter heading suggests. Were this book an attempt at an official harmonic guide-book (from which it is far removed), this would still have to be inserted as an unofficial chapter, justified neither on grounds of method nor precedent, but only on personal experience of the four things named, for these have seemed so indescribably important that they must be considered together before we proceed further.

Most of us know the importance of that which is called a perfect cadence, discussion of which comes later. A cadence clinches key, as we shall see. It is the punctuation of phrases, sections, movements. It is the transaction that carries us to our staying-points. Cadence is the last harmonic word, not the first; the exit, not the entrance; yet the deliberate purpose of this chapter is to detain its readers, to ponder upon cadence together with three interplaying happenings which are of moment to every one on the highway—four things all told, which perpetually work together in so natural a way that mental note of their interrelation beforehand seems desirable.

What is a *leading-note* ? It is the descriptive name commonly given to a note which rises by step of a diatonic semitone into what we may call a staying-note, upon which the mind halts or alights (for a long or a short while) :

The "official" leading-note is the last semitonic stepping-stone leading up to the keynote. It has acquired great significance on the harmonic highway, though in itself the step by which it makes itself known (for what it is) is but the smallest conceivable melodic happening. We must presently try to watch and determine its use in music to-day.

What is here meant by a *leaning-note* ? It is a name the writer has ventured to give (merely for convenience and memorability) to any note which correspondingly *falls* by a diatonic semitone into any staying-note :

(In the last example a quasi leading-note is actually interposed between the leaning-note and its objective.) This kind of note also has acquired an importance all its own ; though definitely far second to that of the leading-note, it is its natural *vis-à-vis*.

What is meant by a *pivot-note*? This, again, is merely a term applied for convenience to a note held in common by two successive chords :

As to the *Cadence* itself, we shall only be concerned here with its two chief forms, still often called authentic and plagal; and chiefly, of course, we are concerned with the later composite perfect cadence as used by Haydn, Beethoven, and others, a cadence which is directly derived from the *Clausula Vera* of modal days.

Few readers can have access to-day to Rockstro's little book of last century called *Rules of Counterpoint*, which so felicitously explains the age-old custom of the *Clausula Vera*, or true close. It will be well to reproduce its teaching on this point; how that when a Plain Song (or *Canto fermo*) reached its last step, which was of course a descent of a tone to the final of the mode: the companion melody, or counterpoint, if any, was required to step *upwards* by a semitone to the same note, whether as a major sixth above: merging into an octave; or as a minor third below: merging into a unison. If there were three voices, the third naturally had to find something else to say. If it found itself, as it most naturally would, on the third above the *Canto fermo*: Rockstro taught that it had to move either to an open fifth or a third above the final:

Tonally sensitive musicians ordained that the third, if present, should be made major:

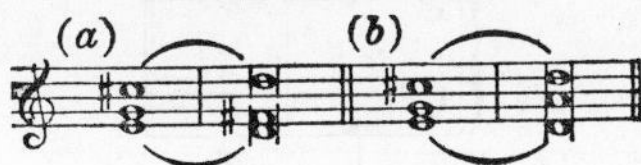

So there came into being what is still called *Tierce de Picardy* in minor modes. But if the chief, or fixed, song were in an upper part, the added or third part could but supply the missing note in the incomplete chord created by the two existing parts: This missing note might stand either above these two parts, or below them: or, if they were in open order (a tenth apart) it might stand between them: and it would in most cases, but not necessarily, naturally move to the final, when it was in an upper part. In the case of the Phrygian Mode, the observance of the identical rules (as shown by Rockstro) gave us the Phrygian cadence in its various simple forms, a thing of beauty still too rarely enjoyed:

At the moment, it is important to notice that the *Clausula Vera,* in its Dorian, Lydian, Mixo-Lydian, and Æolian forms, always gave similar results *:

Compare these two with the Haydn, Mozart, and early Beethoven habits of perfect cadence, and the close affinity is easily seen. When the seventh had been coined and passed into general currency as a chord, and used on what (following Sir Donald Tovey) we shall here refer to as the *home-dominant* :

the result showed a perfect fusion of the older Closes

* See page 291.

into the harmonic perfect Cadence in what afterwards became a sadly debased form. Incidentally it is useful to notice here how this cadence uses all the notes of the major scale except one—the sixth. Its utterance thus became not only incisive, but summary; and still more so when, in later times, the ninth was added: and *all* the notes of the scale were requisitioned in one transaction, as when the lavish little mouth-organist in the street blows and sucks alternately at his too ingenious instrument, flinging out all his scale at his western-bred audience, compressed into this very order:

In this we may hear the typical *leading-note* (C♯ rising to its goal, the keynote), reacting upon a typical *leaning-note* (G falling to the defining third, F♯) and resulting in a typically reiterated *perfect cadence* in one hackneyed transaction. Only the common pivot-note is excluded.

The reader may find it timely and refreshing to look away at this moment, almost at random, to some of the greater classical uses of this eloquent transaction. Here is Beethoven in the *Eroica* making impressive use of it:

The constantly leaning A♭ and the leading-note (B♮) together seem to blend poignancy with weariness in a way that is inescapable, and which could not be conveyed by either note without the other. The rhythmical pivot-note in the last bar contributes a touch of stony stillness.

Or take this cadence of Bach's, from his Organ *Choral*, "O Mensch bewein":

Here A♭ is the leaning-note to G (the most usual of all leaning-notes in a major key), G♭ is made by Bach into a leaning-note to F, then F♭ is made into an unusual and (in such a position) astonishing leaning-note to the key itself, the familiar leading-note being again interposed.

Great and small minds meet in this cadential transaction. This is not surprising, since it would seem that everything that enables a greater mind most readily to tell a smaller whither it is being carried harmonically, is to be found in it. Let us test this. Plant a simple mind upon any note—C, and then upon its common chord:

Next to C, G is the note second in importance upon which the rudimentary mind could first pivot another chord. Could there be any step more natural to all minds than the step to the note G, and then to the G chord?

But in taking this mental step, we can do better for the ear in relating two such chords than to jump a fifth up or a fourth down, in this lumpy disjunct fashion. Here it is that the pivot-note first, and quickly following on its heels our friends the leading-note and the leaning-note, all emerge in aid. Let us not jump a fifth up, but let us take each note in the old chord *to its nearest neighbour-note in the new* :

As we listen to these two, simplest harmonic transactions, we shall find that the cadential importance of four factors begins to be clear. As we are led from any one chord towards another, our mind can receive something like the maximum of composer's consideration, by means of :

(*a*) Moving on a *pivot-note.*
(*b*) Moving semitonically *up.*
(*c*) Moving semitonically *down.*
(*d*) Moving to the most closely related chord, pivoted from octave to fifth, or fifth to octave.

When, therefore, old Haydn loved to write, and we, as children, loved to hear this :

these four rudimentary and intimate aids were epitomized in one friendly strain ; and it is little wonder that Rossini, for example, built prodigious perorations to his popular Overtures upon such a basis. Still less is it matter for surprise that the home tunes of the outstandingly harmonic Fatherland thrived upon it, and that all men, women, and children can feel perfectly at home in it.

Like any linguistic formula of daily life, this cadence takes on innumerable forms. Just as you may say a temporary good-bye for a moment in the course of a day, and a final good-bye at night ; just as you may say good-bye every day for years, and one day may say good-bye for ever ; so there is every shade and grade of cadence in music, as, for example :

It is notable that, if you should be reduced to two-part writing, and so have to cast about to find the two most significant notes to sound—that is, the two notes which would best sum up your key position and intention to your hearers—there can be no doubt that the leading-note, which is the *sharpest* note of the seven, and the leaning-note which happens to be the flattest, will best conspire in action, every time, to leave no hearer in doubt of your meaning. It is true, as we shall presently see, that even when an unadorned or skeleton bass behaves like this (as in the *Eroica*, to be mentioned later) :

long harmonic associations have invested it with a meaning so strong that the mind and ear together treat the four bare unisons in such a statement as if they actually sounded out four major chords—as in fact their natural harmonics do ! Use has taught the musical world to say, " Ah, yes ; that stands for *Tonic, Dominant ; Dominant, Tonic*. But in spite of this easy implication, it remains true that there has not been found a two-part musical remark in the Western world more commonly grasped (consciously or not) by the man in the street than this:

And should it be sounded at any chance moment, anywhere, in any key:

it is the clearest possible announcement that, in the mind of whoever sounded it, a keynote thought has been reached *via* the leading-note, and its major third has been reached *via* a "leaning-note." This sounds an arbitrary statement, but custom has made it a truism. Try it and listen!

But now we must take preliminary note of a further matter of importance. When any note in the whole range of notes in our present system rises by what is called a diatonic * semitone, the higher note is always *a flatter note by five degrees* than the lower, in the natural harmonic ladder of musical keys. Conversely, when a part falls by a diatonic semitone, the lower note is *sharper* than the higher (obviously also by five degrees). This may not at first be clear to my reader. It means that any listener who has grown used to the harmonic highway, thinks of the leading-note as sharp (or acute) compared with its chief: and conversely, the leaning-notes are equally flat (or grave) as compared with their staying-note: Let us see these notes in black and white, so to speak—no, let us go preferably to the keyboard and see them for the moment in white notes only, in the only position in which we can find them in the natural scale of C major: The reader must be referred to the music

* A diatonic semitone is the kind of semitone found in the diatonic scale (as from A to B♭), and therefore always moves to a different degree in that scale. A chromatic semitone is only a chromatic alteration of any particular note (as from A to A♯).

of the masters themselves if he still finds it hard to become aware that the leading-note here is in a real sense the "sharpest" note in the scale. It is, for example, the keynote of B major with a signature of five sharps: That means that all its associate notes and all its diatonic associations are near the extremely sharp side of our ladder of keys. Similarly, the leaning-note, F, proves to be the "flattest" note in the scale, associated with its own key with a signature of one flat: and itself the leading-note of the scale of G♭ major, with six flats:

Now, to the mind accustomed to the Bach-Mozart-Beethoven harmonic usage, such associations grow stronger and stronger with daily experience. Sir Frederick Ouseley long ago gave his pupils the memorably sagacious advice that if they wished to track out the root of any fundamental discord they must search for *the sharpest note*, then think of that as the leading-note, and they would probably be right unfailingly. "Rule of thumb" though this may be, it works extraordinarily well in analysis of all harmonic music up to the time of Wagner, Brahms, and indeed much later. Why? Because degrees of sharpness really *mean* sharpnesses in our minds, and notes lying on the flat side really convey a totally different set of impressions to all frequenters of the classical highway. These associated values, as in the case of any language, are gained by experience and enhanced by study.

Though I have agreed not to embark here either upon historical or technical digressions, yet I may ask permission (risking, perhaps, the momentary estrangement of some readers) to set down a sharp and a flat ladder of keynotes and signatures as a crude reminder of the rudimentary facts, and for later reference if need be. (See page 224.) We can see at a glance the relative sharpness of *all* our twelve degrees. Thus C, the open-hearted "natural" note, is sharpness itself by comparison with D♭ (to which it is leading-note); but, on the other hand, C is so flat a note by comparison with B that it does not even lie in the B scale! We find ourselves on an endless ladder of fifths on both sides of C. On that ladder, C is capable of taking its place centrally, as well as at the extremely sharp end or the extremely flat end of our thoughts. For this reason it seems well to number it as 0 (zero), higher than all flatter notes (or minus numbers) in the endless series, but lower than every sharper note (or plus number). By this means our actual numbering may the more logically bear out the facts. This will be found a useful numbering later on. Beginners on this harmonic highway cannot, and need not, think far along either ladder. Three rungs up the sharp ladder, and three down the flat ladder, were indeed almost enough for the mighty works of Handel himself! Bach ventured the whole way up and down; and, at the two extremes, he beheld and occasionally tentatively entered the fascinating enharmonic world which we shall consider in Chapter 24.

Now it will be clear that this chapter's four factors of communication as to harmonic experiences and whereabouts, as between the most erudite composer and the simplest listener, concern us through all chords, keys, and chordal or key positions. Relatedness through pivot-notes, the *lead* and the *lean* of semitones upwards or downwards to a momentary staying-note of any kind, and the resultant cadential effect, are inseparably eloquent of key and intention. All four factors are ubiquitous. For, of course, leaning-notes are possible wherever there are

(a)
(0)
(−1)
(−2)
(−3)
(−4)
(−5)
(−6)
(b)
(+6)
(+5)
(+4)
(+3)
(+2)
(+1)
(0)

staying-notes of any kind upon which they can lean; and they will always have a comparatively graver sound than the note they approach, as thus:

and therefore will tend to awaken associations further down on the *flat* side of the harmonic ladder. Similarly, leading-notes in the general sense are equally possible a diatonic semitone below any staying-notes up to which they can lead. This, in fact, means that a leading-note is possible below all degrees of the scale:

Speaking generally, it seems accurate to give these the dignity of the name of *Leading-notes*—a name so indelibly associated in text-books with the semitone below the keynote—only when they possess the power in their context to carry the listener to their goal, as though even for a fleeting moment it were the centre of thought. Here, for example:

most listeners would find but one centre, C, and therefore but one leading-note; and neither D♯ nor F♯ would have pull enough to displace it in most experienced listeners' minds. Here, on the other hand:

D♯ rises to the dignity of leading-note. Otherwise such a note remains what we may (alternatively) call a sharp grace-note.

Wherever such notes or any pivot-notes together suggest a perfect cadence, or at least a cadential thought, they lead us to harmonic conclusions, however evanescent. In considering modulation, we shall readily see how "quick as thought" a key can change, and how it is nearly always the result of what we may call the "levitational pull" of the leading-note, aided very often by the gravitational pull of a leaning-note as its *vis-à-vis*.

We may now return to our endless harmonic ladder, and lay firm hold, so far as is possible, upon the central harmonic significance of cadence, before entering the chapters where we shall need to take it for granted.

Notice that the scale of C has every note but one in common with the scale of its nearest neighbour on the sharp side :

F is the only note of difference. Similarly, it holds every note but one in common with the scale of its nearest neighbour on the flat side :

B being the only note of difference. And this is automatically true of all next-door neighbour scales on the endless ladder of key. Just as truly as in social life, propinquity and relationship have potent influences.

But it should be further noticed that if the *keys* which lie next on either side to any given key on the ladder (as G lies to C, or C lies to F) hold most of their scale-notes in common, expectation might be raised that the neighbourly *key-chords* will hold most in common also. Even if there were none but major keys, this would not be literally true ; and if relative *minor* keys are admitted, it is literally untrue. Here is our central or zero key-chord, with its nearest neighbours on either side :

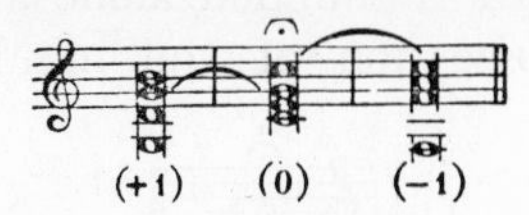

They have, in both cases, one note in common with the centre-chord. Here it is with two minor keys each side :

These hold, in both cases, *two* notes in common with the centre-chord ! And if we go to work " in the letter," we can find other key-chords, major and minor, which hold one or even two notes in common, and in point of ladder-position are in all cases more remote :

It is possible to make beautiful use of this array of chords, literally as nearly related as the nearest neighbour-chords. Brahms, at the end of the Slow Movement in his Third Symphony, makes impressive trombone use of one at * :

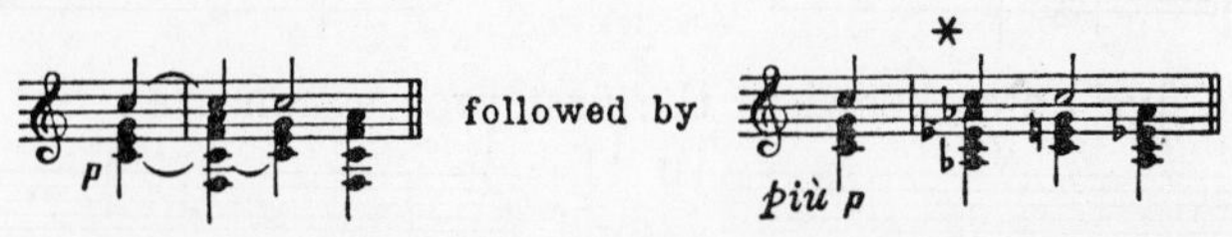

But though, note for note, these relatings (or pivotings of chords together by means of the notes they happen to hold in common) make them appear to be more or less on equal terms, yet it is clear, when one listens to the above example from Brahms, that the second, though as surely riveted as the first, gives a far more distant mental effect, and everything conspires to make the former a chord-relating of the closer kind. How does this come about?

Whatever chord is sounded alone and held in mind tends to take possession of the mind as a centre or key-chord:

The same would be true the next day, hour, or even minute, if the mind is cleared from preconceptions and willing to start *de novo*:

But when once any one chord is in possession, the chords that lie immediately above and below it on the endless ladder tend, both naturally (as we have seen) and from long usage, to become its paramount associates and supporters:

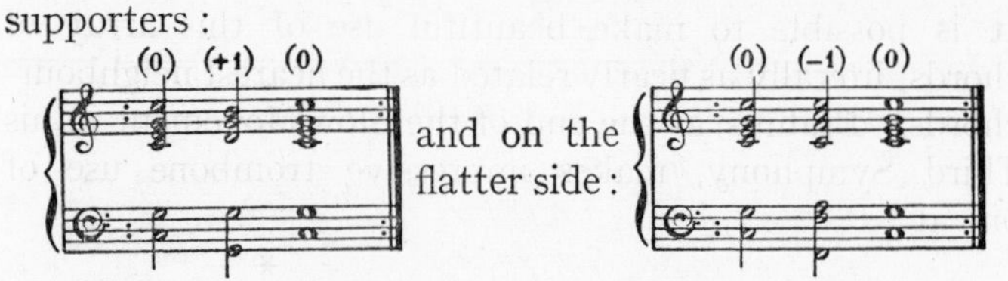

and on the flatter side:

The five notes heard in the first progression are:

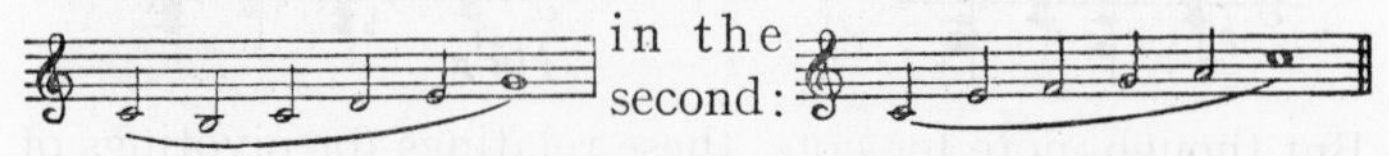

in the second:

and, when added, these together make the diatonic scale.

The above are, in truth, the simplest and perhaps the two most important and far-reaching harmonic transactions in existence, commonly known, when centred upon any one central chord, as *perfect* and *plagal cadence* respectively. And when the ancient *Clausula Vera*, or the modern *perfect cadence,* has told the listener that their staying-point, or, as it used to be called, "the final of the Mode," is attained, can we wonder that the mind lingers round the opposite side of its central chord and adds the plagal to the perfect cadence, thus establishing unequivocal centrality for the key-chord?

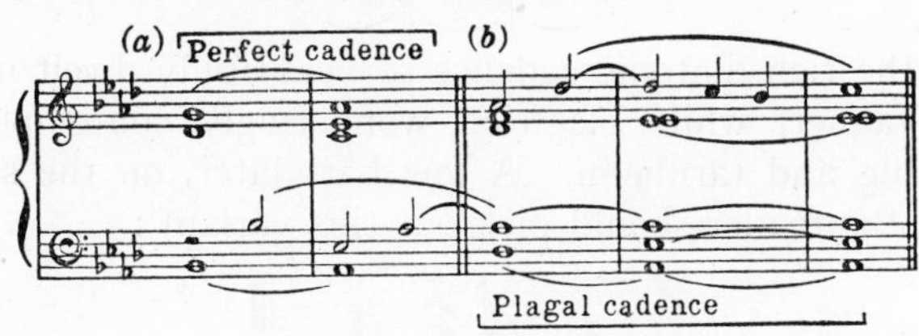

The reader is asked specially to notice how the leading-note is here normally counterbalanced by the most typical leaning-note.

There are many ways in which the reader may increase and make more permanent his mental hold upon the four points here together discussed. First, he should sit at the keyboard and take an intensive course of the above two cadences in every key. He will also find it particularly helpful to study with gramophone records Beethoven's *Eroica* Finale, based as it is on this formula:

The invigorating opening of the *Emperor* Concerto, in the same key, exuberantly sets forth these chords:

before Beethoven sets out upon his concerted enterprise.

Then as to leading-notes and leaning-notes in joint

action, a most illuminating example for study is to be found in *Siegfried*.* Play this first :

It is the rich diatonic cadence so beautifully dwelt upon by Wagner, while Siegfried wonderingly contemplates the ring and tarnhelm. A few bars later, on the same page, the reader should pick out this variant :

in which a supplementary leading-note to the major third appears. But now note the delightful gravity of the sudden introduction of a totally new *leaning* A♭ in the very next bar :

There is, indeed, a strong combined gravitational and levitational pull here, exercised by the leading-notes on the sharp side, and the leaning-note on the flat side, which not only enriches the music, but seems to steady the comprehending mind. Here is a fine example from Vaughan Williams :

And here is a significant instance from Beethoven, in

* Page 206 of the vocal score.

which he exemplifies the greater pull of the true leaning-note as compared with the step of a major second :

for the F♮ suggests new remoteness on the " south " side of the ladder of distances. Here are a few less usual leaning-notes ; their harmonic results should be most carefully " tasted," the reader dwelling on them each in turn long enough to think out their effect upon his mind :

The possible involutions of sharp grace-notes upwards, with flat grace-notes downwards, are numberless, and can both quicken and stabilize thought for any sensitive listener when aptly balanced.

CHAPTER 21

TONAL CENTRALITY AND KEY

THE word *concentration*, and the narrower word *focus*, both come near to conveying the essential idea of Tonality to musicians. At the very outset the reader should carefully observe how all things here discussed are things of the mind. What we call Key is, in fact, tonal centrality. What the vanishing point is to gazers at a landscape this note is, for instance, to listeners to Beethoven's First Symphony: It is the central tone of the whole work. Of course this is the whole point of calling it the keynote, and of saying the Symphony is "in C." Let the reader, at this point, "wash in" on his keyboard a few C major *arpeggios* very softly, with the sustaining pedal continuously down.*

Then strike the keynote once more: If these are sounded alternately several times, and if, at the same time, the reader's eye could look deeply and restingly into some familiar landscape (or better, in this instance, into

* If, in spite of care, any slip of the finger occurs, lift the pedal to clean the tonal slate, then, lowering it, begin again—more carefully!

a seascape), the impression would probably be heightened by analogy, and he would more readily perceive that the sense called key-sense really is the sense of musical *centrality*, realizing also that it is wholly a thing of the mind. It is mental centrality that he enjoys. It is noteworthy that the physical eye can attain visual centrality in its landscape by the mere act of stedfast looking. It makes its own centre, to which all other objects perspectively converge, a "stroke of luck" (the musician might almost enviously cry) for the centre-seeking mind with the *eye* for working partner, and all visible glories in the universe for field of action! No such luck for the centrality-loving mind with the *ear* for physical colleague, and all imaginable audible glories the open waiting field of musical action! No doubt the advantage is on our side when it comes to freedom of the mind to choose. Certain it is that eye and ear must be equally obedient servants to mind. Looking and listening purposefully will alone bring about centrality; and in our harmonic field, while the keynote may be called the musical vanishing-point for just so long as the mind retains one centre, so the key-chord may be likened (curiously enough) not so much to any vertical line as to the horizontal line of sight which lies naturally across the whole picture while it is being contemplated at that key-level.*

This inward musical apprehension of any keynote and its key-chord—whether in major or minor mood—as a central concept, should, we believe, be deliberately, even assiduously, acquired by all music lovers, if they would be ready to make any effectual harmonic excursions up and down the ladder of keys (see page 224), remembering

* Musicians used to reading chords vertically on the page may have to *will* hard to forget the vertical look of them, and to immerse both ear and mind in the sound of them. But this may be done and should prove refreshing practice for a page-weary musician.

that they will be required, as time goes on, to travel far with composers without losing the power to focus or concentre ear and mind. Mental hold upon the key-chord naturally varies with every listener, and probably varies in the same listener twenty times a day. Take a course of early Mozart and no vast range is required. Turn to a late Wagner score, or to Debussy's Preludes, and you will need greater concentration, greater tonal tenacity.

Cumulative experience has determined our highway, and cumulative experience alone can heighten our understanding, enjoyment, and extension of it. It has been well trodden by learned and unlearned alike, up to a point. But it is manifestly adapted to immense expansion, is expanding, and must expand. Unhappily, as experience of chords becomes richer and more lavish, and our aural taste for five-note chords, even for six- and seven-note compounds, develops richly (surely alluring, sensuous charm is to be found in many of the fuller chords—dominant ninths, etc.—cited at the end of the last chapter), our minds may become side-tracked for some time, and grow less diligent to ascend and descend this ladder of endless harmonic adventure—reaching, as it were, from Heaven to Hell, with homely earth midway. This sensuous side-tracking will be familiar to some of my readers. So far as it induces and ministers to imaginative torpor, it is bound to bring temporary confusion and loss, for the extended tonal highway is arduous to tread. Besides, even Bach himself, though he discovered and expounded his cycle-commonwealth of twenty-four keys, and used them all in his immortal Forty-Eight, scarcely ever, in his most elaborate Fugues, ventured more than three thorough removes either way! And furthermore, when men *do* venture all the way, they are destined to discover a spectral enharmonic presence in both the G♭ depths and the F♯ heights, awaiting all who may wish to explore the Dantesque mount of enharmonic thought. But of this we must postpone our thoughts.

The very sound of music can be so full of attraction of all kinds—melodic, chordal, rhythmic, and endless possibilities of all kinds of tasteful, lively delights—that we are easily beset and detained on the harmonic way. But pursuers may not loiter. Let us then try to explore this key or centrality mystery diligently together, forthwith.

Start once again with the natural chord, C major:

and maintain it as centre or key-chord, all the more tenaciously as you venture forth in two directions. First venture your natural one remove in either direction, and see what happens in the kingdom of the resolute mind:

This, however, is a *very* baby-effort to minds that have long possessed a natural scale:

Yet it remains, as we have seen, a satisfying basic harmonic effort to any mind, that of musical babe or adult, unaccustomed to chromatic notes; for it has, in two simple transactions, left us safely and significantly centred. The child in us cries out, "I'm the king of the castle!" The man within protests, "My mind is tethered (like a goat on a very short string) to C!" Both are right. The child is father of the man. There is something both glorious and humiliating in the fact that the above-named two simple transactions soon became fused and stereotyped into one very common formula as follows:

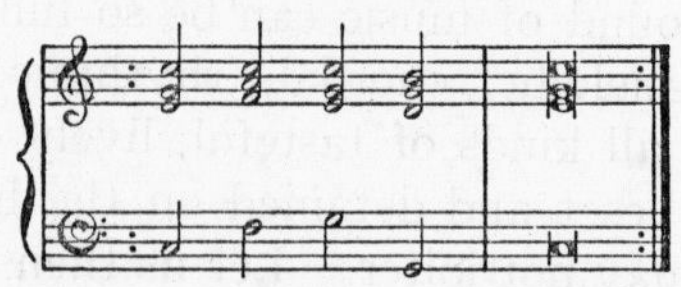

This conveniently epitomizes our natural and reliable starting-point for harmonic centrality; it calls out and confirms our key-sense in music. It was achieved three centuries or so ago. Men like Corelli had a great deal to do with its firm establishment, and with the discovery of its tractability in the common mind of music lovers. Europe may be said to have begun her harmonic education with it.

But long before Corelli or any harmonic systemization arrived on the scene, the natural tendencies (detailed in previous chapter) towards the cadence, the leading-notes, leaning-notes, and pivot-notes were all four at work in the sentient minds of men, shaping musical thoughts and taking on eloquent significance of their own. We cannot safely go a step forward without remembering this. The double pull (gravitational and levitational) of the perfect cadence:

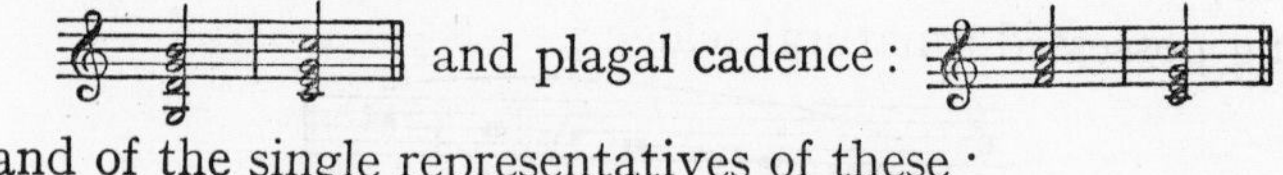

and of the single representatives of these:

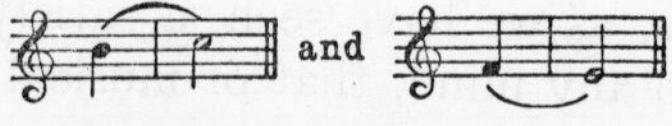

has never yet ceased to work. Readers should here make up any typical fragment at the keyboard to exemplify this for themselves, and then watch the effect on the mind:

Such fragments being interpreted in common chord transactions, *may* have implied alternate, perfect, and plagal cadences to some minds. Thus:

But to the majority of Western minds the implied harmonies, due to our upbringing on the harmonic highway, would certainly be something more like this:

It was probably the influence of the very early arrival of the chord of the seventh: which made it possible to telescope what we have called the "double pull" of key into one experience in the composite cadence, concentrating the powers of both cadences, with their leading-notes and leaning-notes, to draw the mind homewards: This concentration, of itself, has had enormous influence (both for good and ill) ever since. Play the first eight bars of the early C Major Sonata of Beethoven (No. 3), and it is fairly accurate to say that in it may be found a normal specimen amalgam of these chief formative factors in the tonal centralization called Key:

Innumerable fine movements, notably by Haydn, Mozart, and early Beethoven, have been based on this and kindred progressions, consisting of three or four implications of the perfect cadence (with a plentiful hinting of the typical leading-note and its antidote the leaning-note), and with, roughly, one part F major thoughts (under-dominant) to three or four parts G major thoughts (home dominant), and all serving the one end of establishing C as a gravitational centre.*

If we now proceeded to explore by unillumined, mole-like theory, we should perhaps look for our next steps to lie equally in each direction from the centre—two up and two down :

and the next something like this :

But this would be to ignore the lively significance, to

* The perpetual and reiterated, even tedious, use of such harmonic formulæ of centrality in Mozart and his contemporaries, obviously accustomed ordinary men and women, generation after generation, to think in key ways and to acquire the power of harmonic focussing.

musical minds, of the customary harmonic *amalgam* already referred to, and, above all, of this one chord, the dissonant home-dominant first *plus* a seventh :

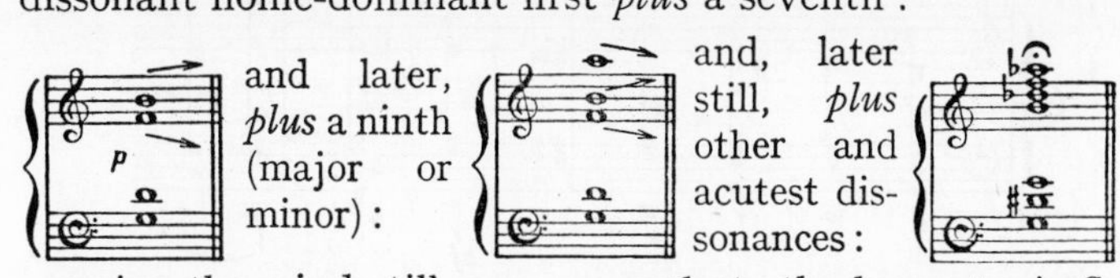

and later, *plus* a ninth (major or minor) : and, later still, *plus* other and acutest dissonances :

pressing the mind still more urgently to the home-tonic C. The reader is here asked to play and ponder over these dominant sevenths, ninths, and any other like dissonances, and at the same time to give them consciously such significances as they have acquired in his own personal experience up to date, though without prejudice against all the ampler meanings which may await him and them. When this is done, the influence of the most commonly used and concentrated forms of home-dominant such as these :

will not even need their fully cadenced forms :

they will soon bring the mind, by implication, to C as centre, without C being heard at all ! Gradually it becomes easier to understand why the natural extension of key-range has actually taken place further along the sharpening series than down along the flattening series. It is as if the keynote (and implicitly the key-chord) had become our mental *terra firma* : and consequently the sense both of climbing and falling from *key-level* has stabilized. It is very important that all lovers of the classics should note this ; it is still more important to be sure that the word *key-level* is no mere theory to read about and ponder, but a reality of mental experience to the reader himself. When Beethoven wrote in C major thus :

he was certainly giving us the experience of harmonic climbing by his leading-notes, though he carefully remains in related minors which keep us in our key (C), while creating the feeling of progressing through keys. Climbing through keys might be amusingly indicated on the page thus :

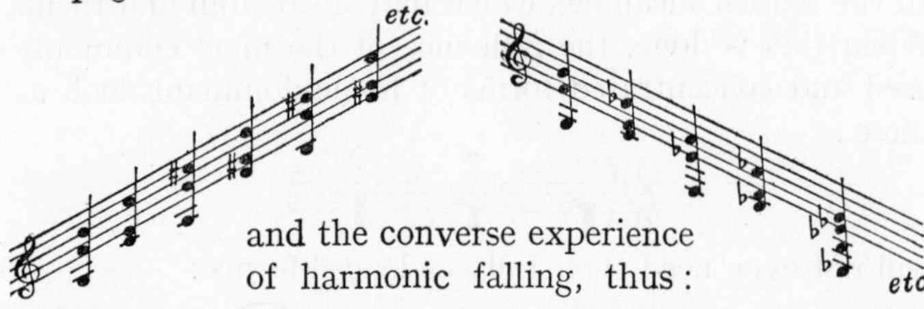

and the converse experience of harmonic falling, thus :

But we must know that the harmonic facts of *specific gravity* and *specific levity* (as we now term the two aspects of one matter) are only in the mind. Such trick-diagrams are useful for presenting at a glance to the eye what remains in effect a mental experience.*

It is the extended personal experience of *cadences, leading-notes*, and *leaning-notes* (discussed in the previous chapter), more than any mere thoughts and theories of

* True, the actual physical sounds in these instances are on the whole tending up in one case and down in the other, and this has its undoubted influence upon the mind. But write this chord here: and this at a high pitch: and we still know it for D♭ far down on the ladder of fifths, upon which the musical mind has come to range its related thoughts.

our endless chord-ladder, that will maintain and strengthen every listener's comprehension of *key*, or, in other words, that will increase the pull and power of tonal centring while bringing our minds to bear upon as delightful chord-concepts and enjoyments of them as we may compass. Experience certainly seems to give an amazingly quicker general grip and use of the sharper chain of chords than of the less sharp ones. This at first seems curious. But the reason for it is clearer when we think of all the notes of the natural scale as themselves potential keynotes, subsidiary to our "potentate," the original keynote :

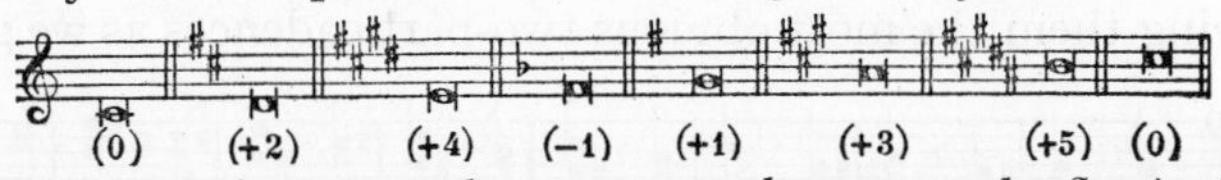

Five out of six prove sharp monarchs, one only flat! No wonder early Beethoven is full of excursions up sharpnesses which do not necessarily take him out of his key! And it seems roughly true to say that, up to the middle of the nineteenth century, for five removes in sharpness above a centre, one remove in flatness was considered a fit balance. When Beethoven later plunged his intelligent hearers at the fifth bar of a new C Major (*Waldstein*) Sonata into a flatness two removes away :

they must have got a momentary mental shock, and wondered to what lengths genius would venture next; only (with his help, and sharing his delight) to find matters subsequently explained, and themselves safely at home and still securely "tethered," as of old.

Yet the harmonic highway is by no means as narrow as it has too often seemed. We shall find that there neither is, nor ever was, anything to destroy the mind's central hold upon C, though it venture *five and more removes among the flatnesses* as well as among sharpnesses. The law of harmonic gravity and the law of harmonic levity are at one in this, that a strongly pulling cadence will, at every stage, *and from both directions*, recall the mind and re-establish the key-chord. A mind experienced in the perfect and plagal cadences, and in the many easy blends of the two, as well as in deftly combined uses of the *leading-notes* and *leaning-notes*, finds no rung of the harmonic ladder in either direction so remote that it cannot instantly relate it to its centre by one or two gliding steps. Let us try to test this by climbing sharply (tonally levitating) and falling gravely (tonally gravitating) through our whole range—chromatically both ways—giving them the most obvious two-part cadences as we go:

The reader may well play all of these cadences in turn, carefully preceding each one with the key-chord itself, and following each in turn with a well-chosen and well-placed cadence in C. Here, as mere samples, are three of the more remote, treated in this rather domestic way. (See page 243.)

We have so far only thought of the natural, or zero-centrality of C, from which the mind may radiate with ever-increasing scope and certitude, enriching its harmonic resources indefinitely in the two directions of greater or lesser sharpnesses. There is, indeed, enough for the mind to marshal and enjoy from this natural centre for a lifetime. We may even believe that we could remain in the key of C major for good were we so disposed, without being bored. And all the other twenty-three major and minor cadences could be as completely and

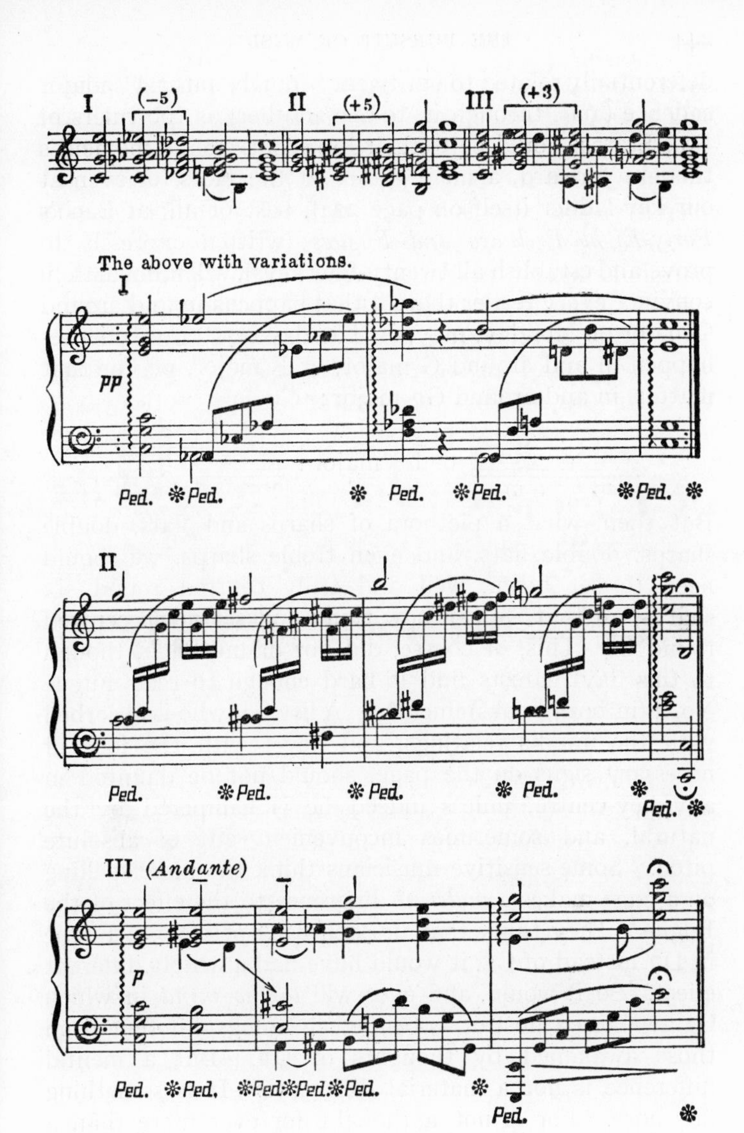
I
(-5)
II
(+5)
III
(+3)
The above with variations.
I
pp
Ped.
Ped.
Ped.
Ped.
Ped.
II
Ped.
Ped.
Ped.
Ped.
Ped.
III (Andante)
p
Ped.
Ped.
Ped
Ped.
Ped.
Ped.

deferentially related to our twenty-fourth, natural C major cadence (and, through it, to one another) as the rulers of Free States should be to their President. But a moment's thought forward, a mere glance at the facts (or even at our key-ladder itself on page 224), best of all, at Bach's *Forty-Eight Preludes and Fugues* (written expressly to prove and establish all twenty-four keys), will immediately convince every reader that all that happens in and around C major on Monday, may, on Tuesday or at any time, re-happen in and around G major, or F major, or, for that matter, in and around G♭ major:

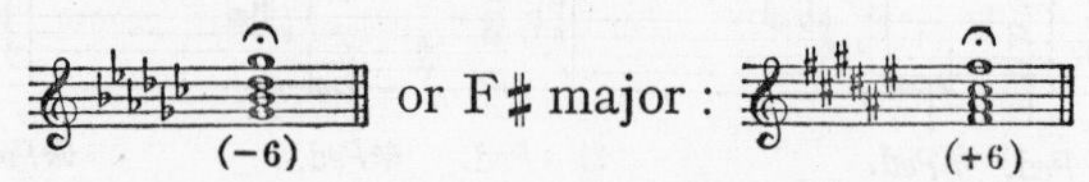

But then, what a plethora of sharps and flats, double sharps, double flats, and even treble sharps, we should need to set down, well and truly centred round six sharps, all that we can now think and set down centred round C! This, of course, did not daunt Bach, though to this day pianists find it hard enough to read Fugue No. 3 (in both books) fluently. A listener who is absorbed with the mind's relatings, and never with the look of necessary signs on the page, should not be daunted in any key-centre, unless indeed he is hampered by the natural, and sometimes inconvenient gift of absolute pitch. Some sensitive musicians think the mere spelling on a page makes a *material* difference to the effect of the Fugue. They think that if Bach had spelt No. 3 Fugue in D♭ instead of C♯, it would have had a wholly different effect. So it would, and ever will *to the mind* in which C♯ awakens a host of associated meanings different from those awakened by thoughts of D♭. But a mental difference is not a material difference. It is something far more. For is not a thought for ever more than a thing? More potent, more far-reaching? My hand can hold a thing called a pearl; my thinking mind can hold worlds called planets and suns called stars! The musician should rejoicingly remember that mind may transcend apparent limitations; and the man to whom C♯ is most profoundly and eloquently and for ever different in meaning from D♭, is the man who can relate all notes in their due order in a Fugue to either one or the other centre, and make triumphant sense of it both ways.

Key, then, is musical centrality; but key-sense irradiates infinitely, as we may believe, from any appointed tonal centre. Key-sense itself when diligently fostered also gives a music-lover power to move his centre or to break with it at will. This is called Modulation, and is a gift into which we must inquire together in our next chapter.

Chapter 22

MODULATION AND HARMONIC PERSPECTIVE

"... Then said they one to another, 'Let us show to the Pilgrims the Gate of the Celestial City, if they have skill to look through our Perspective Glass.' So they had them up to the top of a high hill called *Clear*, and gave them this glass to look ... but they could not look steadily through the Glass.

Yet they thought they saw something like the Gate, and also something of the Glory of the place. ..."

BUNYAN.

LET us imagine our minds now centred effectively upon any tone, C: Its natural chord: has given us our *tonal level*. Beyond or below this, in two main directions, we are conscious of other possible centres at other tonal levels, various mental distances away. These distances can be measured by natural steps, called perfect fourths or fifths (up or down, as we arbitrarily say). Sound them slowly:

If possible, sing them slowly and softly with a friend, closely analysing the mental experience of distances until, in this way, G♭ and F♯ both feel to be six *removes* in opposite directions from the thought-centre. You may feel assured that your experience tallies with the practice of the classics of the harmonic epoch (1600 to 1900). When they wanted mental remoteness, these are the two harmonic "avenues" along which they naturally sought it. Play the series with the natural or implied fifths sounded in full, and with major thirds added :

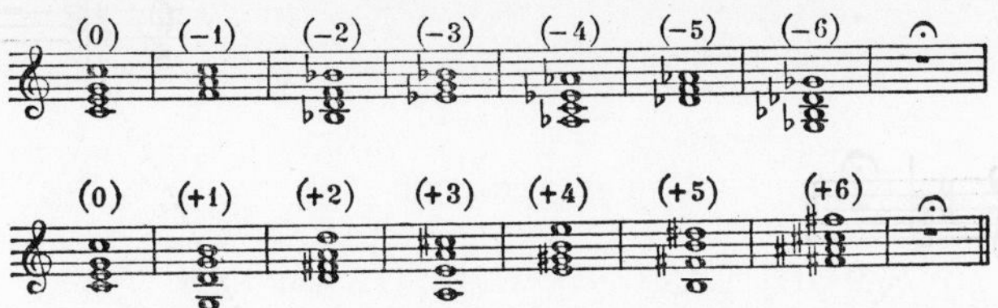

There is now a fuller experience of progress, and the sense of a series of naturally related distances may also grow more convincing as these are ponderingly repeated. Indeed, it seems hard to conceive a better harmonic clearing-house for any devotee of symphonies who may feel his harmonic sense still weak, than to pace these two common avenues for love, deliberately and often.

If we again poise our minds, at rest, for a minute or two on our chosen centring chord: and mentally weave such imaginary harmonic threads as we feel able to conceive from this centre, we shall resemble a spider sitting alertly in the centre of a gossamer web of our mind's own kind. Into this web fall four chance chords. The diagram (page 248) is purposely of the roughest, the chords having tumbled into my mind, and thence on to the page, almost as haphazard as luckless flies may alight in a spider's web. And within the web of harmonic thought you will find it natural to seize with spider-like tenacity upon the outlying chords, and relate or absorb them in your own way, drawing them towards your citadel-centre, as, *e.g.* :

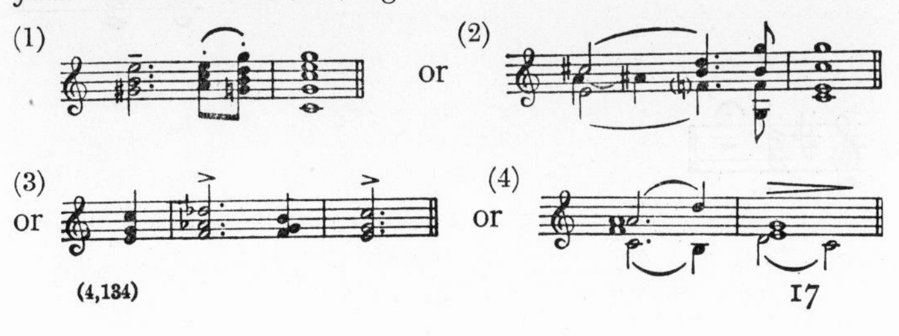

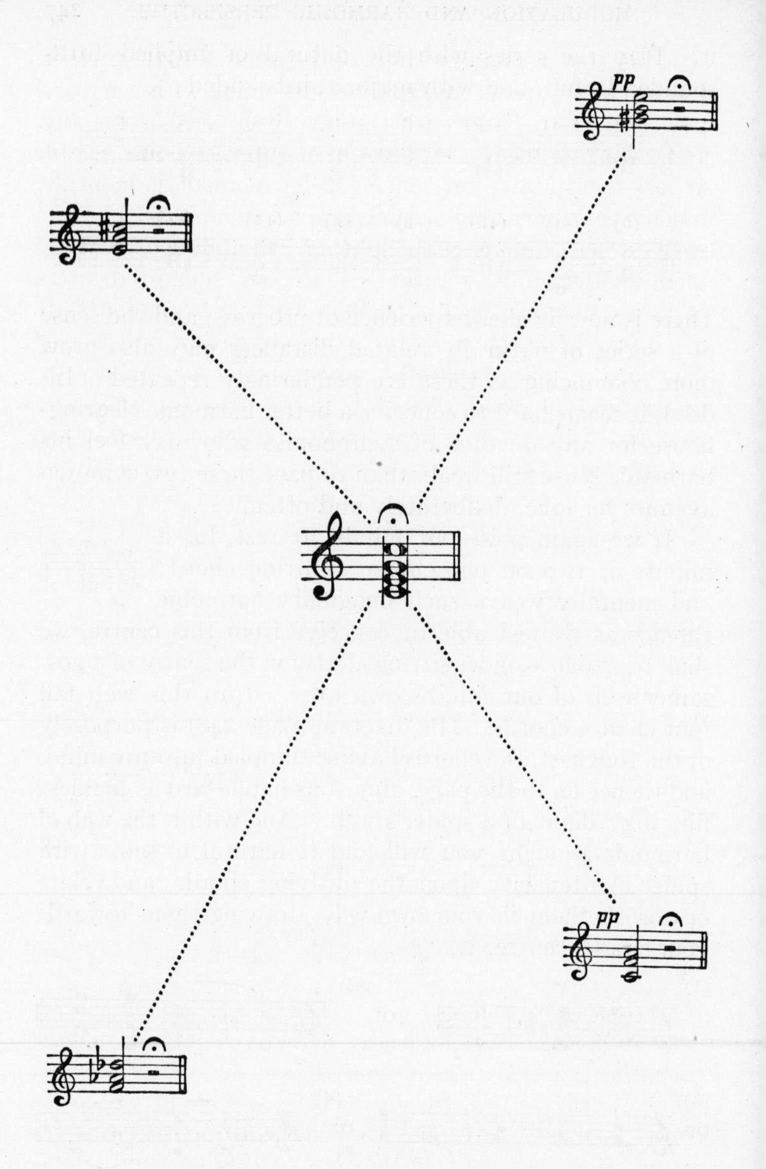

This spider analogy may be pursued a little further. Picture a real spider at work. As he starts with a natural power to weave, and with the law of gravity as his ally, and, swinging from one point to an opposite point, is able at last to establish his centre, so harmonists do mentally much the same thing. They start with minds that can weave tonal threads of thought *ad lib.*, and also, it would seem, with minds subject (as already suggested) to a certain balancing pull of what we may momentarily call tonal gravitation. Until this composite pull is felt, it is hard to follow a Beethoven Sonata at all, or begin to understand his mind. When it is felt, all seems instantly clearer. Indeed he seems continually, and safely, to assume that listeners possess key-sense as naturally as he himself; as, for example, in the opening of the *Appassionata* Sonata, when, after lifting our minds abruptly from:

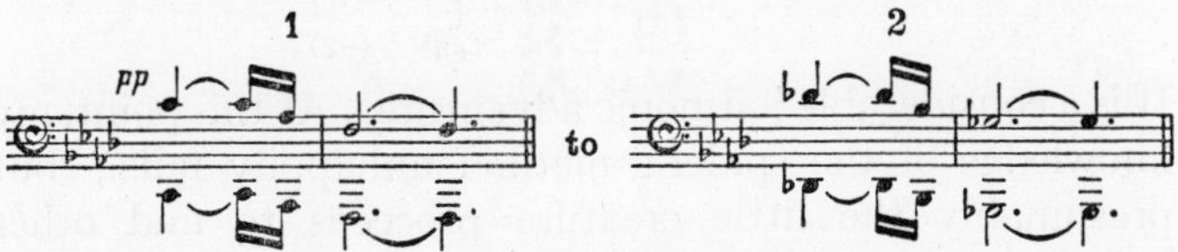

he secures for himself and us the return to our original F minor, by means of the leaning-note reiterated three or four times: and at last:

Realizing that there is one thing a spider can never do—sit in mid-air and begin to weave—let us imagine that the practice of key-sense in music similarly seizes upon *chords that are*, and relates them to an aptly chosen centre. Any one who has sat opposite a sheet of white paper, pen in hand, wondering what he is to write, is momentarily in the impossible position of a thought-spider in mental mid-air. In order to begin, he must take something that *is*, hang on to it, and then he can swing out bravely into mid-air. Imagine your mind set upon C major. You will find all the major chords that are set out on page 289 and numbered—*i.e.* related in what may be called gravitational order to C. Emulating our spider for the moment, let us run out to any chord whatever on the sharp, or *plus*, side: Having affixed our thread of thought, let us swing out in mid-air (with natural laws in our favour) and catch at any opposite chord on the *minus*, or flat, side: Sound on your keyboard what has now happened to any determined C major-centred harmonist:

It is a considerable harmonic adventure. At this point, my knowledge of the spider's method unhappily fails; but presumably the little creature proceeds to find other points and use his natural allies—gravitation and the prevailing breeze—for a few more swings from point to point, till he is at last able to find his desired centralization in space. When his keynote is found and fixed, and the spokes of his natural harmonic wheel conceived of and made, the maze of transverse progressions can be begun. All *we* have achieved so far is our first harmonic swinging adventure:

We must now, spider-like, use our *key-sense*. If the wind of the moment has blown us in the above direction (and if we hold in mind our natural bearings):

we can run along the wall or the tree (of circumstance) to a point but one remove from where we were: (–3) and the breeze (mood) of the moment must with luck blow us on a similarly swinging journey. It does:

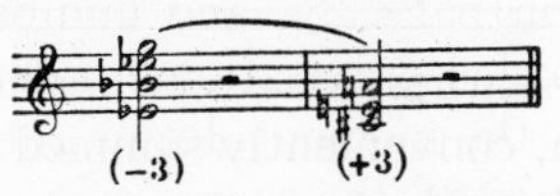

Away we run again (in harmonic *sequences* as they are technically called) and achieve another swing of the same order:

(+2) (–4)

One more such adventure will bring us very near the desired centre, C, upon which the whole of our hopes were placed. It does:

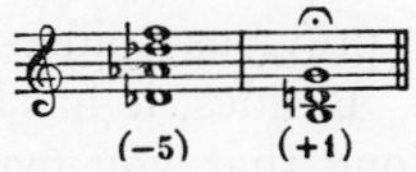

We throw out a composite thread (impossible to the spider?): and we reach our "home-tonic":

We may now set the whole of this harmonic process down, weaving little additional threads, or paths, of pleasant imaginings as we go:

or pianized and slightly ornamented:

Now the very earliest stages of harmonic weaving are, as already shown, conveniently summed up in the following, or any like formula :

Adding a cadence, and observing the time-honoured rule of four, this harmonic progression (endlessly recurrent in usage) is reached :

Compared with our previous spider-like adventure, this sounds complacent. Besides, it has been hackneyed and tritely used for so long that you may very likely find it hard to recapture its primal significance. Heard steadily, however, it proves as important to any student of the classics as a first proposition in Book I. of a Euclid of Music. To this we must return. Learn it, relish it, remember it, and go forward, recollecting (should you feel rather beyond it) how Beethoven himself valued it in the height of his powers :

Its curious importance to us in this chapter is paradoxically two-fold—it will prove an impregnable means of *resisting* modulation, and it will prove the greatest boon in *achieving* it.

But the terms that head this chapter must, without further delay, be defined and inter-related. *Modulation.* This is the word used to describe the power of the mind to *shift its harmonic centre.* That shift is made from one chord-centre to any other, though, of course, the natural stations to which the mind would first expect to modulate are those that lie nearest. This is abundantly proved in practice, and it is here our second chapter-title is needed. *Harmonic Perspective.* This seems the only term at the moment available, borrowed from the visual arts (until the corresponding term *perauditive* or *diauditive* * is coined and permitted), to describe the power of the mind to realize the facts of *harmonic nearness and distance.* Let us now look again into the harmonic territory open before us.

We find twelve possible keynotes that may carry major or minor key-chords. So twenty-four chords are at our disposal as key-chords.† At the very outset it is crucial that we should conceive, and tenaciously hold to, the fact that *harmonic* nearnesses and distances of these, to and from each other, are *mental* nearnesses and distances. If we should omit to establish this fact once for all, the dangers of confusion might be endless. Why? Because there are equally important *physical* nearnesses and distances of chords, and these affect us strongly, as the reader must already have found in the effect upon him of all conjunct movement, especially of our leading and leaning steps of semitones. Let us, once for all, face

* I am told by Professor Rose that the correct word for the art of looking through tonal distances would be *di-auscultation*, a somewhat repellent derivative.

† No more and no less, until the mind of music finds primal delight in the seventh harmonic, and the semitone ceases to be the smallest harmonic concept physically acceptable.

both the facts and the fundamental difference and disparity between the two. For *harmonic* or *mental distance* is often greatest precisely when *melodic* or *physical distance* is at its least! Thus the following three key-chords cover no less than ten removes of harmonic distance:

Play them thus:

and the acme of tonal nearness and smoothness is attained. They are physically as near each other as common chords can possibly get—till, indeed, we come to the mystic land of enharmonics, and find two chords twelve removes from each other, achieving not mere physical nearness, but (in the Bach tuning) physical identity!

Now clearness in listening and musical safety are both found in the recognition of these two unchanging factors. Mental distances were real to Beethoven, and will, I believe, prove to be so to every normal mind assisted by a normal ear, however little we may have as yet realized it. Similarly, physical tonal distances are as real to one age as to another, to great and small alike, and affect all of us enormously. Our recognition of these two facts will be strengthened by recollection of a general truth, namely, that, except in the case of one significant interval (to be noticed presently), harmonic and melodic nearness and farness happen continually to work in inverse ratio! This naturally gives to music an infinitely interesting paradoxical vocabulary, and to composers endless chances of surprising, pleasing, or "mischiefing" their listeners. The exception just referred to is found in the augmented fourth:

or

for if the common chords in their turn be made to stand strictly on parade—at attention, so to speak—it will be seen that the roots of the two chords mentally farthest from C are also physically as far from C as they can be :

Readers may very usefully make a table of all twelve of these chordal distances from C, arranging each example in *three* ways, as below : (*a*) the zero chord of C and the chord in question standing to attention in rigid and unaltered position ; (*b*) each chord so disposed as to favour physical nearness and smooth effect ; (*c*) each so disposed as to favour physical distance and abruptness. Here is E♭ so arranged :

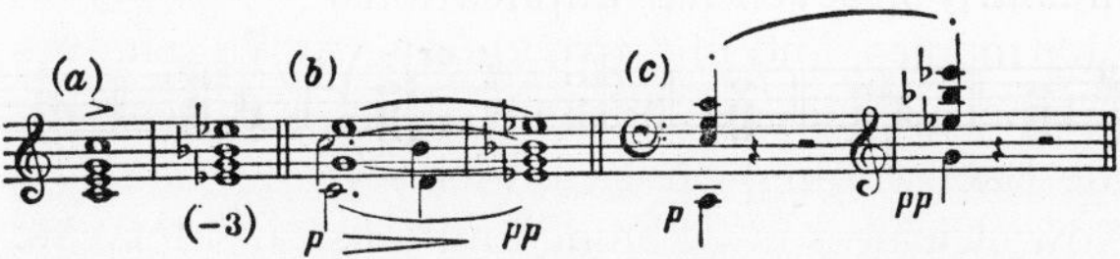

This plan should be followed with the remaining eleven at pleasure. It will be easy for most readers to recall or imagine some of the thrillingly telling progressions composers can create by means of the interplay of these two basic methods of musical appeal. Such interplay is endless.

It is now important to turn for a little to study the effect upon us of *minor chord distances*. As the twelve natural distances from a zero major chord are studied in the way suggested above, the mind is sure to discover what very different effects of distances and nearnesses are brought about when a chord is changed to minor. Thus E major : is four removes from C. But clearly E minor is not : How far is it ? If considered as a relative minor (in the conventional sense) it is the relative minor of G : and is therefore theoretically one remove away from C. If, however, it is thought of as a minor on the so-called mediant of C major itself :  then all its notes lie in the natural scale of C, no new distance need be suggested, and there is consequently no mental remove at all. If, in the third place, any one considers it as in the key of B minor, and thinks of it as two removes away:  who can say him nay? We dare not leave this important issue unexplored any longer.

Let us this time set out the total of twelve minor key-chords—again on a chromatic or parade basis, as we did the major chords on page 255—choosing the spelling which favours simplicity of key (that is, which avoids seven-sharp or seven-flat implications) :

(or)

Now it is very significant that the harmonic minor key still habitually receives a signature as though it were a modal minor of old. Beethoven's *Choral Symphony* begins in a key of which this would be the strictly correct harmonic signature : Schubert's *Unfinished* is actually in this key:  But no one writes it so, nor probably does any one think it so. The leading-note, C♯, is thought each time into place empirically just as it occurs, the major third of the so-called dominant :  In the same way a C minor cadence would be thought into its place, and the modal (Æolian) signature of three flats still stands:  even though the B♭, every time it appears in the course of the piece, has to be contradicted into B♮! Sometimes we find that in eighteenth-century music yet another kind of modal signature, the Dorian, for a long time lingered:  and an A♭ had then to be inserted for every minor sixth. This occurs in the *Messiah.* Indeed it is a telling device capable of useful revival. The burning question for us at this point is, having any major key-chord in mind—say, for example, F♯—what minor chord stands related to it in the closest degree of *harmonic nearness* ?

The truth is richly embarrassing to us all. For there are no less than four minors closely and naturally related to any given major * (and therefore, conversely, four majors correspondingly related to any given minor). But our riches, and the embarrassments thereof, do not end there. For should an isolated minor chord appear, it is capable of implying more than four possible varieties of harmonic distance. Take, for example, the first natural minor key-chord D:  What is its harmonic distance, let us say, from C? That depends each time upon context and mental impression. It can be sounded without even leaving the scale of C itself—that is, no distance away at all, harmonically speaking. It can as easily be the sub-dominant of A minor:  This implies a distance, but *what* distance? Modally, none; but harmonically, G♯ has taken it at least "one remove away." Thirdly, it can be the chord of the sixth of F major:  and so would stand "one remove" in the *minus* direction. Fourthly, it can be the key-chord of D minor itself:  Here B♭ and C♯ have taken it two harmonic removes, but in different directions—a significant leading-note, C♯, has taken it in the acute or *plus* direction of sharpness; a significant leaning-note, B♭ flat, has taken it in the grave or *minus* direction—that is, of less sharpness. (The musical mind may rest

* Thus C major has not only its titular *relative minor* A but also D minor, E minor, and C minor in attendance upon and closely bound to it.

undaunted by this facing-both-ways impression, finding itself not so much pulled two ways, as illumined from two sides; and of course this happens constantly in music.) Fifthly, it can be the mediant or third degree of B♭ major:  two *minus* or flat removes.

Let these facts now be summarized: With the mind polarized thus:  let this chord be sounded: and it transpires that by natural harmonic influence context might make it any one of the following:

(*a*) Part of the C major scale itself (no remove).

(*b*) Part of the A minor scale itself (one sharp remove).

(*c*) Part of the D minor scale itself (two removes, one in each direction).

(*d*) Part of the F major scale itself (one minus or flat remove).

(*e*) Part of the B♭ major scale itself (two minus removes).

In addition to this we have to reckon that, not only to such minds as Schubert's, but to all harmonically-minded listeners, it may strongly imply D major itself (two sharp removes), with the third flattened. For the pull of the perfect fifth upon the harmonic mind seems to be proving, as time goes on, by far the strongest pull of all! The number of times in which Bach himself swings from tonic major to tonic minor without leaving his key-emplacement or harmonic bearings is legion. Schubert seemed to adore this transmutation; and it is open to all, to the great enrichment of music's humanly expressive power. We will now set down the particular chord in question, with the six possible inferences indicated above:

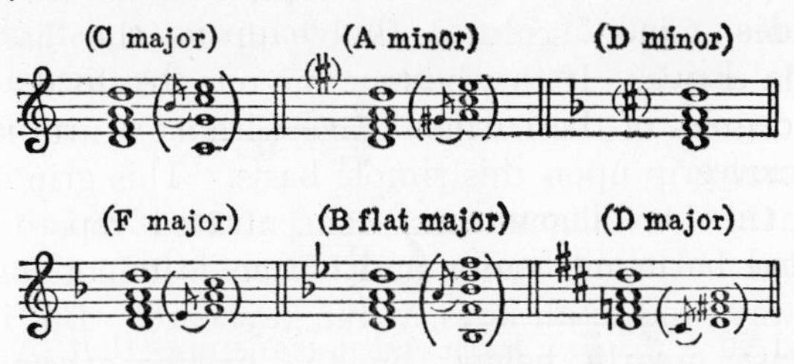

If you have followed this closely you will probably appreciate, first, the enormous embarrassment of riches inherent in key-distances; secondly, the immense resultant importance of *context*, when chords have so many possible meanings; thirdly, the increasing importance of clear thought (and, therefore, of clear indication by context of that thought), when the avenue of harmonic distances is so real, yet so beset with possibilities that could become undesirable ambiguities.

Further consideration of the open question of minor harmonic distances, as related to the avenue of major distances, must here be deferred to Chapter 24. But at this point it will possibly be helpful to compare a few impressions without delay with such readers as are fairly habitual frequenters of the classical harmonic highway; and, at the same time, to offer such advice to beginners as may help them in finding their way through such essentially difficult places. Here are three suggestions:

1. Does it not seem clear that the so-called Harmonic Minor is based as surely as the major upon a chord-formula corresponding with that given on page 252, but with a lesser third and a "leaning" sixth?

The modern (Æolian) signature: is, as already

indicated, a mere survival, not unuseful, but one that should not be allowed to cloud the real nature of the harmonic minor scale derivable from the harmonic formula above. If this be true, no one can listen to the great classics of the harmonic age without a firm mental and aural grip upon this simple basis. This grip can be cultivated by diligent and concentrated repetition of both the harmonic major and harmonic minor formula, in all ways and in all keys, at the keyboard. But it is in any case greatly helped by the masters themselves, especially Beethoven and Brahms, who leave their attentive hearers very little to worry about. They safeguard themselves and us by repeating, often enough for our wants, any important cadences, leading-notes, leaning-notes, and by eloquent use of chromatic semitones as discussed under (3) following. It is worth noticing here that the well-known chords of the major and minor ninth :

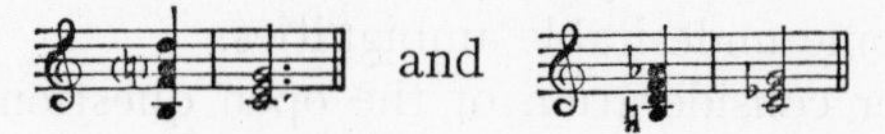

epitomize the perfect cadence in major and minor respectively, though the latter is so frequently used in both that, until the third appears, it is not often clear to the hearer in which context it is being used.

2. Does it not also seem certain that the insistent character of the leading-note in all harmonic music naturally equips it as an unfailing *polarizer* and locator of minor keys as of major ? Perhaps frequenters of the classical highway will agree that no " pointers " to the keynote (or Pole star of the tonal firmament of the moment) can ever be clearer or more obvious than these : in any position ; and that the richest dominant discord is both clearer and more immediately acceptable to the mind when the sharpest note in it stands out and proclaims itself leading-note by natural implications and traditional

"behaviour," provided there be at least one leaning-note counteracting it, thus :

3. Is it not becoming increasingly clear that, to our triple formula already given—that of centre or home-tonic safely rooted with its perfect fifth (whatever its third may be), and rebutted on either side by the attendant dominants rooted a {fifth / fourth} below and above—we should add not only the semitonic steps that give us our leading- and leaning-notes (now unfailing mental pointers as well as expressive inflections), but another and, in practice, a still subtler factor, the *chromatically rising or falling semitone*? These, if taken all together, will act as guides gradually conspiring not only to give us mental distances or perspective, while standing firm on one spot, but to lead us to effective modulations into other keys.

The general significance of the chromatic semitone is based on three facts :

(*a*) To change a *keynote* up or down chromatically gives it no less than eight removes in our avenue of distances :

(*b*) To change a *minor third* to *major* :

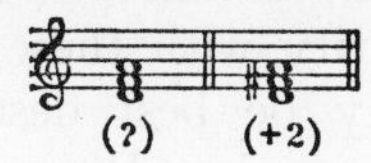

or vice versa, is but a gentle and necessarily ambiguous remove.

(*c*) To change a *perfect fifth* chromatically upward

> or downward is wholly to change its character in one of two ways:
>
> 
>
> And if it happen that the perfect fifth is at the time fifth of the key itself, or of one of the two dominants, then one of three main girders of the key is abruptly taken away or, at least, loosened.

Thus the chromatic rise or fall by a semitone may have varied modulatory or dangerously disintegrating power; it is, to the melodist, inflectively expressive, and to the harmonist always momentously significant. I may perhaps without offence venture to suggest, as illustration, that such use as that in Wagner's early song to the "Star of Eve" (*Tannhäuser*) does more to trouble the harmonic hearer than to please the melodist, by reason of its relentless chromatic contours. Wagner himself was too wonderful a harmonist to expect us to listen unexercised to:

This experience, repeated often, is to me apt to be either shattering or morbid (such are the powers of the chromatic semitone), and neither surely is desirable in the peaceful Invocation to an evening star.

The above suggestions may clear the way for study of much less accustomed and far more modern uses of the harmonic highway. But if they are to do this for us, it will be necessary to turn perpetually to the chromatic avenue of distances (see page 289), and by increasing familiarity with these, to consolidate our hold upon what may be best described as the fully chromaticized diatonic scale. We must, throughout this chapter, for the sake of clearness, draw the line *this* side of all enharmonicism (which will occupy us in Chapter 24). But even the simplest of all modulations involve us in chromatics, whenever and wherever we are on the harmonic highway—that is, when once the perfect and plagal cadences are allowed to appear in relation to any degree of the natural scale other than C itself. So we must urge every reader to practise such limited chromaticisms, by thinking cadences, leading-notes, and leaning-notes into relation with every natural note in turn, and then into relation with chromatic notes themselves. This can be practised in any convenient and comprehensive keyboard formulæ, such as this :

The chromatic scale which this brings into being is complete (and is only enharmonic at one point) :

But when we take a descending formula, leaning-notes with their leading-notes bring us, by a natural process, a richer chromatic palette altogether :

By this our chromatic scale has become much more enharmonic :

This is an assembly of notes, all of which represent harmonic thoughts in the minds of those who have experienced *all these very ordinary cadences.* All notes in the resultant assembly can be thought into relation with each other in ever more subtle ways. Unwonted harmonic journeyings reveal themselves at every turn. Take but one such happening in real life, so to speak. (See page 265.)

It may now be possible to reach a useful conclusion as to Modulation in general, and as to what we have called harmonic distances, or chords in mental perspective.

Modulation can be transitory or permanent. In the first case, it is often aptly renamed mere *transition*, and implies impending return to the old centre. In the second case, it implies new key-bearings altogether, and no return. Whether modulation be to a near or distant remove, whether for a moment or for good, it is always and only achieved by the power of the mind to change its centre to new points in its avenue of harmonic distances, and this is mainly achieved by cadence. As has been shown earlier in this chapter, the perfect cadence by itself at the new point, if pressed home, *may establish the new centre* ; but it is remarkable that, though the cadence is so powerful in its mental effect, a new key is not easily established till the mind has buttressed the new centre chord on both the dominant and underdominant side. This is natural. For example, this :

Quintet in C major (two 'Cellos) **Schubert**

has a fairly decisive suggestion of having modulated from G safely to E♭ major. But this :

brings us more safely, and much more decisively, into B♭ major, having cadenced both its dominant F and its under-dominant, E♭, before finally cadencing B♭ itself.

Though by plain and stalwart journeyings, step by step, we may travel to distant points :

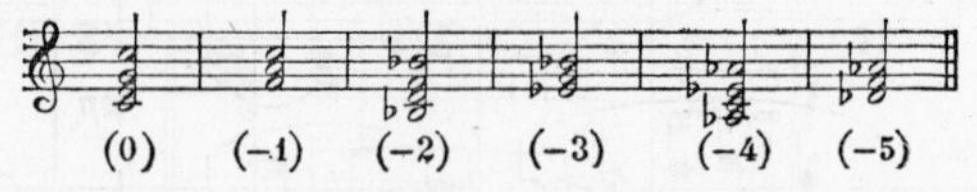

it is not by thus moving to a distance that we can establish headquarters at that distance. This is done by cadences ; and in the process, leading-notes and their *vis-à-vis* the leaning-notes play harmonically decisive and melodically inconspicuous parts. If to these we add the subtle resort of chromatic semitones, as, for example, in such ways as this :

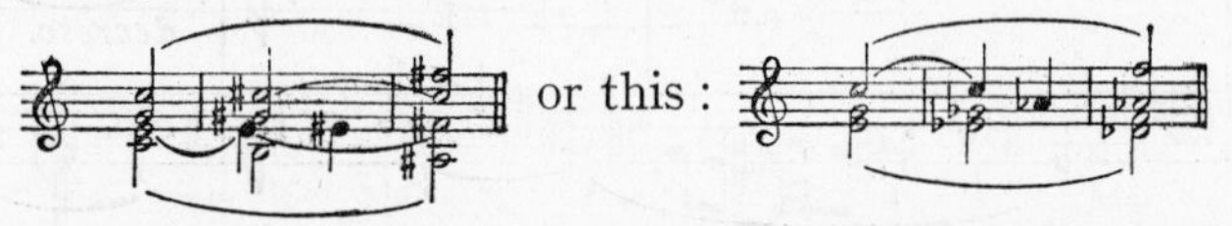

they can spirit us along the harmonic avenue with scarcely a noticeable change in the physical effect ; and we shall find ourselves in possession of simple but comprehensive means of modulation, and of sudden surprises in mental perspective which reveal ever-changing delights on the unchanging harmonic road.

It remains to point out that, by a paradox, the mind's power to modulate is actually increased by its refusing to modulate until it must. Dwell for five minutes (or more) harmoniously on the natural or white notes of the keyboard only. Revel in the available three major and three minor chords, weaving them naturally together in the three ways in which it can be done musically—that is, with no note in common between the succeeding chords, but with strong contrary motion between the outer parts :

next, with one note held in common by neighbour chords :

and next, with two notes in common, as, for example :

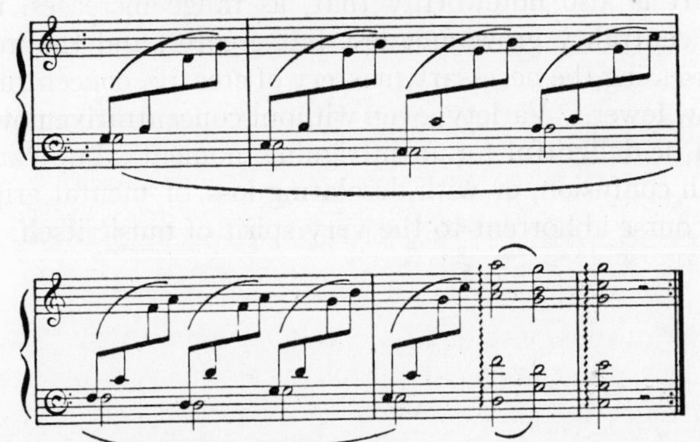

Having played round and about some such series, suddenly make a cadence on any two or three of your six chords *not* the key-chord :

Having done this, return to your meandering on the six natural chords, and vary the experiment at pleasure. You will find that it is possible to allow the first of these cadences to shake your moorings loose and bring you momentarily towards centralizing on G major; the second, in like manner, may draw you to F major; the third, to an A minor centring, and so forth. But this is not the way in which harmonic thought gains power to move when, where, and as it will. You will find it monotonously easy to keep your centrality through all three; and, as we shall hope to see in Chapter 24, the natural advance of the harmonic mind is towards mastery of an ever-widening range, round an impregnably held centre. In other words, the modulating harmonic mind will be set on the attainment of the maximum power of concentring.

It is also noteworthy that, as range increases, need for centrality grows not less but greater, and the minds possessing the necessary mastery of creative concentration grow fewer. Variety, even without concentrative powers, can be delightful for an intriguing moment; but variety with confusion, or with desolating loss of mental grip, is of course abhorrent to the very spirit of music itself.

Chapter 23

ASSOCIATED MEANINGS

"... From the words of the poet men take what meanings please them. . . ."

RABINDRANATH TAGORE.

THERE seems need at this point to give thought to the question of the possible meanings, the human significances, that are accrescent in music round a chord or chords, or even round certain intervals.

"Mi contra fa
Est diabolus in musica,"

ran a monkish jingle, which, being bluntly interpreted, means that this:  is the Devil in music; on the face of it, rather a preposterous diagnosis of an innocent-looking relation.

This is a subject difficult to handle, but impossible to ignore; for it is through natural processes of *selection and association* that music acquires the power to be what we have earlier described as a local language; and this power may be usefully discussed before we try to indicate more fully, and in some measure to sum up, the classical harmonic usages now under consideration, and their bearing on Sonata music and future Sonata prospects. It is but little that we can try now to offer.

We are not, of course, concerned here with any arbitrarily affixed meanings, playfully or over-solemnly determined upon by this man or that school, in any particular moment in musical history. Nor are we concerned with assigned meanings of convenience by which, through Big Ben, for example, the sound of this phrase:  has come to mean to millions of people "quarter past" any hour of the day; or by which the sound of a guard's whistle has come to mean to the passenger, "Now we're off." The only *meanings* we need trouble about are those which link the mind of a composer to the minds of his listeners (*a*) because of some inherent fitness in related tones to carry a particular meaning, and (*b*) because that very fitness has brought about associations none the less powerful for being undefined; associations which are perhaps vaguely accepted, but not yet, even in the vaguest way, openly agreed. Do such meanings matter to the enthusiast at this or at any moment in history? Is there anything to be gained in searching for them? Let us suppose, for a few pages, that there may be.

Let us discuss the question, if possible, without saying a word which might turn the musical beginner away from his confident joy in listening, towards that careful caution which says, "I wonder whether it *means* this or that." All music means all that you and I can ever hear it to mean. But (believing it to be a question of value at this point) let us boldly ask—though it may be but a very small and passing factor in the whole significance of a chord; though it may be comparing an ocean liner with a harbour tug—how far can a chord in a Beethoven Sonata be compared with a word in a Shakespeare Play?

We are concerned to answer only a part of this intriguing question, namely, "Can a chord, like a word, acquire associated meanings at all, and does it actually convey such meanings from composer to listener, as a word does from poet to reader? If the answer should prove to be "Yes," there follows a supplementary question : " If chords have meanings, why cannot there be such a thing as a chord dictionary, in which we may hunt up and confirm those meanings ? "

Before trying to answer, let us pause to consider (for a particular reason) certain ways, *other than through the associated meanings of the words used,* in which a speech or a poem, in English or any other language, seems meaningful or otherwise to us.

1. We are, for instance, affected by the actual quality of the words in a poem ; the vowel sounds of such words as gloom, moon, room, soon ; sheen, preen, gleam, dream, have a *qualitative pull* (quite apart from their anciently agreed *meanings*), a pull which is recognized and used, whether unconsciously or deliberately, by speakers and poets.
2. Pitch of voice, sudden change from high to low speech, can convey vital impressions from speaker to listener, quite apart from the specific words used.
3. Variation in volume and speed of utterance have immense communicative value.
4. Lastly, mere tone of utterance (as indicating depth of thought or sincerity of expression), in both oratory and poetry, makes an appeal quite beyond any single conceivable meaning in the several words used.

The reader may have noticed, and will probably agree, that all these *inter alia* qualities of appeal of the spoken word are exactly those which we are accustomed to consider the chief and far the most clamant ways of music's appeal to mankind. Language and music hold these potent qualities in common. Moreover, music specializes in them. Yet in this chapter it is of the highest importance that we should forget, or rather, momentarily write off, these general ways of conveying meaning, mood, or intention, in order to concentrate on any particular and associated meanings we may discover in music itself.

Let us then reiterate our two questions in the bluntest possible way. Have any chords on the harmonic highway acquired *any* associated meanings that matter to the music lover ? And if so, where is our chord-dictionary to give us the clue to those meanings ? Our replies momentarily can only be: (1) that associated meanings of vital importance have certainly been accumulating for centuries, long before Palestrina and Byrd wrote the examples quoted on pages 49 and 50, and (2) no dictionary of such meanings has, so far as the writer knows, ever yet emerged.

If the first reply is correct, the second should perhaps only stimulate each reader to compile his own private chord-dictionary. The best service any existent dictionary can do any man is, after all, to challenge him to discover what each word is capable of meaning *to him*. Who, for instance, reading Dr. Johnson's monstrous definition of *Art* as "something unnatural," does not immediately rebel, and supplant it with a meaning nearer the truth as he himself has experienced it ? And who would more commend such a reaction than the old lexicographer himself ? It is even more vitally important that this should be the attitude (tenaciously held) of every intelligent man in the intensely personal realm of Sonata music. But there exists no musical Dr. Johnson to challenge us ! So if now we are constrained to draw up our own challenge, conjuring up what is so far an entirely non-existent vocabulary of music, one that can only be consulted imaginatively, we must include only a few tentative probabilities of meaning ; for, from fixities and certitudes of meaning, music (like poetry) is refreshingly free. Moreover (and mercifully), our chord-dictionary will, up to date, still be phenomenally brief. But (less mercifully) it would need endless volumes of quotations. This is obvious ; for all musical meanings must lie in tonal relatings, because all musical interest lies in inspiring tones into action, that is, in comprehensive *Melody*, as defined by Wagner. Each of our chords would need, therefore, some thousand or so of quoted melodies to substantiate their many meanings in usage! Our imagined chord-dictionary would as yet have a very limited list of chords, but with limitless instances for each one. Its compilation would be the task, not of a lifetime, but of an age; not of a man, but of a generation of men. For all that, the inquirer may be astonished to find it within his own modest power to begin that brief catalogue of chords on a moderate working knowledge, say, of a dozen Beethoven Sonatas. His and my volume of instances that are to confirm or modify the imputed meanings can then be collected and collated at leisure through a lifetime of listening. We shall find that a chord—unlike a tune, which is for ever on the move—will obligingly stand still in the mind, for us to contemplate at leisure. And a chord, like a tune, is a tonal relating, vital to music. It is the only relating that "stands still." Though all music, like life, is in perpetual movement, multitudinous in its significances; and though all its human interests are as inextricably interrelated as in life itself; yet, in a chord, living discernible tones are related into a form at rest, much as, in a human face, living discernible features and lineaments are related into a countenance that can be contemplated and have meaning. A chord is a countenance at rest, but full of life.

Let us then challenge ourselves to make a bare beginning with this chord-dictionary, which might read somewhat as follows:

SPECIMEN PAGE OF A MUSIC DICTIONARY ANY ONE MIGHT COMPILE

= a chord generally associated with sadness or depression, but capable of conveying many shades of quite opposite character—*e.g.* depth of gloom, or comparative serenity or peace; emaciated sorrow or defiant endurance of pain, according to context. Used in contrast with its companion major chord (see page *so-and-so*), it can represent the passing from a care-free to an anxious state, or *vice versa*. The following are some of its characteristic shades of meaning:

Lento *pp* = gloomy, fateful, pondering over sorrow, musing over mortality.

Presto = (if light and speedy) taking life lightly, not unaware of sadness, but inclined to mock at it; cynical; devil-may-care; making the best of things; cheering some one who is too sad to bear major chords at the moment.

ff = defiant and enduring; not unhopeful; full of determination to face things.

pp *(pp)* = passing from sadness to hopefulness; inverted, it means the reverse process.

Adagio = expression of resignation; mingled acquiesence and grief. (See Chopin's use in his "Funeral March.")

The five instances show the imaginary compiler's anxiety not to dogmatize as to the general *sadness* connotation which is undoubtedly associated in most minds to-day with the minor chord. He should surely guard equally against the danger of losing its basic meaning in a whirl of vague impressions! The minor triad is in no more danger of losing its inherent and long associated meaning on the harmonic highway to-day, than the meaning of the word "sad" would be endangered if a man entered your room shouting in a loud, excited laughing manner, "I'm so sad, so sad, so very, very sad!" His manner does not change the association of the word, nor necessarily mean that he is *not* sad. "He's a queer fellow," you say. "Has he perhaps a sorrow that he wishes to feel and cannot?" "Is he mad?" It is the same with the major triad. Men are puzzled to know why the "Jolly Miller" in G minor is merry, and the "Dead March" in C major is sad. The reply would seem to lie in the experiment of playing the "Jolly Miller" in G *major*:

and the "Dead March" in C *minor*

It will then appear that, all other things being equal, major and minor still show themselves here as true as ever to their character. For the Miller has become too light-hearted and contented to utter his refrain truly: "I care for nobody," etc., which is now belied by the tune, and the Handel march has lost much of its grit and courage, and *deepened its sadness.* To assess chords rightly, they must be played *minus* all "effects" of speed, colour, volume, light and shade, rhythmic insistences; *minus*, indeed, the whole imposing bag of tonal tricks (no derogation intended by this epithet) which is so generously meted out to the listening public to-day. These can be superadded (sparingly) afterwards, to convey and fulfil the inner intention of the music itself.

The reader will find it easy and beguiling to invent his own specimen page of definitions of the *major* triad. Certain it is that we should all begin our chord-dictionary with these two triads. But how shall we then proceed?

And are we, after all, right in our start? Should we not have begun with the two most significant two-note chords? Thus:

= An open perfect fifth, signifying clearness, confidence, sometimes optimism, faith, and a thousand similar ideas.

= An augmented fourth or tritone, signifying obscurity, uncertainty, sometimes pessimism, doubt, and many similar ideas.

Whether we should or no, let us, under the circumstances, from this latter angle, go forward to consider a few familiar discords on the classical highway; and—again contemplating each chord as we might seek character in the countenance of a man—let us be even a little rashly hypothetical about them.

All chords except the two common chords have for long been classified as "discords" in some degree or other. Now, the most ubiquitous of all discords down the harmonic highway is of course this: How is its associated meaning to be discovered? Recall the story of Sir John Goss, referred to elsewhere, who, when he heard some thoughtless friend spread this chord on the keyboard:

and leave it so, clambered out of bed to get to his piano, played this: and returned to bed. What does this anecdote mean? Returning to our supposititious lexicography:

= a state of almostness, penultimacy, suggesting that another harmonic state is about to follow and fulfil it.

These are quite inadequate definitions, but they must, for the moment, serve. The possible interpretations of such general meanings are again legion. Each of us can best make his own page of instances and supplementary definitions in rhythmic, melodic, harmonic, and qualitative contexts, for such of these as he has himself experienced.

There was a day when another familiar chord: proved to be also of the "almostness" kind; and, had it been spread out on his keyboard, it might have inclined Goss once more to scramble out of bed to add this: yet not so urgently, even at that time; for inherently this chord is far less dissonant. But one of its accrescent meanings was very like that of its companion; for in making a plagal cadence, an added sixth was as natural an approximator:

as was an added seventh in making a perfect cadence:

In compiling our imaginary chord-dictionary, it is a useful plan to view all discords as "added somethings" to the triads themselves. But in trying to discover a working list of inherent and associated meanings (and we are attempting the two together) it is essential to think of the intervals lying within each chord. Here we see at a glance that there *is* a false fifth in the dominant seventh, but there is none between any of the constituent notes of the added sixth. The importance of this distinction seems likely to appear far more clearly as time goes on. Thus, Debussy and others have not only shown us how this major added sixth chord, free as it is from the false fifth, may easily be treated as a concord, or passive point of rest, but they have been able to add the major second or ninth to it, thus * :

What, in this case, could be our definition of this enriched chord to-day? It could be two-fold. First :—

= forward-reaching ; active ; impulsive.

That is its old meaning. Recently, however, it has proved itself inherently capable of being amplified and used, with added second as well as added sixth, in an opposite and restful sense :

pp = pleasantly passive ; contemplative ; contentedly inconclusive.

But how, we ask, can this be ? How can the same chord mean both activity and passivity ? And a second doubt may well arise : If your A is sharpened (making what is called a German sixth) : its sound becomes identical with a dominant seventh ; does its changed *sixthly* meaning merge into a *seventhly* meaning ?

For the moment such doubts look threatening. We might almost incline to abandon our venture, and exclaim, " Every composer means just what he likes, when he likes, as he likes, by any of the chords he uses, and every listener interprets at pleasure." True, this is what happens. But true also, agreeable meanings when agreed upon, so far from restricting freedom on both sides, increase its range. In fact, our doubts, when faced and passed, should bring us on to much more hopeful ground. Let us take the above two specific points of doubt. Take the second or spelling question first. There *is*, as already

* See last chord in Act I. of *Pelléas et Mélisande.*

hinted, a crucial difference in meaning the moment we change the spelling of the chord (how crucial and far-reaching we shall see in Chapter 24); it raises precisely the same problem as did Hood, in his clever verse quoted on page 88. Even when notation is unchanged by composers, harmonic *context* itself may change meaning in a flash. Turn from chordal to verbal meanings. What do I understand you to mean if you suddenly utter the word "box"? There *is* no meaning *until you give the context!* Only then shall I know whether you speak of a tree, a sport, or a wooden or cardboard receptacle. In the same way give this chord:  this context:  and I know your meaning to be different from what you would have meant had you said:  Moreover, if and while you say the latter, I myself, while listening, would have to alter the spelling mentally, to make correct the first sense that entered my head! For this:  (when you first played it) is what came into my head, quicker than I could tell you, and thoughts of B♮ and E♮ compelled me to think their boon companion G♯! Test all this carefully at the piano, and so far from its checking us in our journey of discovery of meanings, it abundantly confirms our hypothesis that chords *already have acquired associated meanings* of a certain binding value to composer and listener, as the acquired meanings of similarly vital words are of binding value to poet and reader.

And now as to the other doubt raised by Debussy's daring extension of the major added sixth:  thickened up by an added second:  in defiance of all its hitherto recognized connotations (whether by old Goss or any more recent, sensitive classicists). How came Debussy to use it as a final consonance of a whole act of his famous opera? Was he wrong, or was he proving his predecessors or any one else wrong? Neither, obviously. Debussy was only going deeper, further, into *inherent* meanings. In music, one connotation does not displace another; far otherwise, exactly as, in literature, added significance only enriches it. Notice the constituent consonant elements of this chord:

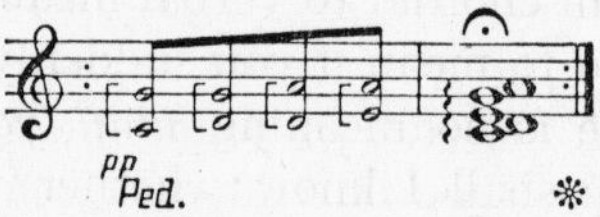

Play them carefully. Again, spread the single constituent tones out in euphonious array:

Or, perhaps better, put down the sustaining pedal, and sound each note in octaves with its most perfectly related neighbour-note within that octave, thus:

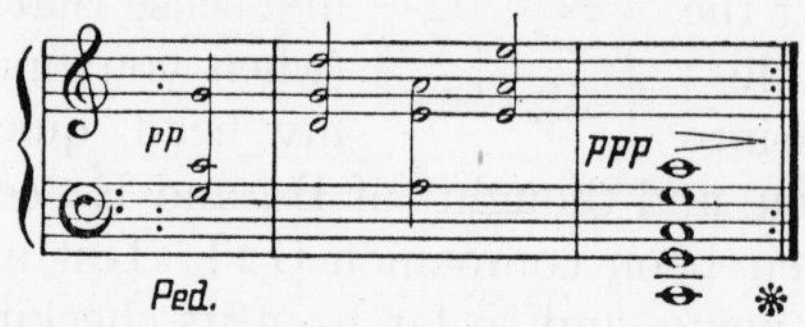

Gradually Debussy's intuitive and visionary use of this (harmonically) all-important five-note concept seems to justify itself; and our associated meaning, in accordance with the inherent qualities of the chord, becomes serviceably (and, by the way, quite logically) extended for good. But it can still keep its lesser and earlier connotation in every suitable context, such, for example, as this:

Our two doubts raised have, after all, increased our certitudes, and so have been fruitful. They have enabled us to go a step further and deeper into analysis of chords themselves, and of inherent possibilities. Let us test the meaning to our own minds of Debussy's other extreme (and even historic) addition to the future chord-vocabulary of musicians, namely, the famous whole-tone chord : What are the inherent or qualitative inferences here ? There is not a single perfect interval in it. But the tritone, or augmented fourth, has full possession. Spreading out the components of this chord in the three ways used for the pentachord * (page 280), we shall be better able to analyse and assess its effect :

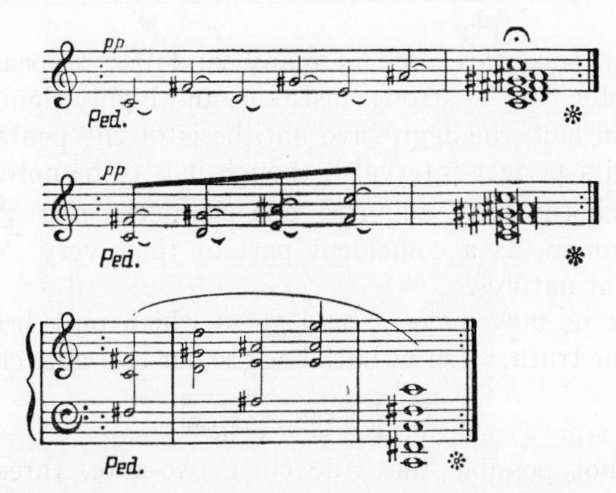

Touched gently, these sound like bells—vague, atmospheric, ambiguous. Treat this chord, however, in the accustomed harmonic manner :

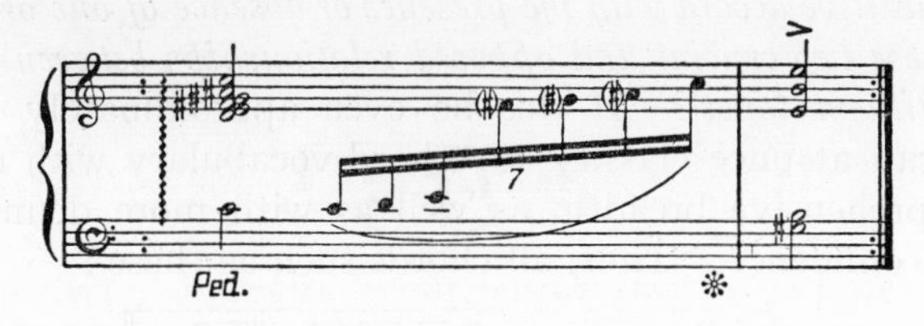

* This seems the obvious name for the perfect five-note chord.

and at once three of its many vital uses appear. Its character can be strong, insistent, and highly significant. It is, in fact, the aggressive antithesis of the pentachord (with its perfect intervals), though it is to be noted that both chords have acquired one characteristic : in common, as a coincident part of their very different natures.

Let us now make a bold guess which may bring us near the truth. Let us hark back to our two-note chords :

and

Is it not possible that the chief two-note, three-note, four-note, five-note, and six-note chords that have already passed into the harmonic language by reason of their associated meanings, have taken on those meanings slowly *in intuitive accord with the presence or absence of one or both of these two crucial and opposed relationships between their constituent tones*? If this be even approximately true, we can at once classify our chord-vocabulary with more comprehensive breadth, as well as with more definition and confidence. Thus, all chords such as these :

with no tritone at any point, would have a general character in common. They might call for a hundred different words to define them in our dictionary. But their inmost character would be essentially that of such English words as Confidence, Clearness, Optimism, Hope, Candour, etc., etc. Similarly, chords such as :

and the complete whole-tone chord, with no single perfect interval in any of them, would, in their turn, hold a common basic meaning, but again with numberless facets ; they imply the opposite of confidence, or clearness, or optimism—boiling down to some form (acute or slight) of *dubiety* or *ambiguity*. Thirdly, popular chords such as these three :

with *both* the perfect interval and the tritone blendingly present in them all, are likely to hold in common the most human qualities of all. We should call them by such names as Reconcilement, Sympathy, Give-and-take, Forbearance, mingling Confidence with Fear ; indeed, so great a host of apt descriptions would occur to the reader in this connection, as cannot possibly be enumerated here. It is no wonder that the last three chords have been most humanly used on the harmonic way.

We turn now from this difficult, speculative, but necessary task of estimating meanings of chords as if they were isolated words, to sum up the position, supposing our guesses at all near the truth. For, even when we have assessed the basic chords (words, in the musical language) in this way or that, we know that from first to last all active significances still depend upon context. Our musical interest is in moving *from state to state* ; our language is dynamic and never static. We shall only, therefore, make sense of a stated chord with a stated meaning by watching its estate come and go. Now we shall hope to see that chords come and go along the mind's avenue of harmonic distances. Their first pull upon the mind is shown there. But each *common* chord in that avenue may, by acquiring additional tones, take on the characters of many of the different discords we have been considering, and become more or less pressing upon our attention accordingly. They may draw us from ease to rigour, from intensity to relaxation. There lies their second great pull upon our minds. Chords, in themselves, like the faces of friends, are living music, apt to quicken rapt contemplation. But along the avenues of our musical thought they can make active music in unlimited ways. For we certainly move upon a harmonic circle or sphere,* often extending our range of harmonic thought, our use of chords, and, it is to be hoped, ever intensifying our aural sensibility ; yet never needing (indeed, are we ever to be able ?) to quit the harmonic sphere as Bach defined it. Doubtless men will discover within that sphere new harmonies only faintly foreshadowed by Bach, chords awaiting discovery by penetrating minds already occupying the harmonic sphere. Harmonic minds are responsively creative in endless ways.

Should any reader, like myself, find musical meanings real yet still elusive, refusing to be defined, it is well to remember that use alone brings the only meanings that matter, and that *Definiteness* has both its lower and its higher opposites—*Indefiniteness*, and *Infiniteness*. Music that refuses to be defined may be of the lower kind ; yet it may be equally of the higher. We may, after all, gain much if we only attain enough of definiteness to be able to put the indefinite to flight. After that we shall be content to listen for infinite things a little less vaguely

* Or is it some heavenly, purgatorial Spiral of the mind ?

each day. Sound, like Light, can be resplendently attractive, yet infinitely vague. To quote from the book of our childhood:

> "'Do you see yonder *Wicket-gate*?' The man said 'No.' Then said the other, 'Do you see yonder shining Light?' He said, 'I think I do.' Then said *Evangelist*, 'Keep that Light in your eye, and go up directly thereto: so shalt thou see the Gate.' . . .
>
> "So I saw in my dream that the man began to run."

We started this chapter with a comparison of Beethoven's use of "words" in a Sonata, and Shakespeare's use of words in a Play. It would be well for the reader to sum up his own thoughts at leisure by comparing very closely—possibly even simultaneously, softly sounding the one while scanning the other—the opening choice of words in *The Merchant of Venice* with the opening choice of chords of Beethoven's E Minor Piano Sonata, Op. 90. The analogy seems by chance astonishingly close in motive, in mood, and even in verbal and chordal values. Such comparisons may prove quite interesting, and even wonderfully illuminating to devotees of both poetry and music.

Chapter 24

THREE LINES OF HARMONIC THINKING

IN order to get as clear and contained a concept as possible of the harmonic territory as it lies before musicians to-day, we must now try to draw together the thoughts of the five preceding chapters. As we do so, three obvious *strata* of harmonic thought will naturally emerge ; of these we may find it helpful to think as of three successive and distinct harmonic veins of treasure still waiting to be worked.

Let us begin by taking up a mental stance at the centre of our now familiar avenue of harmonic distances—that is, at our fixed "zero" point. This may happen through the sound of any tone, at any time, anywhere in the universe. But for simplicity, and especially for practical notational simplicity, it had better still be the natural note C on our keyboard, and its familiar major common chord. In passing, we remind ourselves that it is by no chance theory or caprice of Western musicians that we stand here ; for our choice, and indeed our avenue itself, both indubitably conform to a three-fold witness,—of nature, science, and history.

Think tonal centrality—that is, crown C: and the C chord as *Chief* in your harmonic mind: Glance quickly, as in a previous chapter, one remove on either side of you :

and the thought and establishment of key has once more

begun. Now make again the scale of the sum of notes contained in your three central chords

and all purely diatonic harmony is seen to be instantly possible (to this we shall return later). But recall that this indicates the barest beginning of your hold upon key (or should one say of the hold of key upon you ?). Glance again along your avenue in both directions (see page 289) ; recall how the commonest use of the perfect cadence, with the help of its natural leading- and leaning-notes together, is able to spirit you *presto*, in a flash, along the avenue even to the sixth remove either way :

Seeing how dangerously easy it all seems, with the help of the semitone (this closest melodic nearness), to attain the farthest harmonic distances ; and seeing that the mere *chromatic* change of a semitone can do still more, and carry us seven removes, thus :

(−1) (+6) or (+1) (−6)

we must particularly remind ourselves here of the very obvious inference (already suggested), that if the slenderest whispers of melodic semitones can transport the mind for such harmonic distances, centralization must become more urgent as music develops, and the power to hold our centre must be diligently practised if we are to tread to any purpose the harmonic highway that lies ahead of us.

One more reflection upon the situation now opening before our ears may already have occurred to the reader, and a somewhat startling one it is. If, as is clear, a *diatonic* semitone can carry us five removes along our avenue, and if a *chromatic* semitone carries us seven, then an *enharmonic* transition :

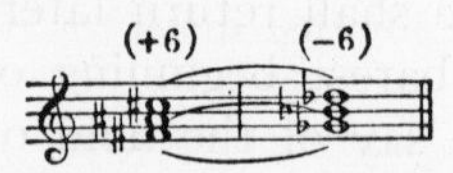

without the slightest flutter of a changing sound (in Bach's harmonic circle) must, though melodically immovable, carry us no less than twelve mental removes ! To the physical ear, enharmonicism is foolishness ; yet to the harmonist it can prove momentous, as we shall try to make a little clearer presently.

Our veins of treasure are then these three : the Diatonic, the Chromatic, and the Enharmonic. And first, we note that they do not lie in different directions of thought at all. Nor, of course, were they suddenly started on their way in the seventeenth century out of nowhere, and developed till the twentieth, now to be dropped into nowhere as a mere dated fashion of three hundred years or so. On the contrary, they arose organically, gradually, and reasonably in the minds of men. And still, in practice, they stand mutually to enhance each other, no one vein ever being back-numbered by another. For *modal* thought need not disappear when *diatonic* thought arrives ; and *chromatic* thought brings greater zest and significance into the use of both its progenitors, as all three are increasingly comprehended. Similarly, as and when we reach the enharmonic *stratum*, as yet little used, all three of its predecessors will have greater, not less eloquence to mastering minds. It can, indeed, not only be reasonably expected, but confirmed by experience, that *the keener the music-lover's awareness of, and sensitivity to, all chords along the whole avenue of distances, the wider will be his total comprehension and evaluation of music.* Our personal concern will therefore be to make our own listening response as quick as thought, whenever finely-wrought music passes our ears.

Here, for convenience, we must set out, both in parade order and in harmonically related order, our whole avenue of major distances for reference :

Avenue of Harmonic Distances

1. In Parade Order

2. In Related Order

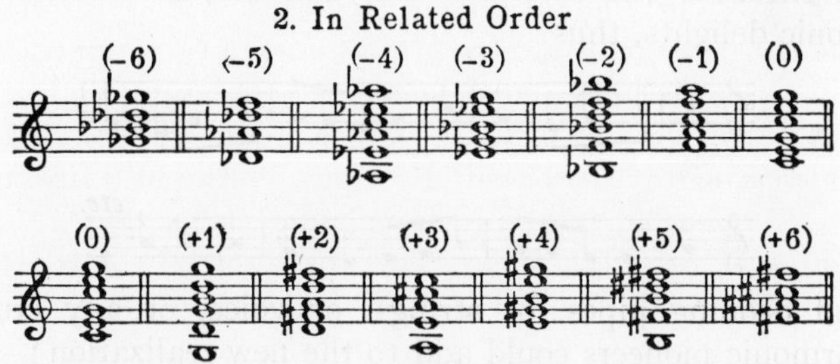

(i) *Diatonic Thought*

Before chord-distances, or even chords themselves, were thought of, the natural or white-note scales held music to an octave of tonal relatedness not only excellently suited for man's age-old wayward melodizing round and about any given note of the seven (called in old days the " final " of the mode), but also (when the time came) perfectly suited for the first gropings of harmonic thought. Even the limited five-note or "gapped" scale (of universal use):

held the (0) possibility of just one major-chord concept: while the natural hexachord of Guido:

held two, (0) and (— 1); and the so-called hard* hexachord:

another two, (0) and (+ 1). But here we must notice that these old primitive melodic scales also brought the more important possibility of related *minor* chord concepts! Within the six-note limit of the hexachord adventurous folk-singers could, and did, foretaste harmonic delights, thus:

and droning pipes, or strings, or voice, or any crude harmonic pioneers could add to the new realization:

Naturally, the incipient harmonic sense had far fuller opportunity to develop apace in the complete seven-note modal or natural series. Whatever the final of the mode,

* The "soft" hexachord in its turn held (— 1) and (— 2).

history leaves us in no doubt that it (the final) became the progenitor of the keynote, and evoker of the cadence. The reader can see two things at a glance: (*a*) that in all modes alike there were available for use in perpetuity the same six natural common chords, of which D, E, and A were minor, and F, G, and C were major; (*b*) that only one of these modes, the Ionian, happened to have a note so installed as centre as to throw the three major chords into their exactly fitting relations for their future logical or "avenue" position.

Look now at our avenue of distances above. The centre three chords, (— 1), (0), and (+ 1), give, as we have already seen, the complete diatonic basis at its simplest. The only three minor chords that we can correspondingly relate to them are these:

Even in modal days, however, chromaticisms began to become inevitable and emerge; the moment a full *Clausula Vera* in all modes was attempted, accidentals naturally arrived, as follows:

This seems a favourable moment in which carefully to differentiate between *chromatically related minors*, *harmonically related minors*, and *modally related minors*, in their bearing upon the avenue of harmonic distances. Here, for example, is a passage suggesting some of Schubert's favourite ways of linking major and minor:

These are chromatically related, and give us a clear foretaste of *chromatic* concepts on our avenue of distances. The following shows a *harmonically related minor* :

and although it involves a black note at the A minor cadence, as all harmonic concepts bring leading-notes, yet it lies in the *diatonic* line of thought, and not in the chromatic. Think, thirdly, of perfect *modal* relatedness between the three natural major and three natural minor chords :

They are all exquisitely and eloquently related, lying gracefully within diatonic thought, showing no sign whatever of being *harmonic* in the accepted technical sense of that word, or of ruffling the preharmonic waters of modal times. Yet one thing is indubitable ; the three natural minor chords here used do stand in the three centre places of our avenue of *minor* distances, which minor avenue ranges itself naturally under the *major* at their related distances (see page 289) as follows :

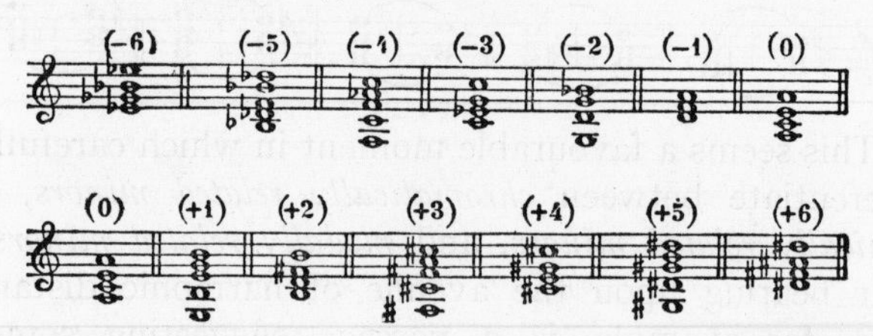

All this helps to explain our perennial and embarrassing riches of related minor keys along the major highway, referred to in a previous chapter. It is abundantly borne out in classic masterpieces that a harmonic composition in the diatonic manner tends to use a little solar system of *six* keys—three major and three minor. The following, for example, are the keys used over and over again by Bach himself in any C major Fugue: C major, G major, A minor, D minor, F major, E minor. And if the reader will glance at both the major and minor avenues, he will see that the three centre chords in both, taken together, constitute the six key-chords of these six keys. Once again run your mind along both avenues, and imagine a Fugue to be written, let us suppose, in E major (+ 4 being its centre). The six keys (three major and three minor) that would then spontaneously but duly appear will be found to bear the numbers (+ 3), (+ 4), (+ 5) respectively. Or if the key were D♭ major, they would bear the numbers (— 4), (— 5), (— 6). No composer, of course, who has the mastery of greater key-distances, is ever limited to these six. As the diatonic led imperceptibly and inevitably to the harmonic, and was merged into its vaster mental spaces, so the harmonic leads imperceptibly to the chromatic. For when Schubert glided from major to minor thus:

he flitted three harmonic removes *chromatically* in an otherwise diatonically conceived style. This brings us to our second line of harmonic thought.

(2) *Chromatic Thought*

Here we must be prepared to face, at last, a comprehensive catalogue of all possible major and minor chords that music or the keyboard gives us, set down, as is fitting, in their simplest spelling, and on parade:

Avenue of Distances.

3. Major and Minor Chords Assembled in Parade Order

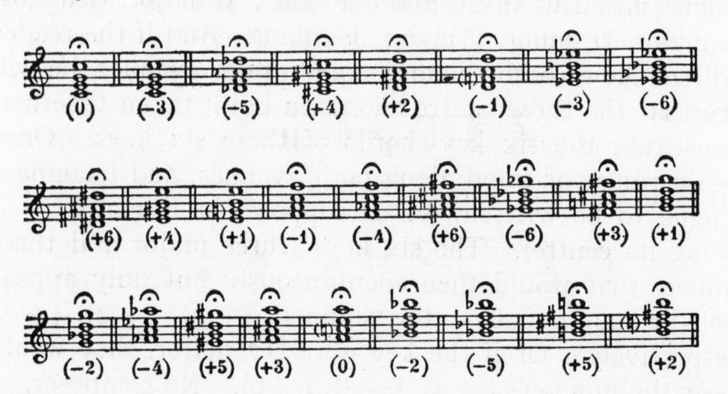

This imposing list is the last of its kind with which the reader need be troubled, because it contains, and suggests at a glance, the maze of *enharmonic* as well as *chromatic* possibilities which await the harmonist. Indeed, it is as hard to keep away from enharmonic thoughts in considering the chromatic, as to disentangle modal from the first harmonic concepts, or diatonic from chromatic. Yet they all can differ profoundly in their effect and appeal.

The above diagram should be sounded softly and slowly many times before proceeding. This list will be especially helpful for reference when, perhaps, some wonderful moment in a Brahms, Franck, Debussy, or Ravel piece has baffled the listener with mysterious harmonic distances suggested only by subtle melodic or enharmonic means.* Chromatic and, still more, enharmonic experiences are only mastered very gradually.

It so happens that most of the discords in classical

* It is well worth while, though often an arduous task, to transpose a puzzling passage into C major (or A minor) in order to see at a more familiar glance what distances have been traversed.

chromatic use on the highway can be first easily derived from, or related to, the diatonic scale. Of course our oldest chromatic friend, the much over-worked diminished seventh, has always needed one black note at least to bring it into being. It was nearly three centuries ago that the dominant sevenths and added sixths arrived naturally:

Bend but one note, in two of these chords, by a diatonic semitone:

or

and there the diminished seventh is, in two most usual key-contexts.

Two things should perhaps be said here, in passing, about this particular chord. If it be played in a chromatic series, softly and rapidly, it can be so sensuously pleasing that thought is apt to be deadened or suspended till the pleasant tonal stream is over:

whereas, in truth, such a progression is a very customary chromatic way for composers to trapse airily along the whole avenue of distances in sequence (implying a series of the very common dominant discords called minor ninths), thus:

and so on, *ad lib.* The second thing about this particular chord is that it has been so thoughtlessly over-used and abused by nineteenth century musicians that at least one learned musical professor has recently written that it is "now practically obsolete." This amusingly shows what real harmonists we all are, that we should first coin a chord, and then weary of it in circulation to such an extent as to imagine that it could now be set aside as dead! In reality it would seem to be as sensible for an artist of any day to say that a certain shape of cloud in the heavens was "now practically obsolete" as for a musician of any day to say that such a chord as this (or indeed any chord) has gone from the face of music! For chords, like clouds, obey laws and not professors. It is the business of every generation to impel them into their proper uses. To use them till we tire of them, and then to suppose them obsolete, seems both too childish and not childlike enough.

Perhaps you may find the greatest guidance in your chromatic thinking through purposely using the step of a semitone, first thinking of it as diatonic, then as chromatic, both rising and falling, in every variety of chromatic progression that you can devise, and by repeating the progression many times, testing its effect upon your mind. Two typical examples of this may be offered to be examined in some detail.

1. One of the most useful progressions in music is to be found by starting on any given note and progressing semitonically at pleasure in contrary directions:

(It is a help to round off every such devisal with any fitting or congenial cadence.) Now this particular progression holds possibilities so vast that a volume could be written to expound them. Yet, played rapidly and softly as they stand, the mind can so pleasingly suspend animation while the ear enjoys the trickle of care-free steps of semitones in two directions that, harmonically, nothing out of the G major way happens at all. We start on G, experience an intriguing sound-happening, and at the cadence our mind remains unruffled in G major. These are indeed merely melodic chromatics within a diatonic thought of the simplest old-world order. Let us now leap to the other extreme, and place a solid fundamental major chord, with such dissonant additions as seem natural to the progression, upon every single note of the series :

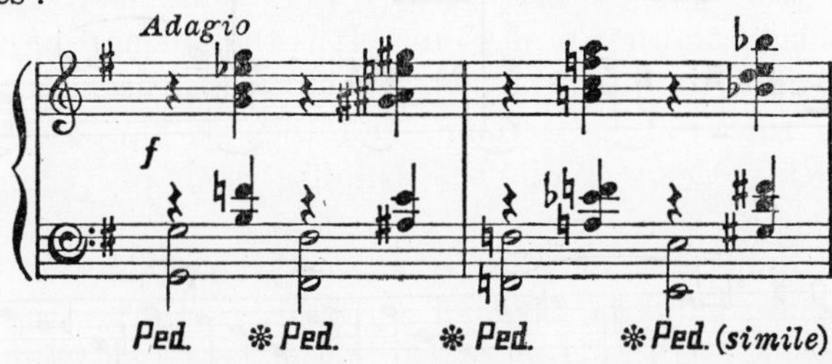

These must be sounded ponderingly, slowly, and often, if their harmonic pull upon us is to be effectually realized. Guided by their leading-notes (the sharpest in each chord) and their under-dominant leaning-notes (found in each case an augmented fourth below the true leading-notes) we may easily locate these most weighty chords in the avenue of distances as follows : (0), (+ 5), (− 2), (+ 3), (− 4), (+ 1), (+ 6), (− 1). Compare this with the first light-hearted version, which might fairly be pictured as follows :

(+ 1) ∿∿∿∿ (+ 1) !

Between these two extremes there are countless harmonic values and instances lying within the two chromatic chains. Here is a delightful one, slightly ornamented :

which you may easily carry forward into a chromatic sequence through the key-centres of A major, E♭, B major, F, C♭ (becoming enharmonically B♮), and at last round to G. Of such harmonic kaleidoscopic fantasy there is literally no end, because the chord-units themselves are endlessly adaptable (see list on page 294). The above example uses none but the most ordinary diatonic four-note chord sounds. The five-note riches have awaited to-day's harmonic explorers far too long; and by explorers I do not mean users of incoherent multiple tonal splashes, but users of newly cogent sounds such as every healthy listener who has listened to Beethoven and his successors for so long could soon apprehend and enjoy.

Before leaving this example it is well to dwell upon

its uses for making simple two-chord harmonic remarks. Thus, here is a fruitful series of dominant-seventh uses that lie within it :

Study will reveal that the chief factor which makes this kind of usage so easy and worth while is the equally divided octave ! We have already seen that if we take any dominant seventh and raise the root by one semitone we have the octave divided into four tempered equal parts :

All such chords turn the octave, in fact, into a recurring decimal of a given number of semitones—in this instance $\dot{3}$, three semitones recurring. The figures $\dot{3}33\dot{3}$ correctly describe the above chord in semitone divisions. It follows that whichever note of the four is now depressed by a semitone will automatically sound like the root of the dominant seventh chord. Play this :

Now follow it with :

and the four transactions, taken together, give all four dominant sevenths that can emerge from the equally divided octave we have called $\dot{3}$:
A similar and obvious series of minor added sixths waits, curiously enough, to be used more fully on the well-trodden harmonic highroad:

The equally divided octave is always by nature chromatic (except in its first and starkest form: (f)) though it is so adaptable for diatonic thoughts. Its three other chord-forms:

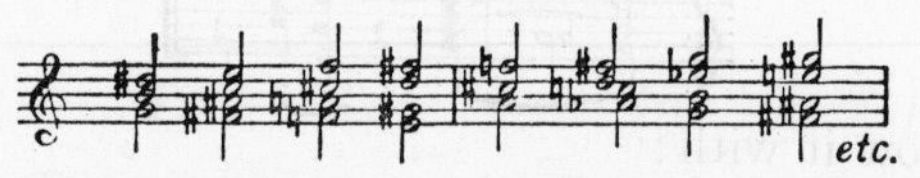

which for calculating purposes may conveniently be christened with their decimal names, $\dot{4}$, $\dot{3}$, $\dot{2}$, will all be found amazingly useful on the above semitonic basis of thought. Of course there is no more obvious use of it than this in connection with chord $\dot{4}4\dot{4}$:

etc.

and though the whole-tone chord ($\dot{2}2222\dot{2}$) offers greater riches along similar lines, and enables the mind to link up six keys in a twinkling, it is of the same nature or chord-formation; it shares the same dangers of complacent over-use for intemperate sensuous effects, rather than a duly tempered use; and adds strength to harmonic thought, for which purpose it seems gloriously capable.

2. Our second example of chromatic usage will take but little space, since it is not only more limited but it is fortunately capable of expansion on lines precisely similar to those already expounded. Its importance here lies rather in the fact that it supplies a framework constructed upon the very intervals which were lacking in the other series, namely, the minor third, perfect fourth and fifth, and major sixth. This is its bare outline, starting at any given point, A, in the avenue of distances :

Here it is, put to use :

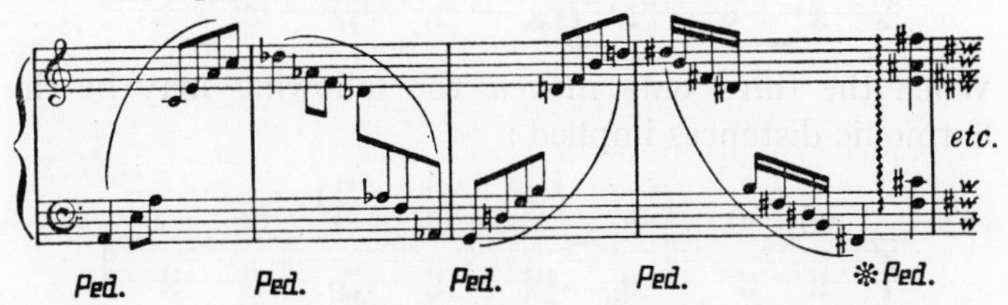

Fascinating fleeting uses may be made of this series, such, for example, as :

And such as these may be found to be as limitless as they are beautiful, and as fruitful, when they spring spontaneously to mind.

By way of summing up this section, it is again suggested that any student who wishes to attain a more practical mastery of the chromatic region might do well to start his serious studies (*at the keyboard*) by committing to more than memory—to his whole mind and imagination—the effect of the rising and falling steps of semitones, diatonic and chromatic, in turn; and this in three ways, (*a*) when it is a *root* note that has risen or fallen bodily by one or the other; (*b*) when it is only the *third* (major or minor); and (*c*) when it is only the *fifth*. Thus when the root (and its chord) rise or fall the harmonic happenings are fairly momentous. The figures record the harmonic distances:

When the third only moves, the following may be the harmonic distances implied:

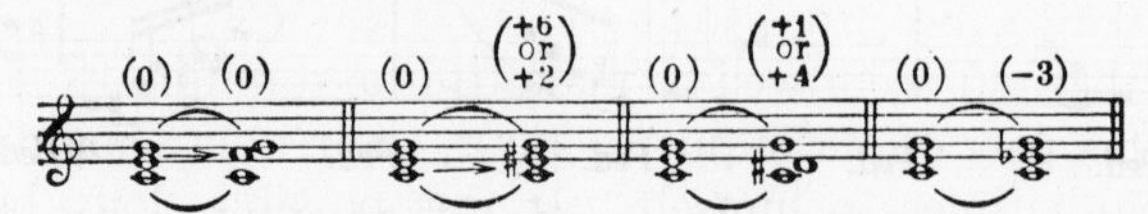

When the fifth is moved, the following is an approximate showing of possible harmonic implications:

In conjunction with these, the mental effect of semitone steps to and from minor thirds, sevenths, added sixths, and other discords should gradually be explored; and the many leaning-notes, as also the many *quasi* leading-notes that lead with effect to any principal note other than the keynote, should be assayed carefully by all zealous listeners. For example, though the harmonic effect upon any musical mind of such an obvious series as the following is striking:

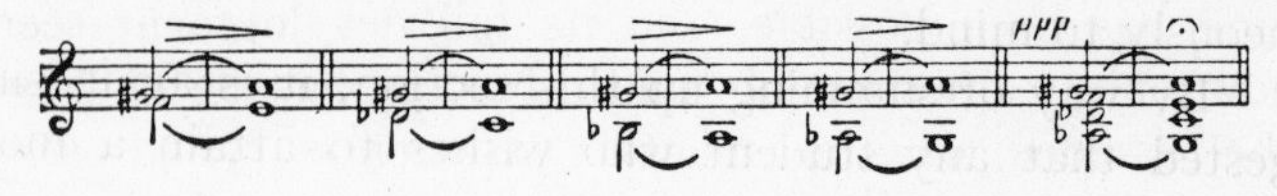

its true assimilation into the harmonic stream of reasonable and beautiful thought and practice seems yet awaited, though any inquirer may straightway enjoy it at his own keyboard.

(3) *Enharmonic Thought*

The axiom that lies at the back of all enharmonic thinking is the truth that a mere change of name (such as changing the note B into the note C ♭) can register a momentous change of thought reflecting upon the whole harmonic context which follows, without the slightest physical change of tone. Doubtless this has already become clear to you, but I have so far stopped short of suggesting any study of its real effect upon music. Here is a classic and most memorable instance of the imaginative use of enharmonic thought (from Schubert's *Unfinished*). (See page 304.)

It would seem well to make this a standing exemplar for this part of our inquiry. First, the reader should play it many times to himself. It was possible, long before Bach's day, to conceive A ♭ and G ♯ in connection with a melody in A minor or in C major ;

was as easy to think in the seventeenth century as :

But it was Bach's marvellous hierarchy, or commonwealth of keys, which, through circumstances, assured to us a fixed cycle of tempered semitones, giving us eleven common euphonies, *physically only approximate*, lying at deliberately equalized distances within the natural octave. Ever since Bach's time, chord-play of a subtle kind has been possible, and its full development seems now only a question of time. For, as has been shown, the essence of the mental experience called word-

The Unfinished Symphony Schubert

play, and as naturally of that called chord-play, is that there should be no teasing change in the physical sound to the ear while the joy of the new meaning dawns.* In the above instance, Schubert clearly approaches F, the note of melodic climax, as the poignant minor sixth of his minor key. He begins to transmute it in his mind at the point marked ∗ (in the example above), where it gradually becomes a wistful and a far more optimistic major third of D♭. The effect rightly defies any final analysis, but yet it is as clear as the day; and such analysis as is possible will show that it is attained by means of a thought of G♯ (in A minor) being at the nick of time transformed into A♭ (a perfect fifth of D♭). Other things happen; the tender, hopeful sequel is left in doubt; the mind sways between minor and major moods to emerge finally into A major, in which some of the gentlest thoughts ever expressed in a Symphony happen. Now, it is the keyboard identity since Bach's day of the chromatic notes, known as G♯ and A♭, that has made this chord-play possible.

If the reader will once again enter the chordal avenue, bent on study of enharmonics at either end, and march from one end to the other, he will arrive at last at identical physical sounds as, for example, in skeleton chords:

He has, however, moved through all his harmonic stations, covering in his mind all removes. If his mind takes breath, so to speak, and then goes forward on the same principle, he will have covered twenty-four removes:

* Precision of thought is fortunately never precluded by physical defect in its presentment. It is necessary to remind ourselves of this very human truism when saying "yes" to Bach's scale and Schubert's use of it.

and the position will have become unthinkable, lamentably untenable, to most of us ! But though this looks like a *reductio ad absurdum,* it is not. It only gives us wholesome and welcome warning of our limitations, and incidentally reminds us how like mental wastrels we should be, if we ran through any *standing* harmonic riches at such a spendthrift rate ! There are apparently two things that may happen to the harmonist *in extremis.* Either his hold on his respective key-centres may evaporate, and only an act of oblivion may give him a clear start ; or he may experience this Schubertian chord-play, and get a depth into his thinking of which he had not dreamed in his exclusively diatonic days. Play the Schubert instance as it stands, over and over to yourself, before you decide that the enharmonic *stratum* of the future holds no new wonderment or treasure for you.

It remains to offer a little practical, diagrammatic help to such patient readers as do not wish at this point summarily to end their inquiry into the musical road of the west. He who feels no further need nor desire for such help may well end this chapter here ; at once proceeding, by much listening and persistent keyboard experiment, to the real musical business of it all—to responsive listening by which he may determine all significances, all values for himself at first hand (or rather, at first ear). Broadcasting and gramophone facilities, if used discerningly and temperately, change the whole face of musical affairs. Adequate means for study is at last dangerously available.

The diagrammatic help proffered below to such as desire it, consists of certain geometric or plane diagrams of Bach's harmonic circle, and of the processes and stages which seem to have led up to it. These are offered, partly because I myself have gained, and still gain, much help from them, and fully expect my readers will do so too ;

partly because it is at all times helpful to the eye to have a system of precisely related diagrams by which the harmonic behaviour of new music may be more readily interpreted than in notation (the look of which, on the page, is often puzzlingly packed with performers' meanings only slowly to be disentangled). But, above all, as long as the twelve-note scale endures, some such forms of diagram may be useful as starting-point from which to depict future harmonic possibilities in forms that logically, and at a glance, relate them to existing harmonies.

Diagrams of Bach's Harmonic Circle

To view our present harmonic system, then, neither in technical terms nor in notation, but in ways which may enable the eye to see the very inter-relatings which the ear hears, the reader is asked to turn first to the diagram of a melodic spiral on page 110.

Imagine that we now are gazing *down* upon that staircase vertically, from a spot immediately over it. Imagine further that it is in reality an endlessly high and endlessly deep circular tonal tower, on the inside wall of which is a limitless spiral staircase, twelve equal steps to a landing. Only about eight of these octave storeys are of interest to men. Below these, the tones offer little more than vague throbs till they die into silence; and above these, they become thin and piercing (like the scratch of a slate-pencil) till they also vanish from conscious hearing; eight "octaves" or so of interesting tones remain, capable of being sensibly and reasonably related by the mind of man, fading at both extremes into silence. Now, as we gaze down the section of the tower or "sound cylinder" which concerns us, we perceive that every twelfth step stands exactly beneath its corresponding step, above and below. Let it be supposed that the C steps all face due north, that the steps rising to the right from this C landing then pass to the E♭ step due east, then to the F♯ step due south, then to the A step due west, and so back to the next C landing, again due north. However far we travel melodically, the C step maintains this same aspect at every landing, and so with all the other eleven. In this way we perceive our complete circle of twelve standardized and ever recurrent semitonic steps within the C to C octave.

The first of our diagrams shows the octave tower with no other step than C itself, picturing a *glissando* up (corresponding to clock-hand movement forward), or down (in the opposite direction) to the octave C.

DIAGRAM I

MELODIC (glissando) OCTAVE

C to C

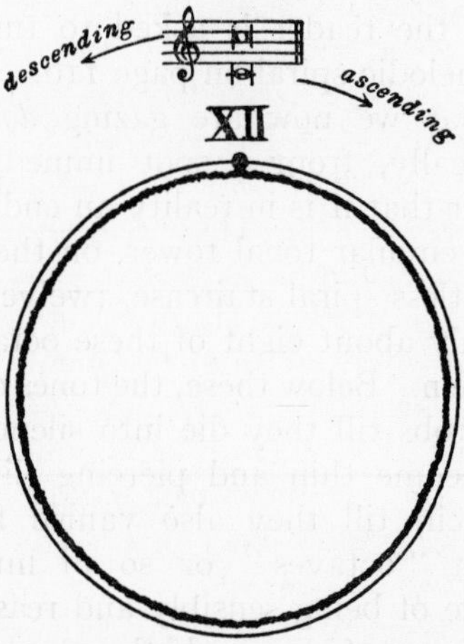

descending

ascending

XII

From this to the final "Bach" diagram (see page 314) it should be carefully observed that all that audibly happens in music happens invariably as pictured here *on the circumference* of all the diagrams. A voice passing by swiftest *portamento* from one note to another is depicted most truly as a curve. The transverse straight lines have no physical counterpart in sound. But like the Euclidean straight line, they exist very definitely in the mind of man. We singingly relate notes by curve. We mentally relate them by direct lines. They are in truth *lines of thought*. They are there only for the purpose of depicting our thoughtful relatings of tones. If this be remembered, the use of the diagrams for realization and classification of all the chord-thoughts possible is the better safeguarded.

One series of stages that naturally lead up to the chromatic scale are here given, exactly corresponding with the process described in Chapter 12 (Diagrams 2 to 9, on pages 310 to 314 inclusive). The seventh and eighth diagrams are included specially to show the appalling complexities which result from the attempt to make all acquired stations in the harmonic sphere stand in perfect tune with their immediate predecessors or *derivators*. Thus, for example, F♯ derived from B (already present) must be flatter than G♭ derived from D♭; then C♭ and C♯ both arrive to be found in conflict on our spiral staircase with B and D♭. These diagrams are given only to show Bach's ultimate tempered solution in its true guise as at once a physical simplification and a practical clarifying step towards an immense mental enrichment of all subsequent harmonic happenings. (It is perhaps still scarcely realized that even Bach's giant contemporary, Handel, wrote for the most part in the five or six elementary distances, while Bach was coursing through the whole cycle of twenty-four !)

There are sixty-six connecting lines in the ultimate or Bach harmonic circle, with myriads of thoughts possible along them. If twelve people were assembled together in a room, and all had friendly relations with all, there would be exactly sixty-six friendships in that room. The same is true of twelve friendly tones. It is of value to bear this analogy in mind, for, when three or four tones form the little *coteries* called chords, the character of the group is much affected by the lines that relate the single members of the group with each other.

Starting with the final diagram of the complete Bach harmonic circle as guide, the student may easily make his own diagrams of any and every interval, chord or scale, new or old. He is advised to draw the different lines of thought in different colours, making the perfect relatings (or "intervals") *red*, the major thirds and their inversions *blue*, the minor thirds *green*, the seconds and sevenths *black*, with the tritone (or *diabolus in musica*) differentiated by a black dotted line. With a compass and ruler, and some coloured pencils, he can spell out every scale and chord there is, beginning with those that interest him most.

DIAGRAM 2

(Showing two fixed tonal points standing in "perfect" relation to C.)

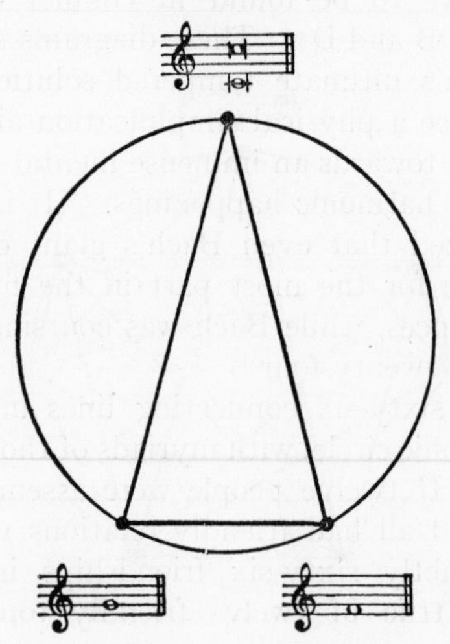

DIAGRAM 3

(Showing two new stations, "derived" from "derivatives" and making the pentatonic group.)

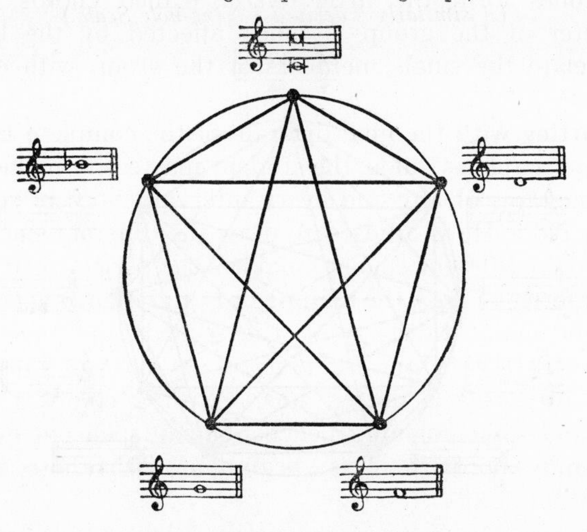

DIAGRAM 4

THE NATURAL DORIAN SCALE.

(With all possible harmonic lines indicated.)

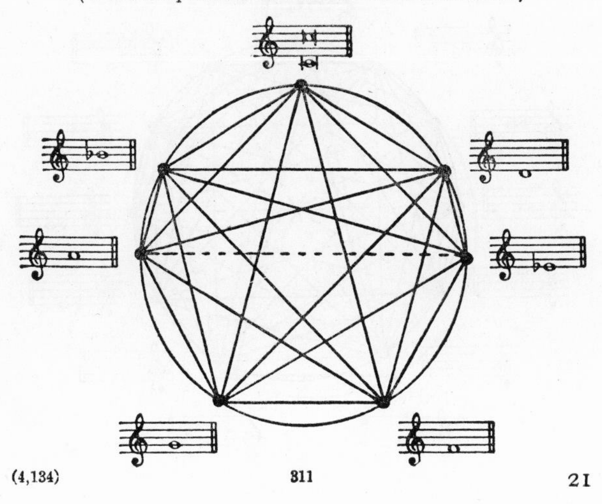

DIAGRAM 5

(*A similarly "derived" Nine-note Scale.*)

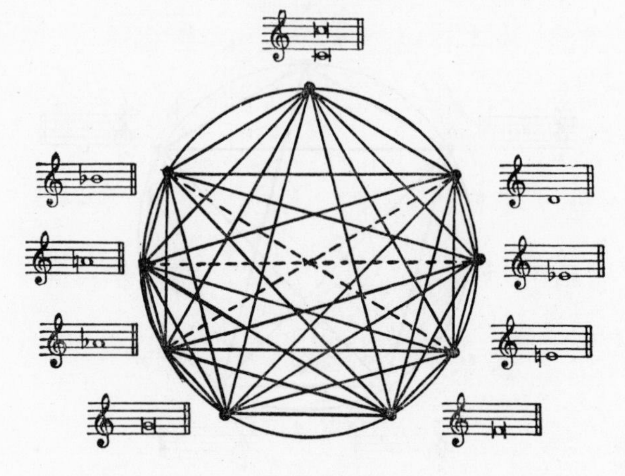

DIAGRAM 6

(*The Eleven-note Scale.*)

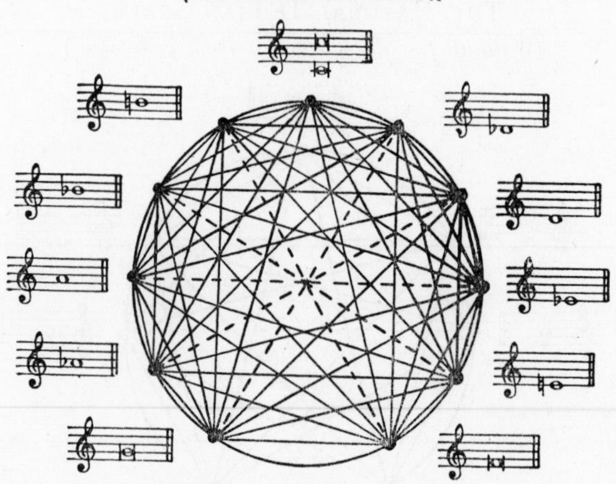

DIAGRAM 7

(*A Thirteen-note result.*)

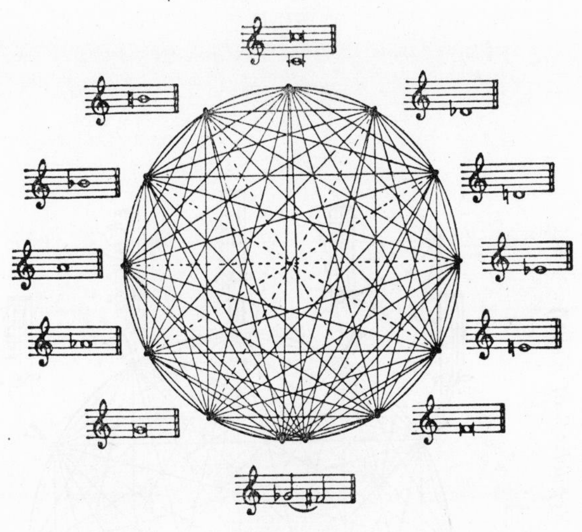

DIAGRAM 8

(*A Fifteen-note result.*)

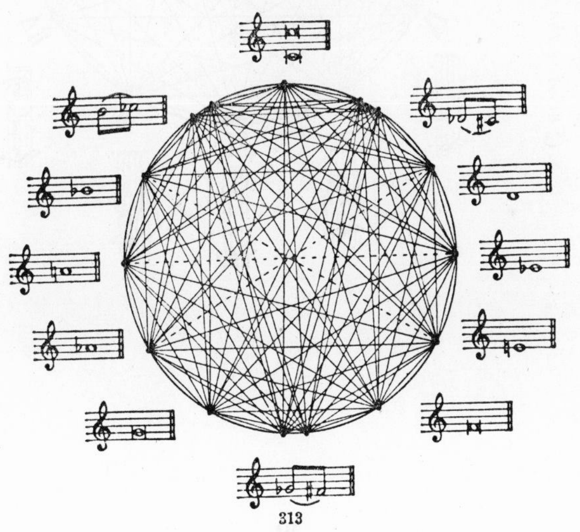

DIAGRAM 9

BACH'S TEMPERED SOLUTION

(*Showing the resultant "Republic" of Keys.*)

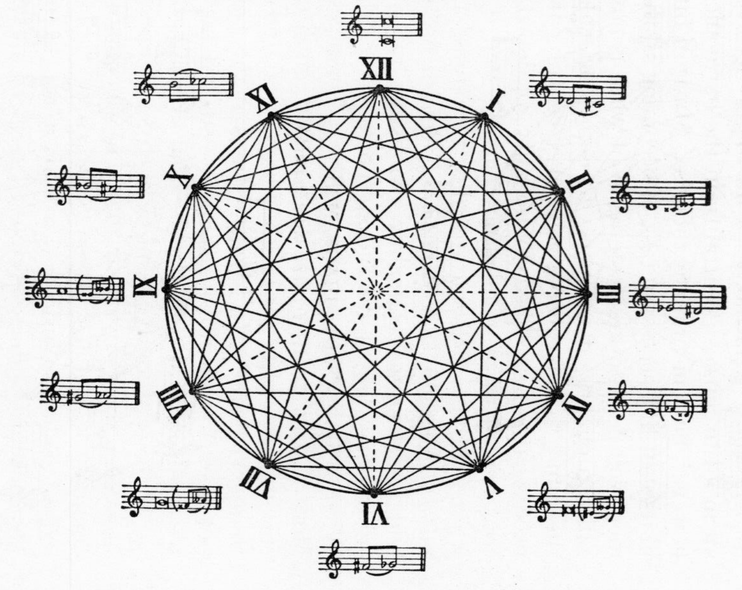

To conclude, we can scarcely doubt that in harmony —whether merely modal or diatonic, whether chromatic or enharmonic—we have imaginative thought at work in the world of sound, in the tonal world, evolving its own exact language of estates (chords) and creative processes (progressions). Harmony, in its comprehensive sense, is all in all to music. Centrality in the harmonic world is, however, but one of many factors ! Music of future days, in its vast but necessary task of becoming all things to all men, will need to take command of what is now vaguely called atonality, if it desires to depict or make audible the mind that is unconscious of a centre ; it will also need what is now called polytonality, to depict the mind conscious of many conflicting centres ; and it will need what may be called mutatonality to express a changing mind. All these may come into relevant use gradually, adding to music's humanly expressive range, without subtracting any of its ancient power of making whole. What will be the natural result ? Tonality as Bach, Mozart, and their peers foresaw and initiated it, will surely prove itself not less but more vital and expansive than ever before. To hazard a guess at this point, had it not been for the work of Beethoven and his followers, we might have found ourselves doubting this to-day.

In face of to-day's musical experiments, we might have been tempted to fear that the principle of harmonic command called Key might conceivably vanish from all except Sonata music (using this term to include all abstract music from the tiniest Design to a Symphony).

Though such composers as Haydn and Gluck gave a striking lead, each on his own very human lines, it was Beethoven who began convincingly to identify real life with music (as in parts of *Fidelio*), and music with real life (as in many a Sonata movement). He did this in so masterly and indubitable a way as to encourage to-day's advance along these lines, towards the consummate reconcilement of the clearest Truth with most visionary Beauty. It is Beethoven again who, beyond all others, causes us to wonder whether the future will prove that the thing now called atonality is a very passing realism, scarcely adapted even to depict the mind scattered or insane. Polytonality may, in its turn, fail to express the Herculean tonal grip upon affairs which its name connotes. It may indeed be that mutatonality alone will be able to tell of the changing mind and of the hurrying kaleidoscope of events. But mutations of tonality are consistent with our experience of both Truth and Beauty, neither abnegating Key, with *atonal* intent, nor making for *polytonal* pretension. Beethoven renders us service incalculable in his Shakespearian grip on life and art. Will not the future Shakespeares of music be likely to resemble our own English poet in this, that never does art seem saner or more concentred in his hands than when it sets out to depict and dramatically to relate abnormal characters and insane happenings? Sanity alone knows enough compassion to depict its tragic opposite. There is wholesome rebellion to-day against tonal fetters. Little wonder, when tonic and dominant have been forged into horrid musical handcuffs. Assuredly it is but the abuse of key, or, worse still, its most complacent use, that drives us poles away from its tyranny. When Drama is so helpless and unresourceful as to make all its characters talk or behave in the same way we deem it poor and ineffective; and one kind of poor music is that which is so bankrupt that it must put all it has to say (and that probably quite untruly to itself) into the same mould of key or keys! But, apart from the helpless follies of its conventional use, key-command remains an essential of the mind. It is the power which, paradoxically, we must for ever seek, in order to forget. Only the completely unconscious exercise of key makes it a reality.

Chapter 25

SONATA FORM

"During it (the contemplation of a work of art) we look neither before nor after; only the now exists for us, freed from all that has been and will be. And we recognize a work of art by its power of giving us this freedom."

CLUTTON-BROCK.

SONATA Form in music remains, at long last, an astonishing mystery. It is, to date perhaps, the culminating achievement of the Harmonic Highway. "Take music at its highest," said Elgar, walking by the Severn with a friend one spring afternoon in 1904 (his first Symphony came out in 1908). "Take Brahms's Third Symphony, for example," he added. Can we all agree with Elgar that Sonata Form is "music at its highest"? Sir Donald Tovey has found it to be music at its most dramatic; certainly it is in this form that the harmonic mind is most free to attain its highest beauty. As soon as music is in harness with other interests, it is manifestly no longer free *of itself* to soar into the highest imaginable regions. True, it might, losing freedom, still reach the heights. There is nothing to prove that some other interest, greater even than music itself, may not finally have power to carry it, in partnership, illimitably high—as the wren, carried on the eagle's back into heights undreamed of, when the mighty wings at last failed, flew out and away into the higher heavens, surpassing the surpasser! But it is not our business, fortunately, to decide whether Sonata music is the highest or not. We have only to try to link it up with what we have hitherto been considering. This should not be difficult; for surely here, if anywhere, we may expect the Nature of music fully to express itself, the Material of music to be put to finest use, and the musical Mind to be ideally heard in Action. For the hand of the composer on his Time-canvas is now given the chance to wield his finest revelations into melody, melody into movements, movements into Sonatas—uniting every diversity of mood, skill, and imagining. Sonata Form integrates all purely musical interests. It seeks Wholeness over the widest range; attaining this, it becomes the last word in musical Form.

But as an embodiment of Fine Form only, Sonata could only fully satisfy the lover of musical design; and it does, in fact, infinitely more. It is so human in its experienced ways that, in listening, we can forget about form altogether. We have just heard it called "dramatic." Is it perhaps drama and design in one—human drama in ethereal design? It obviously could not combine the two unless both are shown to be equally true to life. But a love of form is at root entirely human, just as interest in drama is surely at root interest in the vital pattern that runs through human life—a sense both of the design and fitness of things. Once more these prove inseparable.

Let us reapply our first guiding guess about Art itself, and suppose that the Sonata's supreme attractions will be found to lie always in the interplay of two or more vital interests. It may be again the organic one-ing of *twos* and *threes* that Art is after, even on this vaster scale in the musical field. We watch the one-ing process because we are incurably interested in creative control. This relish for mastery, made manifest, brings peculiar joy to those able to listen responsively to a Sonata.

Let us then take it as a working hypothesis that a perfect Sonata, perfectly enjoyed, blends many human interests in one as it passes our ears ; and let it be supposed that it is primarily a synthesis in tone of the two interests we think of broadly as Design and Drama. We find in actual experience that we can glory in fine form while we revel in human qualities. We rejoice in their oneness and spontaneity. Who has not known the sense of being defrauded when a Sonata begins to grow only formal, when design begins to " show through " ? Conversely, who has not felt disappointment in finding in it merely a series of subjective or autobiographical utterances, with no self-forgetful breadth of vision, no discernible unity of design ? Composers are like this planet earth in being both ego-centric and solar-centric at one and the same time. When I listen to something called Sonata, I find that I expect the reality which blends subjective whim with objective mastery, creaturely caprice with creative control ; for the supreme rapture of a Sonata seems only possible when finest design shows most completely human, and when the most human touches show unconscious perfection of form. Let us turn first, without losing awareness of the human side, briefly to examine design.

I. Design in Sonata Form

Here we should expect at once to trace signs of all primal interests at work, already enumerated in Part I.

As a first step, let us set down, enjoy and ponder this version of a spontaneous yet very formal miniature, a traditional English melody, used in the English Hymnal under the name of " Kingsfold."

This should be played or sung several times before proceeding; softly, of course, and without harmonies. Then it may be analysed in detail, thus:

1. It is an eight-phrase tune. Of the eight two-bar phrases, each successive couple is manifestly inseparable. It is thus also a four-phrase melody. But obviously the first half of the melody makes a complete tune in itself; and the second half fulfils it. So it is a two-fold (or binary) tune as well, each part having its own inner binary balance. Listening microscopically to the whole melody, we soon hear that each half of each two-bar phrase tends also to balance its own counter-half:

So the tune is sixteen-fold! And it is certainly one-fold! It is one-fold, two-fold, four-fold, eight-fold, sixteen-fold. Indeed, listening closely to the ninth and tenth bars:

it is hard to resist an impression of a momentary three-foldness:

This, of course, is no more than if we were discovering details of natural beauty, say, in a leaf or a twig, when a first glance at the balanced beauty of a tree had induced a desire to scrutinize closely the loveliness of structure of twig and leaf and vein. Should you, for love, listen thus microscopically into your favourite Sonata, you will feel surprised and cheated if you do not find it organically and to the last detail at one with itself in the same natural way. It is surely because Mozart never fails us in this respect that he is so readily forgiven his heavily-dated proprieties.

2. Play now the first, fifth, and thirteenth bars of this exemplary tune :

This insistence on one particular note, E, is one of the many natural ways of establishing centrality. For from reiteration : there is no escape in music, any more than in life and literature. When a man repeats a nod of the head, or a single word three-times-three times, he proclaims and establishes the thing repeated as being a sign of something central in his mind. Yet at two of the closes (at the fourth and twelfth bars) this tune leads us to dwell on another note, D : To appreciate the effect of this upon our listening minds, it is well, momentarily, to substitute E for D : both at bars four and twelve. This minute change devastates the tune. Yet how, one asks, can the alteration, by merely one degree, of two notes out of a total of more than seventy, make such a transformation in a tiny, irresponsible, rippling melody of this kind ? Try it on yourself till you are sure of what it means to you.* If it seems to mean nothing, you are merely listening to a lilting tune as you might idly watch a purling brook ; and even that is something to the good. But if it strikes your mind as changing a tune which possessed a subtle mental equipoise into one characterized by monotony, you will know that your mind is one with the mind of the tune ; and may henceforth expect that, in a higher organism,

* The reader is urged to play or hum the tune wholly through many times, both in its original and its mutilated form, in order to probe his experience.

such as a Beethoven Sonata, a single note also may come to make a similar world of difference to you. For this tune only uses notes as Beethoven used chords, inventing melodic devices that throw our minds upon E or D (as the case may be), as Beethoven invents cadences, leading-notes and leaning-notes in the since-discovered ways. The effects upon the total designs, whether of the folk-tune or the Sonata, are equally significant. The mind is carried along, and delights to travel from melodic point to point, as well as from harmonic point to point. The contrasted sway from E to D in this small example is of the very essence of the design. We always know that in melody we may journey to any tonal centre; and we certainly require of every tune that we shall not be left stranded on one tone. We are pleasantly surprised when D is dwelt upon:  But our second impression is touched with magic and astonishment when the mere standing still on E:  at the eighth bar, makes such a difference to us! Now "honours are easy," as it were, between E and D, both claiming our attention, equally safe to interest us. But our minds are like birds flitting from branch to branch of our tonal tree. The ninth bar swings us to D again:  and becomes the most eventful feature of the small melody. But we then find our minds intrigued as to what may happen at the remaining cadences—that is, at the twelfth and sixteenth bars. Let the reader play it again and again, till these details are clear. From all such miniature experiences of musical design we may the more easily surmise how important it may be to us when Beethoven requires us to flit from one harmonic branch to another, from cadence to cadence along our harmonic avenue of distances, in a movement two hundred bars long! For is it not obvious that key centrality and harmonic eventfulness will neither be less exacting nor less enthralling in Sonatas than mere *tonal* centrality and melodic eventfulness in this wayward and lovely little English tune?

3. In order to realize our tune's most delicate unity (wrought chiefly in the final cadence), we have only to play it through once more, *altering the final note itself into D.* The mind seems then left utterly at sea, deprived of its final E. For a like Sonata experience you may well turn to the last eight-bar phrase of the first movement of Beethoven's E Minor Sonata, Op. 90. There again we have but to substitute the chord of G major, or any other major or minor chord lying at hand which is *not* E minor (or even leave a blank in the place of the last chord!), to realize how momentous and inevitable a part one such sound or chord can play in giving a design unity, and how its omission may leave the listener feeling utterly deprived, and at loose ends.

4. We have still to trace the working of a few other natural factors—such as Repetition, Contrast, and rounding Return—in this miniature design. First, take away bars five to eight, and the contrasting melodic throw at the ninth bar would largely lose its significance in design. Conversely, take away this contrasting phrase itself, and the reiteration of the fifth and sixth bars, which has effectively prepared us for adventure into new ground, will have prepared us only for disappointment. This is because *Repetition, with a difference within itself,* turns process into progress, and we call it "development." Repetition, without any change within itself, turns process into a foil provocative of progress in the form of change or event—in other words, it plays into the hands of contrast. The man who makes the same remark twice realizes that he has doubled the chances of being understood; but he has also increased his obligation to "get on," and let the listening mind progress.

There remains one delicious touch to note in this

perfect little melody. If the third to the sixth bars be compared with the eleventh to the fourteenth bars, they will be found to be in essence the same thought, but delicately varied. Such delicate variety, or ornamentation, adds interest without disturbing anything vital to the design. It is as though a friend had slightly varied an amiable remark in repeating it, and in so doing had made its meaning still clearer, still more congenial.

What have we gleaned from this short analysis of a still shorter but exquisite tune? In (1) we saw the whole design permeated with love of Balance. In (2) we saw a subtle tonal design which established one centre; swung us to and from another, twice; and brought us finally back to itself. We thus realized *centrality* and melodic *eventfulness* in equipoise. In (3) we saw that Unity was as loveable and momentous to design as Balance, and, incidentally, we realized in both (2) and (3) that a single note among seventy could matter immeasurably to the design. In (4) we saw chiefly that Repetition in design can both call for Change—challenge it, as it were—and can itself inherently contain or absorb Change, in which case we call it, for convenience, *Development*. In any case, Repetition and Change play into each other's hands, and together secure that, whichever befalls, process shall bring progress. And the above are all Nature's own simple creative ways, and matters of perennial imaginative interest to music.

Little wonder that all we have here heard happen in miniature, happens also in the large, in Sonata form. The magnitude and complexity is increased, the creative processes do not differ.

Of course it is an infinitely greater enterprise to write a Sonata than a folk-tune, just as to design a cathedral or write a drama is greater than to design a doorway or write an eight-lined love poem. It is one thing to be a form master, another to be an inspired President of the

Board of Education ; one thing to give a Flying Display at Hendon, another to organize an International Aerial Tournament that would mobilize the youth of Europe in friendly rivalry, and, incidentally, deal the war-fiend its death-blow. That needs statesmen of genius, greater perhaps than Shakespeare or Bach—who knows ?

It need be little or no more difficult to follow the hand of the composer in action in great works than in small, especially in actual melody or line-drawing. But the mastery that lies behind the phrase at any given time may best, and perhaps only, be enjoyed by intuitively skilled listeners. By experience, by practice in listening, then by ardent pursuit, one may become capable of following ; and the wonderful composers, especially those who are companionably-minded, do themselves help us—as by their disposition and balance of parts, by their repetitions, and, above all, by their staying-points and cadences, their between-while-points, where the listener and composer breathe mentally, the creative minds poise and prepare for further concentration and advance,—most of all by their simply perspicuous motive. Indeed, susceptibility to cadence of all kinds may prove the most urgent requirement for Sonata listening, securing for us our rallying-points in the arduous process of aural receiving. For it must be remembered that we can only receive the parts of a vast musical work *one at a time* ; only through the narrow portals of our physical ears may they be passed by players to the co-ordinating mind. The listener's mental " room " can only be said to be " furnished " (by the parts of the music he has just heard), if he has been able, with tolerable success, to place these in position as they were delivered to his mind ; and this is not, as yet, easy to many. Minds receiving music piece by piece on the aural threshold, resemble a room where tables, chairs, carpets, pictures, etc., are handed in without pause, and may remain for a while in confusion ; and it is not until these are arranged and spaced that we consider the room to be " furnished." So a Sonata is clearly not the music for passive listeners with little or no aural memory, and with what may be called one-dimensional habits of listening.

For this last reason, possibly even the most childish, three-dimensional spatial analogies may sometimes be of help. It may, for example, be found almost absurdly helpful in listening to such tunes as the following :

to imagine the balanced phrases (as they are being heard) placed, one on the *right* hand and one on the *left* of a mental recess, and then to think of the culminating phrases as being placed like an arch *across an imagined mental centre*. Again, the following fragment from Beethoven suggests phrase after phrase placed gradually higher and higher on the walls of the mind, like overlapping curtains or tapestry :

But before we proceed further, it will be well to summarize a few *expectancies* which the very words Sonata Form create in our minds. After which we may perhaps be able to move by one decisive step forward from our tune-analysis to a simple example of Sonata-analysis—or rather of first-movement form (this being the one that matters most). We shall then be free to pass on to consider the human or dramatic side of all Sonata music.

Are there a few reasonable expectancies upon which we can focus, when preparing to listen for Design in Sonata music ? What fruitful lines of anticipation may be suggested ? We all know well enough that individual experience is each listener's best teacher ; yet I venture to offer six quickening memoranda, taken from my own experience :

1. *Expect persistent Balance of statement ;* and respond to it consciously, till expectation of balance and reliance upon it become automatic to you.
2. Expect to be carried at any moment to a second group of ideas and away from your first key-centre.
3. Expect Cadences to bring you to staying-points, or points of momentary rest. Use these as your mental breathing spaces for new concentration.
4. Expect the "unexpected"! Look for surprise developments *as from outside* ; and watch your composer's reaction to them with special care, till you, with him, have mentally compassed them.
5. Expect Returns to first thoughts and to the first centre, however long delayed, and rest welcomingly upon them when they come.
6. Expect unifying cadences and recallings of past forms ; and exercise your memory comfortably over the whole journey, so far as this is favoured by the composer's restful points of cadence.

The above may be of little or no help ; or they may

prove partially helpful, and be improved, expanded, or condensed to suit the individual needs of each Sonata lover, in accordance with his experience.

We may perhaps do well to recall again for a moment the general build of our melody, " Kingsfold," with its sixteen-bar design ; and then think forward from it to our specimen Sonata-movement. (We take here as typical, Beethoven's Sonata in G Major, Op. 14, No. 2, first movement only.)

The following triple order of procedure is recommended :

(*a*) Hearing.
(*b*) Analysis.
(*c*) Re-hearing.

If the reader can first listen to our early tune, followed at once by the whole Beethoven movement ; then compare the two analytically ; then, having paid close attention to every detail of extension in the Sonata form, hear them both played through successively once again, possibly the most serviceable and least tedious means of research into Sonata form will have been found ; and this process may advantageously be repeated before passing on to more complex examples.

Here both melody and Sonata movement should be played. . . . .

Simple as this particular Sonata is, it is not only typical of the form as it stood for a century or more, but is sufficiently developed to be a fit stepping-stone from the simplest classical design to the most complex, and even to the more modern Sonata instances.

Looking back upon the hearing, the listener will have recollections (perhaps only vague) of many a joyous *phrase* of perpetual and pleasurable *balance* (with the rule of four sometimes happily eluded) ; of progress through *developed repetitions*—always maintaining balance of phrases ; and of many a delicious staying-point and lingering *cadence,* contrasted subjects, journeys through various keys—notably through minor keys in the central section ; and of contented resting in major keys in the first and last portions of the movement.

Now let us formulate and make a comparative analysis in a framework that may favour convenient comparison, and bring out the fundamental likeness of the two. We need to use formulæ of some very simple kind in order to set them down with maximum precision and minimum complication. We will set the whole down in each case within one frame, divided into its four natural sections or parts.

A shall stand for the first section ; the second A indicates that the second section is (substantially in the Melody and literally in the Sonata) a repetition, for balance, of the first. B shall signify the new, or third section, and the third A indicates the return of the first section, with its modifications or extensions for the sake of unity and finality. So much for the larger analysis.

Phr. I or Subj. I will stand for phrase, subject, or group of subjects. Phr. II or Subj. II for the second phrase, subject, or group of subjects which stand to contrast with and balance the first—S. I^{d} and S. II^{d} will stand for each of these subjects, or group of subjects, developed anew. C will stand in general for close, cadence, codetta, or coda—that which supplies the resting-point during or at the very end of the design. III in the Sonata analysis indicates the arrival of a new idea or ideas not in any way traceable to I or II, though conceivably derivable from some stray fragment in the process of development, or in the cadences or transitions from key to key, or from subject to subject.

The numerals against each of these signs indicate the number of bars contained in the total section they signify, while the bracketed numbers signify subdivisions of those sections, in which the varied but unfailing balance

KINGSFOLD
(16 bars)

A (4)	Phr. I (2)	Phr. II (2) Close on [D]
A (4)	Phr. I (2)	Phr. II (2) Close on [E]
B (4)	Phrases II and I developed (2)	Phr. II (2) Close on [D]
B (4)	Phr. I^{d} (2)	Phr. II (2) Close on [E]

FIRST MOVEMENT OF SONATA IN G, Op. 14, No. 2—Beethoven

(263 bars)

A (63)	Subj. I (25) 8 + 17 4 + 4 ; 10 + 7 10 = 4 + 6 ; 4 = 2 + 2		Subj. II (22) 7 + 8 + 7 4 + 3 ; 4 + 4 ; 2 + 5 2 2 ; 1 + 1 ; 2 + 3	C (16) 10 + 6 4 + 6 ; 2 + 4
KEYS	G major (suggested A mi.) through to Dom. of D major		D major throughout	D major
A (63)	Subj I. (25) (as above)		Subj. II (22) (as above)	C (16) (as above)
B (61⌒)	Subj. I^d (10) 4 + 6 2 + 2	Subj. II^d (7) 4 + 3	III + I^d (18⌒+8) 10 + 8 5 + 5 ; 4 + 4	Dominant Pedal and I^d (18) 8 + 10 2 + 2 + 2 + 2
KEYS	G minor, C minor, B♭ major, C minor towards		A♭ major, G minor, F minor, B♭ to E♭ major	G minor
A (76)	Subj. I (28) 8 + 13 + 7 4 + 4 ; 8 + 5 4 + 4		Subj. II (22) 7 + 8 + 7 4 + 3 ; 4 + 4 ; 2 + 5 2 + 2 ; 1 + 1 ; 2 + 3	C (26) 13 + 13 8 + 5 ; 10 + 3 4 + 4 ; 4 + 6 ; 1 + 2
KEYS	G major, G major to C major climbing to Dom. of G major		G major throughout	G major

of phrases is shown by the *plus* sign between two figures (as 4 + 4, 4 + 6, 4 + 3, etc.). *Balancing within balancing* is in places shown thus: $\overbrace{\underbrace{10}_{4+6} + \underbrace{6}_{2+4}}^{16}$ In this connection it should be noticed that when balanced figures stand equal (*e.g.* 4 + 4) they indicate an equal or normal form of balance; when the second figure is the smaller (4 + 3) —as at bars twenty-six to thirty-two of the Sonata—it shows a condensation or telescoping of the second phrase for concentrative purposes; and when the second figure is larger (4 + 6) it generally indicates balanced development or extension of the initial phrase. Here then are the two analytical summaries set opposite each other for comparison. (See pages 330–331.)

But a Sonata enthusiast may well be repelled by such a cold multiplex array of figures in squares. What *has* it to do with the exhilaration and refreshment we can feel on hearing the first movement of the *Eroica*, or of Brahms's E Minor? Let us at once agree; it has nothing whatever to do with the vital experience of music; and the sooner we can leave diagrams and figures behind us the better. Yet, we do well to linger a moment to look again even at so repellent a diagram of such an indescribable glory, in order to try the better to comprehend it. Count those *plus* signs, for example, on the Sonata analysis. There is rapture in every one of them. For they all represent the responsive joy of balanced phrasing, balanced thinking. Look again at the mere figures, which give us at a glance length and proportions of the general presentation of ideas, in a total of 263 bars in the Sonata as compared with sixteen in the folk-tune ("Kingsfold"). Are we really concerned, the reader questions, with the space-timing of our greater musical delights? A baby-tune may well be seen as 4 + 4 + 4 + 4; it is as designedly simple and considerate of human memory and imagination in the hearer as is a nursery rhyme or a limerick. But is it of any moment, to Beethoven or to us, that a free Sonata piece of 263 bars should be seen on paper to be spacing its chief sections out so equably as 63 + 63 + 61 (𝄐) + 76 ? Yes, all such details are significant in free fantasy, both in the main sections and subsections. They again tell of balance. It is worth setting down for comparison a like diagram of Ravel at work a century later (in 1905) at his delightful Piano Sonatina. (See page 334.)

Here again the Sonata movement itself should be first heard, then analysed, then reheard.

For the moment let us think of our present small specimen of Sonata Form as a musical *norm*—useful to us as the standpoint from which we may the better survey the Harmonic Highway along which we listen to-day, and we may, by taking such a view, the better keep our heads (and ears) as we listen to still more modern works. But in taking up this limited standpoint we should note carefully that there is nothing sacrosanct about it except the immutable principles which brought it naturally to the help of Beethoven and Ravel and ourselves ; and immutable principles evoke no end of variety ! Thus, joy in balance is an unchanging principle, impelling composers into numberless variant forms. The very squareness which it brought about in this, our *norm*, is a mere detail. Mere squareness may vanish at a touch. Beethoven himself frequently abolished the repeated A. The form often ceased to be square. Later he would return to it again (as, for example, in his last Sonata of all). The truth is that the form A A B A is one *norm* ; the companion form A B A is another. It is the so-called ternary *norm*. (For a perfect example of it, turn to the famous slow movement of the *Pathetic* Sonata.) Of both binary and ternary forms you will read in books. But, better still, spell them out for yourself. For example, the convenient *norm* for Rondo

FIRST MOVEMENT OF SONATINE—Ravel
(109 bars)

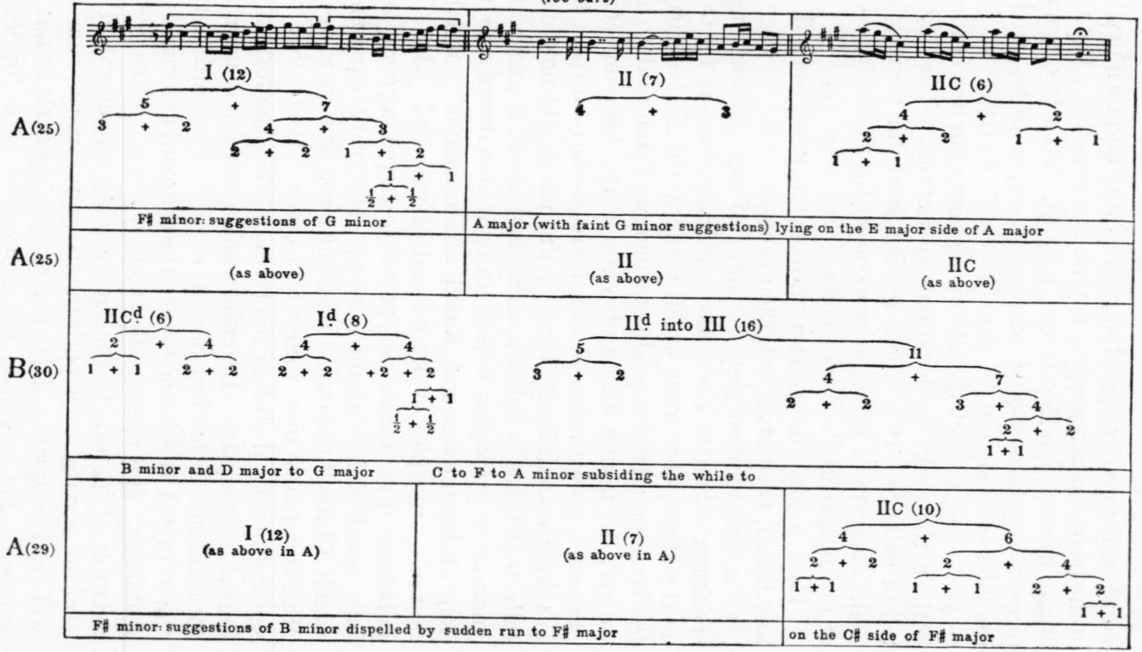

A(25)	I (12) 5 + 7 3 + 2 4 + 3 2 + 2 1 + 2 1 + 1 $\frac{1}{2}$ + $\frac{1}{2}$	II (7) 4 + 3	IIC (6) 4 + 2 2 + 2 1 + 1 1 + 1
	F♯ minor: suggestions of G minor	A major (with faint G minor suggestions) lying on the E major side of A major	
A(25)	I (as above)	II (as above)	IIC (as above)
B(30)	IIC^{d} (6) 2 + 4 1 + 1 2 + 2 I^{d} (8) 4 + 4 2 + 2 +2 + 2 1 + 1 $\frac{1}{2}$ + $\frac{1}{2}$	II^{d} into III (16) 5 + 11 3 + 2	4 + 7 2 + 2 3 + 4 2 + 2 1 + 1
	B minor and D major to G major	C to F to A minor subsiding the while to	
A(29)	I (12) (as above in A)	II (7) (as above in A)	IIC (10) 4 + 6 2 + 2 2 + 4 1 + 1 1 + 1 2 + 2 1 + 1
	F♯ minor: suggestions of B minor dispelled by sudden run to F♯ major		on the C♯ side of F♯ major

form is neither binary nor ternary, but shows traces of both; it may, for example, be A B A C A D A B A. It can also combine in wonderful ways with our first *norm* (A A B A) as follows: $\overbrace{\text{I II}}^{\text{A}}\ \overbrace{\text{I II}}^{\text{A}}\ \overbrace{\text{III II}}^{\text{B}}\ \overbrace{\text{I II}}^{\text{A}}$. Then again, what we may call the Refrain-rondo-form can have for a sound working formula either of these (R standing for refrain):

A R A R B R A R;
A R B R C R D R;
A R A R B R C R;
A R B R C R D R E R . . . A R.

We all may accept such ground-plans and find them amazingly helpful. Whether we devise them or not, they will all be heard, in experience, at some time.

If a panorama of glorious country were only to be seen in motion passing before our eyes, visual memory would have to play the exacting part which aural memory plays in hearing a Symphony or a Sonata; is it not obvious that it would, in such a case, be an advantage to the memory if we knew beforehand that we must look for, say, two main features, round which subsidiary interests would group themselves interestingly? That seems the argument for musical analysis. Just this kind of anticipatory help is needed for the *liaison* of ear with mind in musical enjoyment, as it would be for that of eye with mind in passing panoramic enjoyment.

To sum up, whatever the analytic diagrams we find in books or make for ourselves, out of them all we may deduce, and within them all we may continually trace the supreme influence of *two* unvarying and overmastering orders of Sonata form:

(*a*) The two-fold form of balance known as binary, which may be pictured as A B, A B, *ad infinitum*; and

(*b*) The ternary, or three-fold form of Subject, Contrast, and Return: A B A.

These two, in interplay, are persistent, giving music her needed limitless field of action. When we think of them then, together with the indomitable love of *wholeness* (for all forms whatsoever remain unitary), we are the better able to understand the wonderful and often wistful *codas* which are a distinguishing mark of many of the greatest Sonata movements. We are also able the more easily to discount the bombastic *genre* of *finale* which does not know that *assertion* of finality is not finality—that a manufactured wholeness is a bogus wholeness, the more futile the more it protests (perhaps in repeated brilliant cadences) that it has triumphed and is about to " resume its seat."

2. The " Dramatic " in Sonata Form

We now turn to consider the more markedly human side of Sonata Form, with examples, chiefly from Beethoven, upon which we may dwell wonderingly, and just long enough in each case to glean the human content. For the word "dramatic" we are indebted to Sir Donald Tovey, to whose writings and broadcast utterances on Sonata Form the reader is gratefully referred for help.

The *Drama* depicts life, doing so by visible means and by words. The *Sonata* does it by audible means alone. Can its sounds be as humanly interpretative as sights and words ? In drama, the sights depicted must be true to life, and the words chosen must intelligently fit the situation seen. Put briefly, the case for Sonata is similar : the sounds heard must be true to the mind's experience of life, and the chords chosen must intelligently fit the situation heard. For it is certain that to see a drama without understanding the words of it may be partially enjoyable ; and, in just that sense, to hear a Sonata without understanding the chords may be partly enjoyable also. Indeed, we may go further, and say that—given plenty of practice in either case, but especially in that of music—time and active listening will enable us gradually to pick up the very inherent sense of words and chords, through long association with the corresponding sights seen and sounds heard, respectively. Look closely now at three examples in Sonata music, two from Beethoven, one from Brahms. Play the Sonata in E♭, Op. 7, No. 4, last movement, and stop thirty bars from the end :

Those who know nothing of the harmonic avenue of distances may come to know that Beethoven is experiencing real distances by the manner in which he pauses and softens, and then meditates. In the same way no one could hear the 35th and 36th bars of the Sonata in E Minor, Op. 90, No. 27, as follows :

without getting a vague sense of the harmonic distances which are as real as real life can be to Beethoven and to all who have experienced the accustomed Highway. A third amazing example may be found in Brahms's B♭ Piano Concerto, slow movement, at a certain moment, where B♭ minor suddenly gives place to a chord of C♭ minor (or B minor, if we think it so enharmonically) :

and the " tonal behaviour of the crowd " (so to speak) on the dramatic " stage " of music at this point is such (as ordered by the composer) that no one can doubt what a mysterious and ominous harmonic change of outlook this single dramatic " word " has brought about. Brahms makes very clear by the subsequent context what a vast and new harmonic vista it opened to him.

The more you are able to hear and dwell upon first-movements of the greater Sonatas (and you can hardly do better than stick to Beethoven at early stages), the more clear is it likely to become that the two listenings—with the ear to the sequence of sounds physically high and low, rapid and slow, loud and soft, and with the mind to the sequence of harmonies—will be as distinctly two tasks as those of the spectator-auditor in drama, who knows that to take in with the eye the sequence of sights, and with the mind the sequence of words, are two tasks, entirely complementary to each other. True, Sonata music is bound to be obscure whenever the interest in what may be called the sensible (" spectacular ") side of sounds outpaces the more intellectual interest ; still more so if the harmonic intelligibility of the Sonata drama is treated as unimportant, either by a composer who sees fit to be inscrutable or a listener who sees fit to remain indifferent. Some would have us believe that this indifference is specially true of our time. But, as suggested previously, it is much more likely that a sudden access of new potential significances, and the trend of music when used in harness with other arts and interests (see Part 5), have together temporarily handicapped our powers to *listen* to the *music*

SCHERZO
Allegro molto ♩ = 69
etc.
SLOW MOVEMENT
Adagio ♪ = 50
pp
pp
cresc.
f
pp
pp
cresc.
sonore
mf
cresc.
ff
etc.

(that is, *watch* the *drama*) and to follow the harmonic text at one and the same time. One thing emerges clearly: our power to enjoy the *Sonata* on its human or dramatic side can only be complete when we both hear all the happenings and follow all the composer's harmonic text. This, being interpreted, refreshingly means: study to master your avenues of harmonic distances and the chief chords used upon them. All other rules of the game—balance, centrality, and the rest—are so customary to man, that the power to listen to all balanced and concentred music will prosper with the using.

It is not within the scope of this book to pursue Sonata Form further. Its endless musical possibilities beckon men to a timeless pursuit. Think how humanly you can change a tune, for example, by retarding it! Note the subject of Elgar's *scherzo* to his First Symphony, followed by its transformation into the slow movement. (See page 339.)

Here is Brahms making this simple musical remark:

in an enthrallingly acrobatic way:

Here is Beethoven, playing hide-and-seek or blind-man's buff with a playful subject:

and here deriding it by making it stand on its head :

But even the purely musical devices known as inversion, reversion, augmentation, diminution, imitation, canon, *stretti*, etc., all are entirely human if humanly used and heard on the Sonata-stage of life. And there is hardly need to remind the reader that the more elementary tonal impulses of mere slowening and quickening, loudening and softening, rising and falling, and all qualitative changes of tone, are lifelike things, to be used, and thrillingly so, in complete deference to the text—that is, the Music itself.

We started this chapter with the thought of *Sonata* as an astonishing mystery, one type of the burning quest that haunts all art as it " seeks to hold a mirror up to life," and which perhaps haunts music most of all. Who can say ? Can the two joys—Design and Drama—be fully apprehended at one and the same time ? Can they prove *one* ? Can design unite beauty and truth in one and the same musical work ? It seems to be so. Beethoven at least believed it ; and when he was neither faultily formal nor, as Grove used to say, " boisterously " human, he seems to have attained such unity ; thereby pointing out one permanent musical way for men of all time. There are little children living to-day who will be listeners, sixty-six years of age or so, in the year 2000. If Keats was not wildly wrong in saying " Beauty is truth, truth Beauty," Sonata music may in that year fulfil this decree, and be wonderful indeed—fantastic, orderly, free, balanced, not without its centring " rules of the game," with all harmonic glories and enharmonic horizons. But we must realize that the Sonata of A.D. 2000 may possibly have but slender historic traces of our old-fashioned fourfold diagram of a few pages back, showing Beethoven's simpler ground plan in 1800, and Ravel's possibly playful emulation in 1900. On the other hand the form of A.D. 2000 may be as like Ravel's of 1900 as Ravel's was like Beethoven's of 1800! Be that as it may, by-laws certainly will come and go, and perhaps come again —who knows? Instances vary. Intelligible principles of Design and of all human Wonderment remain, creatively at work, behind all by-laws and instances, for the joy of all ages. They seem as universal as they are simple.

PART 5

MUSIC IN DOUBLE HARNESS

" My heart danceth in the delight of a hundred arts
And the Creator is well pleased."

KABIR.

CHAPTER 26

MUSIC AND POETRY

" Wed your divine sounds, and mixt powers employ
Dead things with inbreath'd sense able to pierce."
MILTON.

IN beginning our study of Music in Double Harness with its alliance to Poetry, there seems at first sight no partnership more fitting, since there is none more natural, familiar, or popular. Yet we know this ideal partnership to be attended with formidable difficulties and dangers to both ; and just because verse and music, when perfectly fused, may gain immeasurably each from the other, it is the more necessary for us here to consider the possible reasons for their frequent failure to unite.

A famous poet quite recently remarked to a musician, " Of course we always say you musicians spoil our verse." Richter once exhorted Elgar, in a memorable inscription on *Gerontius*, to " Let drop words, let drop everybody, but let not drop the wings of your original genius." Again, of recent years, the long-distance listening public has heaped mountains of abuse on luckless singers, to this effect : " We cannot hear a single word sung by women, and very few of those sung by men." But is this the fault * of singers ? Even a slender experiment may here

* Incidentally, there is also a widespread but unverified theory that broadcast words are especially handicapped by natural defects in wireless transmission. Yet there is no complaint that the speaking voice is especially handicapped. The root problem seems to be that to sing is to sustain vocal tone, and when a vowel is lengthened a consonant is handicapped.

convince us of their difficulties, and of the lovers' quarrels liable to crop up in the still inseparable friendship of Music and Poetry. Play this delicious phrase :

then play its almost equally happy rhyming reply :

Then sing the words, "It was a lover and his lass," light-heartedly several times to both tunes. Now try to sing as liltingly, yet with speedy clearness, the poet's second line, "That o'er the green cornfields did pass," to either phrase, but especially to its own (the second), syllable by syllable. Having done this many times, and having probably failed to find the poetic and melodic appeal lying easily at one, turn to the refrain of the song,* and notice the complete success of the fusion of light-hearted interjectory words with this melody :

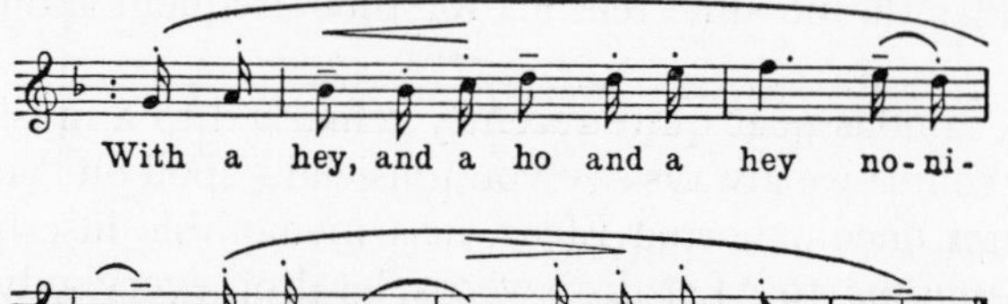

And lest this should leave an impression that music is chiefly successful when the words are pleasing nonsense, sing another fragment of rhyming tune :

* Thomas Morley's delightful contemporary setting of Shakespeare's words.

where the words convey important poetic sense, and yet the fitness of words and music is wellnigh perfect. From this example it is easier to search into the nature of fit and misfit, and to glean three root-facts about music in harness with any art, together with a few special facts about the particular partnership discussed in this chapter. The root-facts first.

Is it not a triple truism to say of this, as of all combinations of two interests, that music should (1) *fit*, (2) *give*, and (3) *take*? It must amplify, not merely duplicate; adorn, not merely clothe; and this with unfailing tact. Fulfilling these conditions, it acquires new intelligibility, new stores of meaning; having *fitted* and *given*, it *takes* benefit to itself.

Turn momentarily, for a sidelight, to another alliance. If, while watching a sunset, you were to hear a strain, say, from Schubert's "Abendroth":

if it were as beautifully rendered as the sunset itself, might not the combined effect of music and sunset stir you more deeply than one of them alone? This could only be if the three conditions had been fulfilled by the music—that is, if it were *fitting* (to the scene), and tactful (which is only to say that its *contact* was perfect); (2) if it *gave* by its beauty new meaning to the sunset; and (3) if it *took* new meaning from the beauty seen by you while it was being sounded. The appeal of beauty heard must not only endorse that of beauty seen, but the two appeals must fuse into an ampler unity, inclining you to feel that "you never before understood music so clearly," or that you "never knew the full meaning of a sunset" until Schubert, through another medium, chanced one evening to muse upon it with you. In succeeding chapters we shall look into what Milton describes as this "able to pierce" quality of two audible arts in one act. But before more closely examining music and poetry in simultaneous action, we must pause upon another notable fact about the fitting of any two particular arts.

There seems to be a unique and added pleasurable interest, not accidental but inherent and permanent (as we believe), *in perceiving the ingenious version given by one art, of a theme previously shown to us by another.* Never does a clown more surely raise a laugh than when giving his version of an episode or a remark, or even of an individual, by which his audience has *already* (perhaps more soberly) been entertained. His movements and his art in itself may already be quite admirable ; but it is the *recognition of the subject* of his whimsicality—some imitation, it may be, of the mannerisms of a mutual acquaintance, or some public man—it is this discovery itself, *sui generis,* that brings added and often keenest enjoyment. You have double amusement in relating the oddities you were already aware of, with the clown's clever impersonation of the same ; and recognition brings its special titillation. It seems, indeed, that the discovery of *relation* between things hitherto apparently unrelated is one of the deepest of human satisfactions. It may not be so, but if it is so, then music, in companionship with other arts, may here find its widest range of appeal to the vast majority. Fitness will then be of first importance.

Let us try to get more light on what this fitness involves. Let us, for example, ask each art, in turn, to enact in its own way some human quality or characteristic of interest to us all—say, nobility of mind, as manifested in some hero. In what way would poetry proceed to show this? Certainly not in a torrent of words. Volubility is the very last way in which to depict nobility. A few lines of verse, choice and reticently aspiring, would probably show us all we ask. In painting, we should be given a portrait with delineations portraying quietude, yet resolute, compassionate energy. On the stage, controlled gesture, lofty and restrained speech, would convey the same nobility. Turning to music, would Elgar ever have written the word *nobilmente* against a bustling semiquaver figure, however otherwise finely wrought? Poetry, Painting, Drama, Music, each has its own fitting way of suggesting such an idea, and each, within its limitations, would strive to make clear its meaning. Let us now propose a less simple test. Let us ask them each to show us (*a*) human sorrow tinged with mirth, or (*b*) human mirth tinged with despair. And here we begin to see their several propensities for fitness in more detail. Poetry has here an advantage over the other arts, that of a vast vocabulary already "understanded of the people." Subtleties of feeling would be amenable to well-chosen words. Painting would again have to rely on lines of countenance, posture, and perhaps suggestive background; Drama would fare better, human gesture having acquired agreed significances, linguistic *without* the help of words, and *with* them, of course, fully expressive. But Music is, perhaps, best equipped of all four. Even its elemental means of expressiveness are many. What is more, all of these are naturally significant, and intelligibly so—that is, its varieties of tonal volume, speed, spacing, pitch, quality, and elementary rhythm will speak clearly enough to all normal auditors. Then sorrow may be expressed merely by little volume and slow pace:

by, as it were, a weary tread. At the same time a tinge of hope may be expressed by an added rise in pitch, and slight access of volume :

Mirth could be conveyed in quick pace, and by the addition of some frivolous little figure in the treble :

At the same moment the leaven of despair might be suggested by lower and lower pitch, or an additional drooping musical figure :

But all this barely hints at the numberless possibilities of music to give and take—possibilities which can be limitlessly developed. For all the natural significances to the mind of music itself, of melody, chords, harmony, and counterpoint ; all the agreed harmonic significances of the classics up to date ; and all the cumulative significances daily added (and still to come) may be used to convey from mind to mind every shade of human interest and joy. Thus the particular tasks just proposed, of depicting sorrow with mirth and mirth with despair, are child's play to music. Watch, for example, Schubert at work in the *Unfinished*. Not only can he make as much sound or as little, as high or as low, as rapid sound or as slow, and all the possible permutations of these, as he wishes; but he can express innermost human experience far more subtly and uniquely when he finds, for example, this (associated since the day of Monteverde with sorrow):

transmute itself into this (as habitually associated with contentment):

to momentous purpose in this most human Symphony.*

We may now readily see that it is important to be aware of the particular *aptitudes* of the several arts—apt, sometimes, in unspoken, vast, inexpressible ways of impressing, appealing to and conveying interests, dealing in urgent masses of colours or of sounds; apt at other times in familiar, homely, expressive ways. Music will be found dangerously rich both in broad and in subtle ways. It can be melodramatically massive and exciting in its appeal to the ear, or dramatically subtle and intimate in its appeal to the mind; and obviously, when care is not taken, drama has a way of evoking musical aid of a kind so eloquently sensational on its elemental side as to be unbearably disparate, and dramatically quite unreasonable.

To return now to the specific companionship of poetry and music, it is clear that, as in the case of other arts,

* As shown on page 304.

they will prove to possess (*a*) *complementary* aptitudes, and (*b*) *overlapping* aptitudes. Aptitude is not fitness. It is the capacity for fitness. Arts apt to collaborate may yet fail to fit. We dare not expect give-and-take between music and poetry by processes of *overlapping*. This means that in this partnership the complementaries must fittingly amplify each other and illumine the hearer; and (2) the overlapping aptitudes (which we may portmanteau, as Lewis Carroll would certainly have done, into *overlaptitudes*) must be carefully cut to size, with what we may nickname a fifty-fifty consideration in the cut. But what *are* the complementaries, and what are the "overlaptitudes"? Let us try to descry them.

Arne was a fine setter of words to music. Let the reader *say* the two words "Rule, Britannia" *aloud*, to himself. Now let him play or sing this fragment without words:

Putting them together, the speech-rhythm and the tune-rhythm are heard to be admirably cut to size. They are also completely satisfying apart, *qua* words and *qua* music. But together they are better, producing (in a far less personal degree) something of the thrill imagined when the sunset and Schubert's musical reaction to it were blended. Yet Arne could make mistakes. Read this, again *aloud*, and with relish of its human mood:

"Blow, blow, thou winter wind,
Thou art not so unkind
As man's ingratitude . . .

"Freeze, freeze, thou bitter sky,
Thou dost not bite so nigh
As benefits forgot . . ."

Now play this Haydnesque tune :

Could any verse and music sound more at variance? But sing the poem to the tune; and even if you try to concede, for purpose of argument, that Arne's melody really is a "complementary" called for by Shakespeare's words and intention (as revealed in the context of the play), it must be owned that the "overlaps" are hopelessly wrong. The relative lengths and strengths refute each other. Try them again. Then turn to Roger Quilter's :

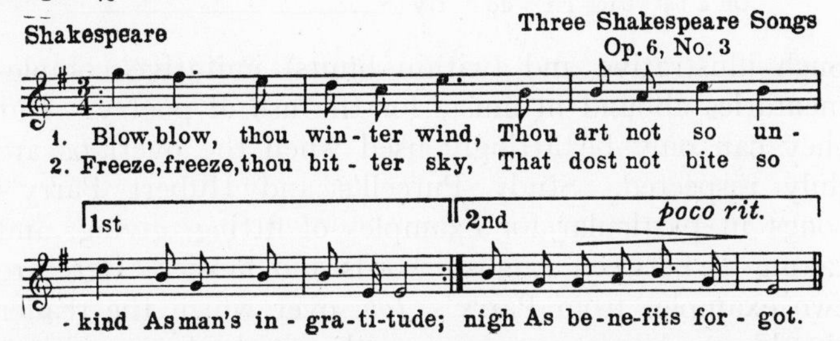

Here, whatever the quality of the melody, as melody, the overlaps are admirably adjusted. Poetry and melody utter themselves at one. But watch Arne once more setting Shakespeare :

And here is another fragment from the same setting :

Could anything, this time, be more exactly right? But a new kind of "complementary" now comes to light. Cowslips are not to be tonally *depicted* thus:

Yet this graceful little drop and rise, in terms of pure melody, is an appropriately added musical adornment to the poetic fancy. The mind's eye more clearly visualizes the delicate flower, in the modest grace of the music which complements it at this point in the poem. A similar but more extensive complementary emerges a moment later:

Such illustrative and (within limits) imitative complementaries abound in music for the use of poetry. But they can only be fittingly used when the overlaps are duly respected. Study Purcell's and Hubert Parry's songs in particular for examples of fitting, giving, and taking as between English words and music. Here are two examples from Parry's *Job*, over which the reader should ponder (accompanying the final phrase with a *pianissimo* cadence into F major):

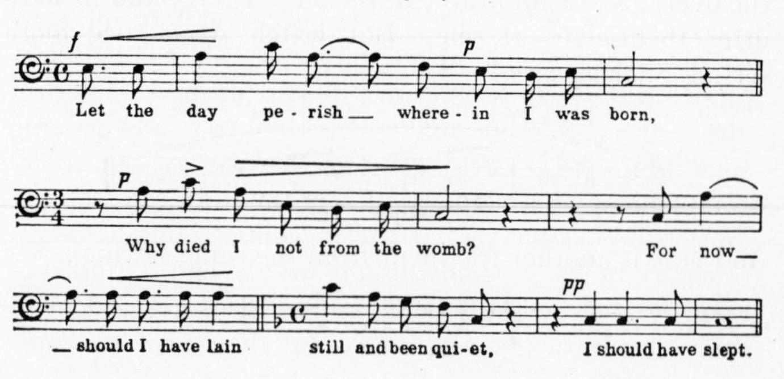

And here are three interesting Purcell examples :

These examples will, it is hoped, stimulate the reader to look out many more for himself. (Purcell's " fit " is often thrilling, and sometimes disappointing.) They may also suffice to enable us here to think out and assemble something like a working list of the overlapping and the complementary aptitudes. For ultimately the true fit of music and poetry, and their powers to illuminate each other to the hearer's advantage, will depend, as indicated, upon (*a*) the overlaps being cut to measure, and (*b*) the complementaries being fused. But the reader may question, how are overlappings to be distinguished from complementaries ?

It is surely fairly easy to determine that the overlappings mostly, if not all, lie in *dimensional* ways. They are matters of tonal magnitudes or measurements, already considered in Part 2. For words, like notes in music, have relative shapes and sizes in utterance. They reach the ear in differing *loudnesses*, *lengths*, and *pitch*. Words, in utterance, are as subject to *speed* and *spacing* as are notes in utterance, and have like *qualitative* character. When a word of a poem is set or sung to measurements which completely ruin its value and meaning in context, the effect on the attentive hearer can only be one of painful frustration. When, for instance, its position and significance in a poem require it to be interpreted and uttered with softness, shortness, mellow pitch of voice, deliberation, careful spacing—that is, given a moment of white silence before utterance—and if it is then given instead (for musical ends) loudness, a great deal of length, high pitch, blurred enunciation, and a loud background of accompaniment to boot !—is it wonderful that the poet should complain to the musician that " you musicians always spoil our verse " ? How very frequently this happens, the reader knows. Is it not due chiefly to a failure to apply common sense to the task of adjusting magnitudes ? This adjustment does not mean that melody should be reduced to the all-round size of speech—though, indeed, singing words (in their speech-sizes) have ineffable beauty compared with high-pressure vocalizing carried in our own day, as every reader may well testify, to sickening excess. Already it becomes possible to believe with thankfulness that, in a not too-distant future, the customary hectic singing of our day will be remembered only as some astonishing error of judgment, for which no one in particular was responsible, because it was a complacent, generational error shared by us all ! Music, it is true, may be used with moderation to magnify and intensify every detail of poetic speech to scale, much as a lantern magnifies a slide ; but such enlargement should never be greater than is fitting. That the dimension of song must not be as great for a small room as for a concert hall is a fact easy to perceive, but too often ignored. In broadcasting, a new thing has come about, for whispers of speech and melody can now be even more perfectly detected than louder sounds. Speech-inflections, speech-volumes, speech-rhythms, speeds of utterance, spacing of words at important points, and vocal qualitative needs can all be brought out in proportioned and reasonable counterparts of melodic-inflections, tonal lights and shades, rhythms, speeds, spacings, and qualities.

Let us turn now to the *complementaries* of Poetry and Music. These may be better appraised if we stay to make a few comparisons between the actual appeal and effect of words and musical notes upon us.

It is fairly clear that while both use sound to *communicate,* and to *communicate attractively*—to carry thoughts and to please—yet the primary purpose of utterance in speech is to use any unit of sound in its *communicative* aspect ; whereas the primary purpose in music is to use sound in its *attractive* aspect. A word *communicates* and sets us thinking, more than a chord does ; whereas a chord attracts us and sets us *contemplating,* more than a word does. So the unit of communicative thought in words is a verbal sentence, generally causing us to think ; whereas a unit of contemplation in chords is a harmonic sentence, generally causing us to meditate. Other helpful comparisons will naturally arise from these, and tend to make clearer the power of words and music to play into each other's hands, thus : (1) *Verbal meanings* are apt to be bounded, precise, particular, local, definite ; whereas *musical meanings* are apt to be unbounded, vast and vague, general, universal, infinite. (2) In the matter of quality or " colour " (if this is not too indefinite a name for the distinctive charm in tones of voice or instrument) the tables are turned; for whereas qualities of *words* are vague and uncertain, those of *chords* are precise, clear, and minutely differentiable to any practised ear. (3) *Repetition* (of phrases) is used by both arts alike, but with a different bias or leaning, for verbal recurrences seem to be used chiefly for emotional emphasis, and secondarily for structural purposes; and musical recurrences chiefly for purposes of design, and secondarily for emotional emphasis.

These three are, so far as we can judge, the main conditions and facts of the contrast between the two arts. To ignore them would be further to delay our desired ideal of a perfect union of the two.

When the overlaps are perfectly adjusted (as they very nearly are in, for example, the exquisite Morley-Shakespeare song quoted earlier), then these complementaries have their chance. Remembering Stevenson's delighted remark, " To my ear a fourth is delicious," we can hardly imagine his inimitable line, " Bright is the ring of words when the right man rings them," without the ring of a perfect fourth; or set instead to the clang of major sevenths and minor seconds:  Again, in " I know that my Redeemer liveth," could Handel or Bach have set the words " I know " with *augmented* fourths:  Both of them intuitively chose a rising *perfect* fourth. There is no end to the particular and fulfilling service which the language of words and the language of chords can give each other when conditions are favourable.

But having clearly seen this, there are yet two formidable facts remaining to be faced by all who would understand the difficulties as well as the glories, the limitations as well as the glowing prospects of this alliance. Let us, to conclude, observe them.

Dean Beeching once said that there are poems so wholly beautiful that they do not bear reading aloud, but make their perfect appeal direct from the silent page to the mind. Musicians could as truly claim that there are certain musical moments in the classics so delicately poised as to exclude tones of any volume, and which directly, in silence, absorb the mind that is fully sensitive to harmonic contemplation. Between these extremes there is a boundary-land where words and music not only can synchronize in utterance, but each fulfil the other. (Arne's second little song, quoted above, is a very slight example of this perfection of unity.) There are vast intermediate tracts of appeal where great poetry prompts great music, yet where the result of attempting the union is to break the poem to pieces. We may generalize and say that within this great tract words which evoke music are of three kinds : (1) those in which exact agreement (of magnitudes and intention) makes simultaneous utterance a joy and a success ; (2) those in which the words refuse to expand to the magnitude of the music they evoke, and so have to be instantly repeated, as in Bach's greatest choruses—*e.g.* the *Kyrie, Gloria, Sanctus,* etc., from the great Mass (and when words will bear repetition, all is well) ; and (3) finally, there are words which prompt music, but which simply will not run in harness with it. These can then only form a motto to be put in mind beforehand, and remembered during the progress of the music they have called to life ; or they may be recited, or musically spoken, in alternation with, or during, the said music, in cases where both arts prove amenable to such a plan.

The second fact arises from the third generalization above. The reader may have noticed, when attending to a play, that when an actor has a momentous word or speech to utter, the delivery of it is often astonishingly reticent. It may indeed be stated as a principle, that the more momentous the word, or words, the less fitting does it become to *spread* their utterance in any way whatever. The exact opposite is true of momentous music. The greater the idea behind it, the more expansive the music tends to become. To this fact we shall return in Chapter 29. But in every partnership between Poetry and Music, the actual utterance of the most momentous word will be likely stoutly to refuse to fit with the utterance of the momentous music that it has of necessity evoked in the most sensitive musical mind.

CHAPTER 27

MUSIC AND SCENERY

" See deep enough and you see musically ; the heart of Nature being everywhere Music."—CARLYLE.

SOMEBODY has said that one must be able to *hear* a landscape to enjoy it fully. I suppose this meant that, whatever the splendours of the picture, pigment is too silent and still to be anything but a makeshift. Along such a line we might naturally go further and demand ability to *breathe* the fresh air and fragrances of the landscape as well as to hear the wind in its trees, its singing birds, murmuring brooks, and the rest. This brings us face to face with the old problem of the realist, and all the exacting requirements of realism. Let us " have the real thing ! " True, dear realist. Art is in search of the real thing in order to bring it before your and my very eyes and ears (and nose if need be), and thence to our imaginative mind. A few daubs of pigment in a frame on our walls is thus both more and less real than the sunset it brings to our mind. To the senses it is contemptibly less. To the mind it can even be more—we are not *alone*. We are in company with a creative imagination. We had seen a sunset yesterday, and yesterday week, and yester-year—dozens of thrilling sunsets in our time—alone. What we imagined to be the reality about the sunset is now endorsed and enriched by Turner (if Turner happens to be our artist). Or, put the other way round, what he, the artist, found real enough to utter in art-form is now at hand for your and my endorsement. In the mouth of two, *it*—the open secret of all Beauty—becomes established. If you and Turner are utterly sure about it, you will find other witness needless. It will be whole, and will wholly meet you. You will ask for no incidental music ; no poem about it, no nature-sounds or scents. You will never really even need to see another sunset again. Yet, on the other hand, you will more than ever seek to see sunsets ; and will find the more reality in every subsequent experience of sunset (or, for that matter, in every sunrise too), because you and Turner did once make sure of it between you. Art is significantly more than scenery in this, that it is the dispeller of lonely wonder. For lonely wonderment, one does not go to the Tate Gallery, but to nature, lingering, say, on Victoria Embankment to watch the Thames, the clouds, the traffic, and the lonely ones. If, however, you want witnesses as to *it*, go to the most trusty art you can find. If one witness, Turner, or whoever the artist may be, leaves you still in doubt, then seek two. If their witness tallies, you will at least experience a less timorous delight. But should you find that your Turner is all along an utterly convincing companion, you will tend to grow as regardless of other witnesses as two children of one father might show disregard if some one offered to prove to them that their father was a real good sort. They know already.

So the Arts, all of them, at their most real, are most independent of each other *except for one*, the companion-witness. The Turner you love may suffice to fill your moment to overflowing. The Beethoven you most admire may need no picture, nor poem, nor programme, nor any word from any fellow admirer to throw light where all is light already. But whenever you linger at the other extreme in the land of doubts—and which of us does not often suffer art-darkness and puzzlement ? —you may possibly find a cloud of witnesses still insufficient for your needs. With experience comes, of course, more confidence, more grasp, and less need of confirmatory witnesses. As your conviction of reality grows stronger, doubts fall away, till at last it may actually come to pass that even a mere six strokes of one artist's brush, or six lines of a poem, or six or eight bars of a Sonata suffice to thrill * you.

But, more often, even fine art leaves us in need of assurance from one direction or another. We are half stirred, but wonder, " Is he making it up ? " or " Am I imagining it ? " Yes, we *are* imagining it, and we only want to be sure that what we are imagining is reality. So did the artist or composer in his turn. He probably wants your word for it too.

All this serves to show how permissible it is for one artist in one kind to witness to the reality of a fellow-artist's utterance in another kind ; and it also suggests that the combining is especially useful to us in the early stages of our wonderment, when we have not caught the drift of the second artist's mind owing to unfamiliarity with his language. In this respect music especially gains owing to the subtle nature of its own particular orthography and syntax. It so often *needs* timely interpretation in early stages. Only let us try to keep clear of the easy fallacy that three or four arts can be expected to do more for us than one. Experience up to date has proved to men that one art at its fullest can tell them 100 per cent. of that which all would tell and we all would experience.

* By " thrill " I mean a sudden feeling of " yes " : of certitude—something that is the same for all. It seems an experience quite incommunicably personal, yet quite common to all ; that never changes. It seems quite timeless —that is, one feels exactly the same every time it happens. Every such experience seems to revive *all* its predecessor moments of the same kind in the past, and to raise expectancy that they will recur countlessly in the future. The physical symptoms of this sudden event of mind are sufficiently ordinary and involuntary to suggest that they are shared by all men—a sudden tear, a sudden gulpiness in the throat or shiveriness in the spine, and an unwillingness to move and inability to speak. The only way to describe the thrill of which these are often the somewhat humiliating symptoms, is to compare it with a sudden arrival at a longed-for place—a " home-at-last " feeling.

True, the senses can be pleased with a piling on of sense-impressions. Arts four-abreast (as in opera) may bring a sense of overflowing exhilaration. Who would belittle the good uses of such exhilaration? But when we remember that the senses all remain, for good, the agreed and agreeable messengers of the mind, then we call in a third or fourth witness to advantage only if two or three others have failed to move us (possibly through our slow response or through the inconclusiveness of one art in particular). In short, we bear in mind that the moment Art (like Life and Nature herself) is satisfyingly real—when she communicates Reality—she stands in no need of Realisms.

We shall therefore only consider the uniting of Music and Scenery (or Pictures, or Stage tableaux) in simultaneous appeal to the mind through eye and ear, not for sensational purposes or an indolent desire for realism, but expressly to complement and fulfil each other's appeal, as and where and when they, and we, are mutual gainers. In short, we must inquire for a second time how two arts can *fit*-and-*give*-and-*take*.

A musical broadcast recently caused an Anglo-Indian listener to write home saying that by fitting an Indian sunset to a Delius record, he could, at will, "induce nostalgia." This letter interestingly implied that one of these two joys alone could not do it; in the mouth of two witnesses response was assured. Let us explore this ground in some detail.

First, ask a friend to look stedfastly, say for the space of a whole minute, at a fine scene, landscape, or picture; and yourself stand by to watch closely the behaviour of his eyes as he looks. You will find that the eyes are continually on the move; and if you ask him to keep them dead still (for a few seconds even) he will find it an impossible command. The eye of the lover of pictures, in fact, is always *melodizing*. It moves from point to point quite unconsciously, relating line with line, colour with colour, or happening with happening. This affords only one example, but a telling one, of the truth (mentioned on page 12) that the eye moves to enjoy the picture that stands still in space, whereas the ear stands still to enjoy the music which moves in time. How then can eye and ear best act in consort when music and landscape are combined?

Let us try to think of an orchestral piece that most completely resembles a landscape. Is there one? If so, we may get an automatic *fitting* of sight and sound. Here we are at once confronted with one or two obvious conditions. The orchestral piece, for example, must not be *intenser* than the picture, nor more *subdued*; for a very bright orchestral piece would never fit a landscape of subdued purples, and *vice versa.* Again, an orchestral piece full of *angular* melodies would not fit a scene full of *rounded* forms. But here we will stop short and turn back, because obviously we are being led along a premature line of thought. For even if you find music with the fitting rounded melodic lines, and just the right glow for the picture, how are you to enable men to use their melodizing eye on the landscape in such a way as to fit with your preordered melodizing in the music? How is a man's ear, at *your* command, to be made to synchronize with his eye at *his own* command? Synchronizing is, in fact, the chief difficulty. Besides, to be practical, we should first settle whether the fitting of heard *movement* to seen *stillness* is possible in itself. If music is, very broadly speaking, *all* movement, and the landscape *all* stillness, can it be done?

Now set up an imaginary landscape before your eye, and listen with your mind's ear. Would not the strict orchestral analogue of it be just one long-drawn, stand-still composite orchestral chord? It would probably be a very soft chord, because loud music is too immediately excitating and tiring, and a picture is neither, till the observer makes it so. Yes, this "stillness chord" is the obvious answer, for the moment, to our second point.

Granted then that the eye and ear have quite different methods of assimilating their arts; and granted that the only orchestral piece that would behave like a landscape would be a mere composite sound or chord, held still and within hearing for as long as the picture is within sight (which seems a most unpromising musical effort); let us, in the third place, proceed to reduce both eye and ear appeal as it were, to "zero," in our minds, start them together, and see what happens. Throw, then, upon the screen of your mind, a picture, say, of a "morning at sea"; a calm, blue sea, and a still bluer, unclouded sky; no breeze, no movement of any kind. Now go to the keyboard and sound any contented major chord:

lunga

ppp

Ped. *

Look at your mental picture and listen to your sustained chord as long as both are possible. You can now try varied chords of this kind (high up, low down, dark or bright), and adapt your imagined moving scene, as nearly as you can, to each variety.

So far so good. We have a useful analogue as a starting-point. Now if the picture were Turner's, and the chord Beethoven's, we realize at once that the former requires our eye to take in the picture—all of it—and not passively to gaze at one spot. Our eyes must move melodiously. The artist leaves us, in fact, to compass the extent of his concept with our own eyes. Beethoven's method, on the other hand, departs here from Turner's. He requires our ear not to *ex*tend over the whole musical concept, but, on the contrary, to stand still, and, as we may well put it, be *in*tent. It is he who must do the rest—*i.e.* direct our ear from point to point of the chord, or of the harmonic concept. He cannot do it in absolute stillness, it is his melody that does it. Music itself moves; and it is at this point that our absolute analogue disappears. But still the composer can do the melodizing in relative stillness, disturbing us as little as possible in the movement of his brush on the time-canvas:

(Compare the opening of the *Choral Symphony* and many another still moment in Beethoven's, with the above guiding gestures of melody.) There is nothing in the rules of art to insist upon your looking at any particular points of the picture in any particular way. Every observer is personally free, in eye and mind, and personally busy according to his own responsibility (that is, his ability to respond). But with our heard analogue of the chord we have not this freedom. Our " ability to respond " remains, but our responsibility changes; and we are called upon to go with ear and mind to whatever points Beethoven takes us, and in doing this we *give our creative response or sanction* in a different manner. There is nothing in the rules of either art to prevent you, or Beethoven, or Raphael, or John Jones, from *looking* upwards when the melodic line makes one *listen* upwards, and down when the melodic line makes one listen downwards. You may find this fitting, and John Jones may not. Or, the whole world may find such analogous movement of eye and ear an inherently natural one to follow. Speaking generally, this seems really probable. Try it carefully and testingly in this " zero " case, and it will have the advantage of clearing up your own possible relatings between eye and ear habits and the eye and ear appeals of two arts ; but bear carefully in mind that all this is but a passing and unessential guess at what happens.

A more important aspect now deserves our close attention. We have so far imagined no *movement* in the music. Our thought has been of a chord of three euphonious tones at rest, in the one case ; and of a horizon line, a sea-depth below it, a heaven above it (an equally euphonious trinity of impression to the eye), in the other. The music, we say, is bound to move. But the picture is in reality bound to move too ! Nothing real can stand still. A still picture stands there to tell us all it can of things for ever in motion. That first " zero " scene is as clearly and merely a *starting-point* for enjoyment as that one chord is. But then, for Turner, it is the finishing-point too ! He can move nothing further. So it is true that the works of loveliness in the National Gallery of Art remain stark stillness year after year, whereas in Queen's Hall, that other gallery of audible art, all is movement. And by this it may be readily admitted that music and pictures cannot *run* in harness at all. Yet they can co-exist and co-appeal. Why ?

Because they can be complementary.* *And they can start together*. So the one may stir up our minds to enjoy the other ; one may stand passively and quite congenially, as a helpful background for the other. The fitness of scenery and music is an *initial* reality, even while the picture is all stillness. It is only a *perpetual* reality when that which is seen is seen to move with the music. That is why it is so clear to-day that the Cinematograph and Music have a great future of collaboration before them ; and it is good to find their intimate union beginning to be

* In the sense discussed in the previous chapter.

apprehended, seriously attempted, and now and then beautifully realized.

Look back therefore, once more, at our still scene and our still chord, dwelling earnestly on both for a few seconds; then imagine the kind of thing that is certain to happen in reality; imagine that the horizon or sea-level line shows a ripple, and music gains at once a first glimpse of its greater and more vital chances as a "complementary."

Stillness continues in the held upper chord of the music, and in the picture's cloudless heaven. But apt movement of every delicious variety round and about the note G, which we may conceive as an aural horizon-tone or line of sight, can depict to the ear what the eye is experiencing in ripples on the water.* When the scene, for any reason, is withdrawn from our attention, and the music alone remains sensibly present, even a faintly remembered sight can continue to enrich our musical experience imaginatively. There may have been some meaning of this kind in Beethoven's cryptic remark that he "composed to a picture."

If, then, we are guessing aright, music heard and stillness seen may have deep affinity. When they start to deliver their appeal to eye and ear in their own natural ways, they do not lose affinity, they only lose power to extend it in identical ways; for stillness is ever still, movement for ever moves, and the scene is left behind if we are to travel with the music. Yet "left behind" need only mean "still standing in the background." So a scene can be a fitting (or unfitting) background to music,

* Such subsidiary musical rippling is doubtless the origin of the famous title "Moonlight" for the C♯ Minor Sonata. It was originally compared to "Moonlight *on the Lake of Lucerne*," and so got its nickname.

as it can be to life itself. Conversely, music may be a fitting or unfitting foreground to any scene of loveliness. Foreground it is bound to be, so long as it is the moving partner ; for movement (as is well known) has always the pull upon us mortals. (How poor a chance the most heavenly string quartet has when some slight movement occurs on the platform to distract the attention of the audience.) Music and scenery possess an initial affinity which never disappears ; and the movement of the one with the stillness of the other can uniquely combine to complement and intensify the appeal of each to the mind in a perfect give and take, the two artists collaborating in as real a way as in the case of poet and composer.

The moment there is *movement* in the picture our two artists are still more like poet and composer. They have more than complementary powers and problems. They then have their own *overlaptitudes*, mentioned in the previous chapter. Music and Action—that is, heard rhythm and seen rhythm—need to cut their complementary output to measure again. How this may be done will be our concern in the next chapter.

Before leaving the subject it is important to notice that, though all music moves, and though our one-chord Orchestral Scene may seem absurd, or at least impracticable, movement in music is still only relative ; and such tranquil, *legato*, melodic movements as those indicated on page 367, or (to think of a famous instance or two) those in Brahms's Violin Concerto :

or in the opening bars of the *Ring*, or in certain lovely passages in Vaughan Williams's "Lark Ascending" (see page 42)—all these movings are so akin to stillness that it may safely be laid down, as a general guiding statement for those interested in the allied joys of eye and ear, that all music preponderantly tranquil resembles, and is indeed akin to, scenic joys, while all stirring and distinctively rhythmic music is the reverse of scenic; it is dynamic, life-like, forceful, energetic—whatever other adjective suits your mind. In the one kind, the composer guides our minds by gentle melodic movements to dwell upon this and that aspect or related point of sound in a general scheme of chords in quiet succession; in the other kind, the composer is not so much the friendly passive suggester as the active aural challenger. The difference is not always clear, and the actual border-line is indefinable or even non-existent; yet it remains true that the point at which Delius (for example) ceases to be "scenic" and becomes "dramatic" is very far above our observed *zero* chord-point.

Long life, then, to the natural partnership between still loveliness seen and lovely music heard in stillness; they will ever be held together by their deep affinity, undisturbed by problems of synchronization. But we do well to think of this partnership as the starting-point for one far more vital, more difficult, but perhaps at last more permanently serviceable, now to be considered.

CHAPTER 28

MUSIC AND ACTION

HERE unification of rhythmic motive seen and heard is imperative. Fortunately, it is not hard to attain when once we are aware of its simple postulates ; for there is no formidable problem of synchronization to be surmounted as in the case of music and words. Fortunately also (since few men, women, or children seem to be gifted with an equal capacity of eye and ear), the partnership is of a give-and-take order that is of the most obvious service to both arts.

There are vast tracts of this partnership so accessible to all that we need do no more than mention them. Sound but this on your piano :

or this :

and mark it (with Handel) as *a tempo ordinario,* and with your mind's eye you will see people marching. If you take these fragments either at twice or half this rate, you will at once change your inward picture :

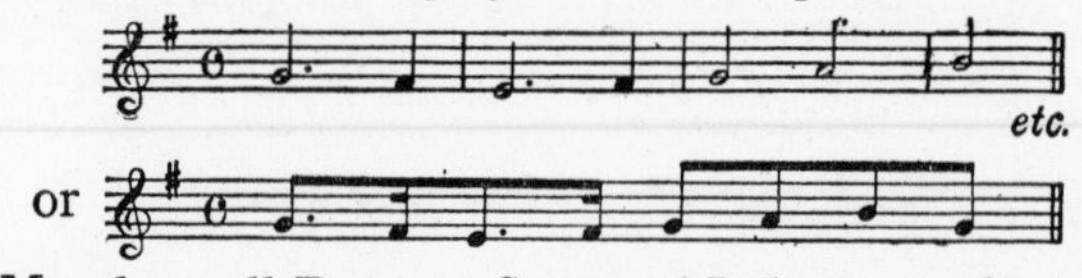

or

All Marches, all Dances, Songs of Labour, such as rowing-songs or sea-chanties, or the famous Volga (timber-hauling) song, can tell their own rhythmic story, and make natural and effectual contact with the corresponding seen rhythms; at first inherently, and later by persistent association.

We may safely take for granted all such broad unities of rhythmic music with specific movement, and give our attention to the possibilities of more delicate, subtle, and significant uses of rhythm seen and heard synchronically. It may be well to note, too, in passing, that the mere mention (in words) of movement—as in a play with music, or even in a title or motto of a set composition, or in the course of words sung—may start the association of music with action. Thus, mention of such movements as *strolling*, *lingering*, *rushing*, *flying* and the like, may evoke the utterance of musical rhythms to match. These instances are discussed in the two following chapters. Here we are solely concerned with the simultaneous appeal of inter-related movement through eye and ear; and, as in the other cases of double appeal, we wonder how they may best be fittingly, givingly, and takingly consummated.

And first it is noteworthy and astonishing — seeing that even Brahms's Fourth Symphony has been translated recently into superb and most impressive Ballet form—that many obvious and elementary requirements in this partnership still seem often to escape notice. For instance, I saw, not very long ago, the following subject from Schumann's " Carnival ":

translated into Ballet. If there are two things clear in this phrase, they are (1) that the sudden *lunge* which projects itself into the music (at the third and fourth bars) is the most prominent feature or event in the little movement, and (2) that this lunge recurs at the fourth and fifth bars, and several times later. Watching and listening simultaneously, however, one found in the Ballet no trace at all of this main scheme of the music! Time, of course, was kept religiously; but events in the Ballet proceeded with a seeming indifference and disregard of the ordered and calculated design of the music! On the other hand, when Chopin's little Prelude in A Major was danced:

it was delicious to get, at the sixth phrase:

the conceptions of exaltation and tenseness as thrillingly attained and communicated through the eye as through the ear. Furthermore, as you will readily see, the musical design itself at that point not only brings the dancer's body to tiptoe with his fingers raised as near the roof (one vividly remembers) as they can get, but brings his mind also to harmonic "tiptoe," when the chord stands at what may be styled the farthest "northern" distance from his key-chord. So, once again, out of the mouth of two arts is the thrill established.

We now begin to catch glimpses of musical possibilities vastly beyond our present grasp. They make us wonder how and when, if ever, men on this planet may learn to combine with spontaneous ease and veracity the glories of melody, harmony, and heard rhythms, with those of line, colour, and seen rhythms. It is the memory of that Chopin chord: and of the dancer's amazingly disciplined limbs interpreting it, that is both exciting

and troublesome, raising as it does the vaster issue. Can there exist visual interpretations for all our aural experiences in the avenue of harmonic distances? Is there possibility of some day linking these up even with the poet's avenue of imaginative distances, communicated to us in words?

It might well be unhelpful to the reader to ask him to dwell on far distant possibilities which, though imaginable, are at present indefinable. But the time is surely far less distant when Ballet will thus illumine and be in its turn illumined; and even those of us who are already climbing our seventh decade may live to *see* with our eyes the happening that we have so often *heard* with our ears at such supreme moments as the ninth bar of Schubert's A Minor miracle, already quoted twice in this book. Meanwhile, we cannot do better than look diligently into the combining materials at our disposal, and our obligation to use them with common sense, according to the principles already discussed. Certain materials are at music's disposal, certain common obligations exist (dictates of artistic decency) as to their use in partnership with visual art.

Picture now a large stage, on which no word is to be *spoken*, but on which anything may *happen*. Imagine also, not only an unlimited modern orchestra, but a chorus of all kinds of voices at music's disposal; with these, conceive that every appeal of colour, line, and movement which may be assembled to attract the eye is possible.

As a barest beginning of spontaneous alliance, and starting with an empty stage and silent orchestra, let the stage be very slowly lighted up until it be flooded with cheerful daylight. Has the orchestra power to produce the same effect in sound? We will imagine its parallel to be a sustained crescent chord (on strings?) of this gradual kind:

Now where mere lights and shades, blends or hues, are concerned, we note that there are numberless musical counterparts of these at our disposal in orchestral chord-effects of every strength and euphonious (or cacophonous) complexity. The tonal material here is endless. What are the common-sense obligations as to its use? Just as it would not be common sense to set a delicate love-song to *fortissimo* music, with an accompaniment of trumpets, trombones, and drums, so there is an equal obligation to use available orchestral qualities and intensities with propriety, where simultaneous appeal to eye and ear is concerned. The important thing to notice is that there are at least hundreds of orchestral hues and intensities available, and the range from the most subdued to the most triumphant must obviously be used with perfect freedom of choice, but with consideration for the seeing listener, as well as for the hearing beholder.

To return to our empty stage; it is now illuminated, and the orchestra is holding a brightish chord. Suddenly a small figure appears—that of a cupid, a page boy, a little prince, an angel or an imp—and moves rapidly to the centre of the stage, then stops. Where is the musical counterpart, and how does it proceed? The chord, of course, continues; but through it, moving appropriately, is heard a correspondingly small musical figure—played perhaps on a flute, a clarinet, a solo violin; or a solo string quartet, a bassoon or side-drum—*fitted*, in movement and quality of sound, to the figure seen. Here again there are hundreds of different instrumental qualities of tone and manners of emitting it, and literally thousands of rhythmic figures available in music wherewith to match with personally free whim, but universally recognizable aptness, any figure moving in any manner that could be staged. Here, for example, is one :

If our stage now begins to be filled with moving figures of varying kinds, it is certain that we shall see nothing that cannot be matched by the musician from his counterpoints of moving figures. The movements of three or four people on a stage could have their analogue in three- or four-part counterpoint ; and in both, prominent features, in movement (rhythm) first, but also in colour and line, could be agreeably interpreted both to ear and eye. But with further crowding there would come a point at which sight and hearing would be over-worked ; and Manifoldness, whether of scene or score, becomes Singleness in the sense that many humans make one crowd. General effect obliterates particular appeal, and the mind, in self-defence, gives up the struggle to master detail in multiplicity, calls the many *one,* and awaits some arresting feature, figure, or sign, to bring a new interest, a new two-or-more-ness.

Thinking along these lines, we shall probably conclude that in every way—in the mass as in diversity of detail—there should be a " differentiable " sound for every " differentiable " sight ; and within the vast range of both there is a manifest ability and a common obligation on the part of any artist in partnership, to match the colour complexities and intensities with tonal complexities and intensities ; further, to match also all movements, magnitudes, and character of appeal in either art. What if the whole visible universe has an audible universe to match it, which the power of man's mind may gradually bring into being ?

Picture for a moment the gifted musician of the near future as a kind of creative potter, with not only all kinds, consistencies, and colours of clay at his disposal, to shape as he will, but with the greater power to bring his forms into movement, into life, to speed them this way and that, and at a touch to "magic" them from one state or consistency to another—fluid, solid, or aeroform. Would there then be any visible loveliness in the world which he could not with imaginative diligence re-create ? This seems a not too far-fetched illustration of the future possibilities of musical material.

But so far we have only concerned ourselves with the obligation to apply musical material fittingly to another art, and have ignored what may matter most in the music we most love. If we are bent on measuring up how we stand in comparison with another art, merely in order to match or endorse what *it* expresses of the seen world in *our* own world of hearing, shall we not abrogate our very first pursuit of Beauty made audible, as well as our pursuit of a tonal language for our own innermost mind ? May not our pursuit of music as in itself a universal language be thus narrowed into the conception of it as being exclusively an *interpreter*, however universal, of other languages ?

There are two encouraging replies to such fundamental questioning of the whole of music's aim, as we have attempted to trace it in preceding parts of this book. Let us note them. (1) Music in double harness no more ceases to be good music in every known sense than does a man, in aiding his neighbour, cease to be a good man. On the contrary, ethics tell us that his neighbourliness *proves* his goodness. "What is your father, my little man ?" asked the magistrate of the waif in a

Children's Court. " He's a Christian, sir ; but my mother says he isn't doing much at it at present." What is your abstract music ? It may be ordinary music, waiting to become good music by friendly alliance. Five working alliances are before us in this Part Five of our pursuit of music. There are others. Our second encouraging fact is this : (2) When any art at any time depicts any related movements, what the artist is most concerned with is the wholeness of the result to his and our responsive minds. Thus, if in a Ballet every movement seen by the eye endorses, and is endorsed by, every concurrent musical movement, then the total result to the auditor-spectator must still be wholeness. Wholeness may be thus doubly and splendidly assured. But how disastrous if the effect be merely one of well-meaning redundancy or irrelevance ! It is for us to see to it that we get our arts singly *if they serve us better singly*. Has the reader, present at grand opera, never inwardly exclaimed, " Oh, do please leave off singing, and let me enjoy these heavenly harmonies in peace ! " If not, then he is certainly promisingly amenable to appeal from four arts at once.

One thing more remains to be touched upon in this chapter. Along the purely Harmonic highway, and presumably along its future extensions, melody moves in a certain assured way, and for the most part smoothly. We have seen how sedately harmonic composers may bring about startling changes in our harmonic whereabouts. They can spirit us enharmonically at a touch of new context to new worlds of thought, and the melodic and therefore rhythmic movement grows less, and significantly more refined, and—one may even say—confined ; limited in its appeal as the harmonic depth of appeal and interest increases. Again, the highway is the very creation and expression of orderly thought, of fantasy that is both logical and fancy-free, bound to reasonability, however whimsical. Now it is most clear that our Harmonic highway is still but a small part of universal music. It is even likely that it is but the first essay of the mind at this early date in the human story to release loveliness into audible form. It is also more than likely that music as a neighbour or partner of visible art, and susceptible to the whole field of action and its own neighbourly requirements, will shortly discover new loveliness as yet outside the ken of the most learned devotees of the great classical highway. Imagination kindled brings new music continually, some of it adding permanently, we may believe, to human vocabulary, some of it dying out as soon as heard. Listen to Marenzio, in 1599, adding glories then inscrutable (and since unsurpassed on the Harmonic highway) to be available permanently from 1599 *ad infinitum*; and we can only marvel that things so stable and convincingly lovely have had to wait three or four hundred years before they pass into the current language:

Let us, then, eagerly expect an immense but wholly intelligible extension of the harmonic field for all purposes of music in partnership. In doing so, it is good to realize that the very perfection, simplicity, and logicality of our classical harmonic system seems likely to give it central significance in future music. In that case music will not merely illustrate action in tone, but will influence and even dominate action. And in Music-drama of the year 2000, for example, it will be surprising if the great moment of a last act is musically less simple, less beautiful, or in any material way alien to or far removed from the sublime simplicity of Beethoven's last piano Sonata, or the concluding page of the *Matthew Passion*.

What Action will be found to match these?

Chapter 29

MUSIC AND DRAMA

". . . There are certain limits within which one art may lawfully help another. . . . The arts are all fine ladies, and they cannot replace each other or lay down the law for each other, but they may exchange courtesies now and again. . . ."

MARY COLERIDGE.

THERE is perhaps no greater problem awaiting music than that of its working in double harness with drama ; nor one of which the solution offers more entrancing possibilities. Grand Opera, as it stands to-day, seems still an astonishing and phenomenal enormity.*

Yet scenery and music, as well as action and music, have proved themselves capable of being delightfully at one ; as we know, not only from daily experience, but from contemporary Ballet. They are ready for the reasonable collaboration we desire and expect, as between Music and vital Drama. When dramatist and melodist find a working solution of their mutual problem, we shall be within measurable distance of uniting the creative energies, wills, and utterances of poet, painter, actor, and musician in one consummate deed. This can only come about through a completely sensitive awareness and yielding on the part of each of the four, and on the part of at least three out of the four at any given moment when one of them may be moved to " take the stage." Such awareness will ensure that no two of the four will between them create confusion of appeal by giving

* This must, I fear, sound arrogantly assertive ; but that which makes me differ from experts in opera is inescapably clear to me.

forth, in forgetful enthusiasm, simultaneous contributions which detract the one from the other. For it is obvious that agreement of *intention* of appeal is essential, but insufficient. Agreement of individual utterances at any given moment is equally essential. The cup of joy must be full, and must be well mixed. But no public must be asked to lift two cups simultaneously to its lips.

No one can make light of the problems of Music-drama. Those who have a particular love and specially intimate understanding of any single one of the four co-working arts must realize that their own deep and particular intimacy must go, that their favoured art and they themselves will be called upon to " take counsel with their beloved " in an altogether new way. The " beloved " will no longer be, for example, the poet alone ; it will no longer be a case, say, of Dean Donne, the sixteenth-century poet, conversing with Dean Beeching, the twentieth-century lover of poetry, in words of such sweet counsel, so aptly final and perfect, that the lover can only bear to read the words on the silent page, feeling audible rendering of them an unhappy intrusion. No longer can it be the personal musical intimacy of Samuel Wesley, the champion of Bach in nineteenth-century England, conversing profoundly with his hero in what he called the " Saints in Glory " Fugue. But Music-drama can be intimate too, though it is with a more formidable universal intimacy. It is four stages more personally impersonal, and, one might add, four-times-four more difficulties may be expected to lie in the way of its unified attainment.

Yet, whatever happens, the quest for a perfect Music-drama seems likely to be perpetuated as music advances, not only in a laudable desire to call out the most complete creative response possible from the intelligent and highly sensitized auditor-spectator ; but, still more, for the sake of the light the combined appeal may throw upon the path of less intelligent though eager responders. Those who only half understand the words, or are partly baffled by the music, when they hear the two half realized arts working *concurrently* with wholly intelligible scenes and actions all inspiringly interrelated, will come into a new and guiding knowledge of the ways and meanings of both poetry and music—a knowledge unattainable by other means than this of fullness and simultaneity of appeal to eye and ear. Music-drama seems likely to become a permanent ideal, with two such irresistible motives—these of consummating to the intelligent, and making clearer to the partially intelligent, the joy of the whole creative deed that men call Art.

And here, it seems specially desirable to keep within the musical province. This book is on music bent. We are not in pursuit of Drama, as Drama, so it behoves us to try to take it as we find it, refraining, as far as possible, from the suggestion that it, in company with the other arts, should concede points to music here and there, in order to make Music-drama an immediate reality. We must particularly refrain from attempting to show drama how to make room for music. This forbearance may not be easy; and we expect reciprocal courtesy from those "in pursuit of drama." They, as well as we, may well cogitate how best the two arts may illumine each other. Yet our most fruitful question will be as to how music may illumine drama *in statu quo*; for the more music does of the giving, the more we shall discover of her adaptability to bend without breaking.

We are together aware of her own expressive and impressive powers. We know her power to *express* the movings of the mind, and may believe her the subtlest existent interpreter of its intimate workings. We find her, too, possessed of another prodigious and picturesque gift—that of being able to *impress* or represent in counterpart all sorts and sizes of outside or objective energies, events, and moods of nature, vividly in her own sound-technique. We believe, moreover, that both in her subjective or expressive, and in her objective or impressive powers, she can never cease to prove a more and more adequate servant of the mind of man as time goes on, depicting life's infinitely varied energies and events in ever more effectual terms of tonal energy and event. With these facts in mind, are we not likely to err rather on the side of claiming too much than too little for music itself ? So let us the more carefully assume that ours is the art which, at the moment, must submit itself to develop unending resourcefulness and flexibility to the needs and abilities of the companion arts. Let us also, incidentally, realize that it is not a case of double-harness here, or of a mere fifty-fifty compact. For in drama itself the arts of the poet, painter, and actor (in word, scene, and action) are already running in triple harness ! Thus our art is the fourth comer of four, not the second comer of two. And why does it come in at all ? Believing that it comes for the two overpowering reasons just mentioned —the one subjective, the other objective ; realizing the difficulties (sometimes humiliating, sometimes amusing) of the partnership, let us try to foresee future developments by a careful inquiry into the facts on both sides.

What are the salient facts on the subjective side ? They seem rather complex,—hard to disentangle and not easy to co-ordinate.

We find music already equipped (and these are early days !) with her wonderfully evolved and ever evolving harmonic significances to tell more than words can tell of the subtle workings of the human mind. These are all-important to every dramatic plot. But it is not enough to suggest that Music can uniquely expound the Mind of Drama. For a moment's thought of Music-drama puts us at once in a dilemma (or a trilemma, quadrilemma, multilemma !). It causes us to ask : Whose Mind ? Whose Mind can music thus expound ? Let us exemplify the problem. A five-minute Overture by Verdi might suffice to tell *Shakespeare's* mind, as it seeks to illustrate one of his dramas ; but the Overture being written by *Verdi* must primarily communicate *his* mind to us on the subject in question. Again, the mind of one or more of the *characters of the play* may also be speaking to us through the Overture ! When we come to the play itself, we know that a deftly wrought succession of harmonies may tell us more, in an incredibly short space, of the situation of each person in the plot, than any number of words or speeches. Thus, the orderly mind of a Brutus, the distraught mind of a Hamlet, the grotesquely exuberant mind of a Bottom, and that of the whimsical Puck, may all be clearly expressed for us *in music*. So that the subjective powers of music have, at the very least, three uses, though, paradoxically, they may prove powers of an objective subjectivity. And as music grows into an increasingly perfect language, we shall increasingly find it (*a*) expressing the mind of the composer ; (*b*) expressing (or perhaps interpreting or matching) the playwright's mind ; (*c*) expressing (semi-objectively) the minds of the characters in the play.

With all these our *own* mind must make such an alive and discerning fourth partner in the musical transactions that it is a case of spontaneous and instant amalgam of four minds,* in which we must meet, realize, unify, and be moved (or " emotioned," as Delius put it). This united resultant act or movement is of *Mind*—theirs, yours, and ours,—in analysis distinct, but in action at one. Yet even in action, say, in listening to *Boris Godounov*, we may catch ourselves now and again thinking isolatedly, as we hear grouping harmonies, " Ah ! there is *Boris* in a mood of gloomy foreboding." Or with equal pleasure (because it gives us equal companionship), we may think, " There's *Moussorgsky's* masterly

* Or five or six or more ! for the scenic and acting minds are *all* involved.

mind at work ; how aptly he interprets the king's mind at such a moment ! " It is both unavoidable and pardonable, because creatively companionable, to give a nod of "Yes, that's it ! " to Chaliapin, or to the mastery of the scenic artist ; and in practice we may do this kind of sectional " Yessing," or companioning, while keeping our heads to apprehend the whole. For in any case, whoever the particular man may be who has in a flash made us thus exclaim, we are still saying " Yes " to *the Mind of the whole*. It is noteworthy at this point that whether the arts are functioning initiatively or interpretatively—that is, as beginners or seconders of the composite work—they are each at work on origins. In this sense, the contributory musician, actor, and painter all have to attain their own first-hand *originality*, as had the dramatist who started the show ! The same standpoint, for that matter, is ideally required also for *original listening*.

What, now, are the chief or guiding facts on the objective side ? Here also we recognize that music is already marvellously equipped (and again—these are early days) with such instrumental, vocal, and imitative sound—such material as is equal to all demands of drama. This is the most salient objective fact. In other words, apart altogether from her expressive powers, she has shown so rapidly expanding a power of impression that she offers us a whole potential world in sound. It is, however, a world only to be brought into existence any time, any where, fortuitously by the minds of men in actual performance, to die down and be re-created endlessly. That is why we have to call it a *potential* world. Tonal objects, tonal realities, can be called into being by any man, woman, or child with the means to make the willed sound, be it a baby boy beating a drum, or Toscanini wielding an orchestra (to Mozart's prescription). In this audible world we find music can erect every shape and kind of tonal object. So she will more and more seek to serve her sister drama, because of her apt power to set up audible appearances, energies, and happenings which may endorse and reinforce the visible appearances, energies, and happenings on the stage. But (once more) we have to question closely this objective power, as we had to do in the case of the subjective power. Is it enough to say that, when music is not busy *ex*pressing subtle things of the mind, she will busy herself by *im*pressing external scenes or events ? By no means. To begin with, we know that there is a well-marked difference between objective music that *imitates*, and objective music that *illustrates*.

In the world of natural sounds that are not music (that is, the audible world that man does not create, but only enjoys, or endures), things like waterfalls, hurricanes, steam-engines, etc., are realities often relevant to a play. Music can depict these with entertaining success (and sometimes with equally entertaining shortcoming). And generally the least musical orchestral contraptions (such as cymbals or wind-machines) are most successful in this department of apt mimicry.

But there is an objectively *illustrative* music that has a far wider and more fruitful field. It is that which depicts not natural sounds but natural volumes, intensities, qualities, and characteristics of all sounds or sights, of all sorts of happenings outside our minds, seen or heard, or put into quickening words. This is music's objective field that really matters ; it is truly endless and attractive. And when we look more closely into it, we again find (provokingly enough, perhaps) that there is no clean-cut possibility here, any more than there was in our subjective field. Think ! An artist cannot choose and depict any object in the world without *giving himself away* (as we say) by the way in which he chooses and depicts it ; and a poet cannot choose and depict any thing or happening outside himself without doing the same. Just so musicians put *themselves* inevitably into the choice they make, into the way they choose to depict objects, especially those of visible beauty or visible ugliness (both of which are, of course, relevant to drama). In short, as we were driven to the horrible term objective subjectivity in the first case, so we are here driven to its companion horror—subjective objectivity. Yet there is nothing to repel the reader beyond the clumsy wording itself. It is our job to keep the two powers of music in mind *as two*. But it is well, having them in mind, to put ourselves to the pains of thinking out their indivisible interplay, in concept, fact, and action. The natural threads that may bind them into one work of art become clearer if we are prepared to discern how strangely and yet naturally their very differences mingle from first to last. This must be the writer's apology for detaining the reader so long (and, it is to be feared, not too comfortably) over two simple points, which, however, are not always obvious though they are always crucial.

And now we may throw our minds forward for a few years, perhaps to the year 1960, and attempt a little guess-work.

A music-drama (in England, for choice) is just about to take place, and the stage is cleared. Poet, painter, dramatist, and composer " to a man," have taken up their fitting functions. In fact, we might well imagine them all as one man—the composer his own poet, the actor-manager his own composer, and so on—some English Michelangelo or Leonardo of the day. We find there is no Overture *before* the curtain goes up ; for will it not still be true, twenty-five years hence, that it is useless to ask people to be straightway interested in a Music-drama which, ostensibly, is to exercise and appeal to their seeing, hearing, imagining, and thinking faculties if we dole it out to these four piecemeal ? An Overture ! An integral part of the great Art-contract ; yet for several minutes nothing is offered to the eyes but a darkling auditorium, and shadows of late-comers and the back view of a conductor's head to distract us. "Ridiculous!" says Common-sense in 1960. "Draw up the curtain if you want the Music-drama really to begin." It is worth while reminding ourselves here of Sullivan's refusal to write incidental music to a play. "No," said he; "when the curtain's up my music will interrupt the play, and when the curtain is down it will interrupt the conversation." In 1960 all musicians will have learnt Sullivan's common sense. The bell will ring, the curtain will go up, the stage may be impressively empty, the orchestra and chorus silent, yet the work has begun. And eyes and ears are attentive and focussed. Coming out of the silence, a *pianissimo* figure is heard (in the viola part, shall we guess?):

and as it is heard (if and when the contemplative Preluding is over) the eye is held by the corresponding event on the stage, whatever that may happen to be. Judging by the music, it may possibly be the subdued figure of a rather forlorn child, wandering from the wings across the centre of the stage. Yes, there he is! What a perfect fitting, giving and taking of sight and sound! For when he pauses the music does so, of course; and when it moves again, the child has moved on. When he looks this way, then that—in one of a thousand natural ways of looking this way and that, all thousand of them human, all natural, all entirely intelligible to all men—the viola figure does the same in any one of a thousand natural intelligible musically human ways:

But here perhaps the gaze of the child (and the viola) are seen and heard to become fixed, stony, transfixed, at a sight in the wings ; seen only by the child in wonderment, only *heard* by the audience, for the sight is planned to remain a mystery for them :

What is it the child sees ? But the musico-dramatist is far too wise to show it to us till, let us say, Act IV., Scene v.

Has not one of Wagner's most ardent champions, Mr. Ernest Newman, somewhere tellingly pointed out a rudimentary redundancy of Grand Opera as exemplified in simultaneously showing a sword on the stage, speaking about a sword in the Book, singing about a sword, and introducing a prearranged and labelled sword-motive in the orchestral part ? In 1960 this, surely, will long ago have proved simply too insulting to the imagination of the least educated spectator-auditor.

But now let us, from these slenderest of conjectural beginnings, presume to picture what may substantially follow in this supposititious Music-drama.

We may venture to suggest, at the outset, that the fabric of all Music-drama, from the rise of the curtain to its fall, will then be continuous on all counts—continuous, that is, with a conjoint poetic, scenic, acting, and musical continuity. Secondly, its intention will *never pull contradictory ways* ; the auditor-spectators will, in consequence, never be called upon to give a divided attention. In the third place, it seems safe to predict that, where the appeal of one art becomes of necessity predominantly intense (it may be the words, or it may be the music, or some vital happening at the back of the stage, or even the scene itself in its stillness), then the appeal of the other three will be deferentially in abeyance. No one art will ever be in competition against the others.

But it is here that the gravest questionings arise. How, we ask, can music, when required to be silent, yet remain continuous? Could a stage be darkened and yet the appeal of sight remain continuous? A good answer is found in Sir Walter Parratt's direction to his organ-pupils: "Remember to play your *rests*." There is a silence that is meaningless and dead, and that will snap all four threads; and there is a dynamic musical silence that is as alive as music. In the same way, there is a poetic silence, and a stage darkness that illumines the play, or (in other words) vitally informs the eye, and is actually an integral part of the appeal to the sense of sight. Is the hero necessarily out of mind when he leaves the stage? Is the thread of his interest for us snapped? By no means. And precisely in this way significant silence never yet snapped a musical thread. A few such thoughts as these reassure us that the Music-drama of 1960 may answer the three-fold requirement of maintaining the verbal, scenic, actional musical threads simultaneously, (1) all unbroken from first to last, (2) all unconflicting, and (3) at the same time never allowing them together to intensify the sum of claims beyond bearing—that is, beyond the one hundred per cent. capacity of united appeal and unified response.

The result, in effect, may surely be simple. The four Arts will be assembled as four enthusiasts might be assembled to tell of some great experience they have shared. They will, none of them, "leave the room" till this has been told. But they will observe the ordinary practical courtesies of any four enthusiasts, all bending their aim to one fine purpose. Each will contribute his utmost, while none will fail to give place to the vital contribution of the others. What will this mean?

They will confirm each other's testimony at every point without confusion. They will together have endorsed or *yessed* everything in their own ways of expressing themselves. But one thing will not have happened which, in 1935, is still happening blatantly. Not one will cover up or confuse what another was saying by simultaneously saying the same thing louder, or longer, or in some incompatible way peculiar to itself. This brings us to the real crux of "Grand Opera" as we see and hear it to-day, the confusion of audible appeal as between the *Book* and the *Music*. Many people accept the confusion of appeals set up simultaneously as something inevitable; they deem it a conventional price to pay for the "richness of the entertainment." Musicians and poets will not indefinitely continue to accept confusions and absurdities as the price they must pay for the privilege of working together. The more fully they come to understand each other, the more intolerable will such confusion become. The more eloquent music grows, the more impossible will be this irrelevancy of appeal. Some have hoped that as a compromise half the play could be sung and half spoken, the confusion being at least more and more reduced. But this involves the *snapping* of poetic and musical threads (which were to be *interwoven*) in order to oblige special aptitudes. It is as if an arrangement were made that one of our incompatible enthusiasts should leave the room while another addressed the audience; to be allowed in again only when the other had concluded his message and was similarly turned out. It is perfectly easy to do this for comic effect, or in a comic play. Not only is the incongruity acceptable in comic situations, but to have a merry fellow sing his dialogue melodramatically where ordinarily people would speak, adds to the merriment and scope of the partnership. But we may hope that in 1960 Music-drama will have shed Grand Opera's major mistakes, and all its distortion of the Book in the supposed interests of the Opera. All must be done without sacrifice of any single essential to the ideal partnership of the two. Why should it not ? What is the difficulty ? It is one that stares us in the face, or rather in the ears. The difficulty between the Book and the Music resolves itself to-day into one huge and practical problem of adjusting *dimensions* in sound. We have seen that music is fast achieving an endless capacity both to express and impress the mind. She must and will refuse to hurt drama itself in her impulse to illumine and glorify it ; she may then safely go ahead in collaboration from first to last, throughout the play, as with the visible arts ; and there seems no insurmountable barrier to her kindly field of creative ability in closest relation with her three companions.

But at this point we may well ask : if it really is as simple and attainable as all this, what has hindered it having been done long ago in the case of Grand Opera ? Only the angels know ! It *has* been done occasionally—for example, in *Boris,* in innumerable moments of the *Ring* (vocalism permitting), in *Falstaff,* in *Pelléas,* as well as anew by Holst and others in our own time. Still the very latest accepted methods continue to perpetrate the old amazing and depressing enormities of incongruity, unresented. It is little use to inveigh against these here. To say " Thou shalt not " is, we know, as perverse, unhelpful, wrong-headed, and quite out-of-date in the realm of music as in Christendom itself. If a musician still feels in 1935 that he must make his heroine in all seriousness scream her love at the top of her vocal powers (against a full orchestra), and must also make all other characters behave vocally to pattern ; and if delightful people still want this to happen at whatever cost, even that of distorted art, as it seems to me to do, the quickest cure is a " Yes, do it, and continue to do it, harder and harder," till at last the inevitable thirst for Reality and Beauty, and drama of a truer order, forces itself upon those who had too easily tolerated the hectic way. None the less, I dare not hide my conviction here that by such means the art we cherish *is* constantly and terribly degraded to-day. Hubert Parry wrote in his last diary (of 1917–18) that "Opera is the shallowest fraud man ever achieved in the name of art." This fierce saying (coming from so genial a friend of all music and musicians at the end of a life of perpetual devotion to music and musicians) had been first scribbled in pencil then deliberately inked in with a clearer script. Through his long life he believed in the future of Opera, and even made it one of his dreams to build an opera theatre at the Royal College of Music (which has since been done in his name). It is clear that he referred to what has so far stood for Opera, and not to what may yet be. Let us inquire, with the reader's forbearance, a little further.

The stark difficulty before Drama and Music in consort is clearly the reconcilement of two *manners and magnitudes of utterance* as they attempt their simultaneous appeal to one faculty—that of hearing. Of our four arts, two appeal simultaneously, through sight—namely, the scenic and the actional, and two through hearing—the poetic and the musical. We are not troubled with overlappings and confusions of the first two appeals. But they are conceivable. For example, if an artist had designed exquisitely fitting scenes, say, for *Julius Cæsar* or any other drama, and the stage manager had so contrived the action that, at the moment when the scene was most vital to the work, it was completely eclipsed by characters, groupings, and movements on the stage, then steps would have to be taken to adjust the respective appeals in accordance with common sense and reason. But there is perhaps little likelihood of any disagreement there. Common understanding is against it. By the nature of things, it will be seen that *the* perennial danger to Music-drama lies between the third and fourth appeals, where one may either tend to impoverish or overload the other. It also should be noticed that neither of two arts in *one* category (that of sight) finds any inherent difficulty in synchronizing and happily agreeing singly with either or both the two in the *other* category (that of *hearing*). In the simultaneous appeal, synchronization as between eye and ear is obviously easy, never confusing and ever complementary, if fitly managed. It is only in the simultaneous appeal of two arts *through one channel of sense* that one has ever to cry out to the other : " We are in each other's way ; what can we do about it ? " Here at the root of the problem of Music-drama two notable trends appear.

1. It may not have occurred very vividly to the reader that, as has been elsewhere suggested, words, in Drama as in life, as they are used to convey more and more important things, inevitably require more and more reticence in utterance. If a word is going to decide, for example, a man's life or death—say, in a court of law ; or through the mouth of a doctor, who is to communicate dreaded news—one cannot doubt that, the finer the feeling of the judge or the doctor, the more subdued, and bereft of all idea of effect, would be his utterance of this momentous word. Words evoke mental reactions. They touch electric buttons in the mind. If the reactional current is likely to be terrific, discernment will touch the spot with great care, certainly not with any histrionic *bravura*. Now, at the back of all drama we descry the same necessity of discernment, the same fine feeling.

2. It is, perhaps, far more likely to have occurred to most readers that music, on the other hand, as it deals with and attempts to express more momentous issues, tends to become more and more expansive ! This does not, however, mean that, on the one hand, words never

expand ; nor, on the other, that music is never reticent exactly as words often are. Both are both ! It means on the contrary that if music is to be fired off coincidently with the words that evoked it, and if the great moment of the Music-drama arrives, and both arts are in attendance upon the mind, for example, the noblest of heroes is to die, and the equally admirable heroine is to decide not to outlive him, then two natural things happen :

(*a*) Any *words* that pass between them in the drama (as in the instances just quoted above) will be few and restrained in utterance ; they would else belie the heroism.

(*b*) Any *music* that is to express adequately the human pathos and depth of reality in such momentous matters as life and death may well be capable of filling the time-canvas for ten minutes, when the natural utterance of the very words that brought this music into the mind will barely fill ten seconds!

Who can suppose that music in 1960, reasonably and mercifully prevented from a fratricidal forcing of the words out of the true, will be compelled, not only to abrogate nine minutes and fifty seconds of its duration and its eloquent magnitudes in order to cut the two audible appeals exactly to measure, but also to deny its (by that time) prodigious abilities, naturally and eloquently to express the situation in tonal volume and vastness, in breadth, depth, and height (as it were), as well as in length ? The Slow Movement in Beethoven's *Eroica* is a noble Reverie on life and death. But it would not be bearable if it had a concurrent chain of sung words to it—all about life and death ! The reality of Grand Opera, as we know it to-day, is apt to be at its greatest when no speaking or singing problem is raised, as in the *Götterdämmerung March.* The unreality, yes, and the agonizing confusion and absurdity, are all at their height when momentous things are being communicated in words, *plus* the momentous musical ideas evoked by those very words. This hysterical unreality has, we may fervently hope, come very near the end of its unreal days. I believe it is already potentially rejected. It has been astonishing to witness the tolerance shown to so unloveable an enormity by most loveable men in our own time.

One cannot help surmising that the public discouragement of National Grand Opera is not mere culpable apathy. It may be largely an instinctive refusal to finance any unproved benefits. It's a big show. But it is often wearisomely incomprehensible. Show and reason should go normally hand in hand. Possibly the first step to the National Music-drama which we can all fervently desire, rests with composers (and such faithful inspirers as will encourage and support them). If ten or a dozen English Music-dramas were forthcoming in which *not a single word was strained,* or inaudible, pulled out of the true or rendered ineffectual for music's purpose, nor a note of music's contribution *impoverished for the words' sake;* if each of the four arts conspired in due relation to fit, give, and take, it might prove not merely the sensible and reasonable way, but the only way in which to move our fellow-countrymen.

We may try to guess a little further how it may be done. First, this problem of comparative magnitudes will be admitted by all interested, because it is something real, deep in the nature of things, therefore to be willingly reckoned with by all; and not as a fact compelling reluctant capitulation. This realized, all possible ways of maintaining agreed and indivisible continuity of appeal unbroken in all four essential strands, will become the unceasing concern both of composer and dramatist, not merely of one of them! To admit a single point at which one is out of the running is clearly unthinkable. The stage scene does not disappear when the play is in progress. It is an integral part of the play; if and when scenery is not relevant to what is happening, it can be changed or darkened. When action is not relevant, the players do not necessarily disappear, they can remain motionless. And in the same way, music, when not taking a prominent part in the proceedings, may sink into the background. For, as already suggested, it is no more necessary either to drop music in order to give words greater scope, or to pull words into all shapes and sizes to fit the music, than it is necessary to cease action in order to give significance to certain scenery, or to distort scenery to fit it to action.

Ahead of us lies a glorious chance. As I see it, there gleam three possible lines of advance along which there may lie the long overdue solution of the chief problem. If the problem of verbal and musical magnitudes could be solved, there seems no lesser problem which these three (the third of them in particular) might not virtually straighten out: (1) the practical reconcilement of natural speech-rhythms, inflections, *tessiture* and volumes, with musical rhythms, harmonies, and volumes; (2) the addition of vocal resources to those of the orchestra *off* the stage; (3) the development of frank alternation of prominences of appeal, without snapping threads.

1. The Cultivation of Musically Reconcilable Speech

Every word in our predicated Music-drama of the future, if it is a word normally integral to the drama, *i.e.* normally essential to be heard, must be uttered as normally as in any other drama. Moreover, " normal " here excludes the translation of the whole utterance of words to any abnormal level of pitch, any abnormal loudness, or any abnormal syllabic *sostenuto*. Mozart is reported to have been much enamoured of the thing then called Melodrama, since known, here in England, as Cantillation, which was natural speech accompanied by a background of loosely-fitting music. English *musical speech* is already a tentatively explored reality. What is to prevent our using it in Music-drama ? " Her voice is so musical," you exclaim of a friend, and you are perfectly right ; moreover, that musical speaking voice is none the less natural for being musical. It is only unfortunate that we have got so little way towards its recognition that it will at first be hard for a musician of the finest ear and skill to accompany it with any but the most accidental and elusive harmonic fitting. That does not mean that an analysis of its natural loveliness is not easily possible, and a very little close analysis and study of English—in the natural voices of men, women, and children, from various parts of the country—would, I believe, yield quick results upon which to base a sounder start for true English Music-drama. *Parlando* song and *cantando* speech are already a proved reality, awaiting us.

A few years ago it would not have been possible to write so optimistically. But to-day, of course, speech-rhythms, speech-inflections, and speech-*tessiture*, can all be taken on gramophone and Blättnerphone records, studied minutely, and fitted with experimental harmonies over and over again till working euphonious results are secure. And it should be remembered that there now is no note in music that cannot be incorporated in any fundamental chord of any composer's choosing, with perfect lucidity.

It is worth noting here that, as in drama itself, it is a question whether intimate Music-drama can ever be normally presented in any auditorium which, by its size, forces any voice for a single moment out of the normal. A forced change of pitch, length, or loudness in the utterance of a significant word *does* change the utterance! It ceases to mean what it did mean. And, alas for

Grand Opera, it cannot *cease* to mean volumes! You cannot raise or drop your voice on the stage and hope it will mean nothing at all from the dramatic angle! It *means* something humanly and inescapably different from the unforced natural lie of pitch, natural lengths, and natural loudnesses of each word in the natural course of each character's contribution. Now, if present contingencies force the voices of an eager hero and a calm heroine in dialogue both up an octave, it may, in doing this, throw both their respective meanings, not only abnormally high, but incidentally (their temperaments being differently affected by the " octave higher than speech ") it may also throw their innermost relationship quite out of the true. It is useless to plead that the octave up is *necessary*. Why? To get them into musical range above all that the orchestra is naturally impelled by the situation to utter? Quite useless, because a violation of the true. Still more useless is it to plead that " if they are used naturally they would not be heard." There is an exacting demand on art, the inexorable demand for Fine-feeling and Reality. When men have begun to recognize this inexorability, a small auditorium* may be conceded to every serious drama that needs it according to all the rules of common sense—whether it be Music-drama or not.

The speech-rhythms and English speech-inflections, not only of our every mood, but of every district—those of Yorkshire, Norfolk, Devonshire, Wales, and so on—will some day be studied " with a view " musically. The *tessiture* used for musically reconcilable speech will remain the same as that for unmusical speech.

In that day one very important result will probably follow: no Music-drama will prove amenable to trans-

* Glyndebourne, thanks to Mr. John Christy, has brought us a great boon in this respect. It is not too much to hope that English Music-drama will come into its own there, as Mozart recently has.

lation into another country's language without having to be entirely rewritten! This seems true already of such thrilling pioneer works as Debussy's *Pelléas*, and others which already largely approximate the normal ideal of musical speech—that is, dialogue—of which every syllable is relatable to musical concepts or chords in the total of musical thought underlying the Drama.

2. The Addition of Vocal Forces to Orchestral off the Stage

In this there is nothing revolutionary, nor indeed new. But I can never forget a moment, years ago, in the production of the able musical setting of the *Vicar of Wakefield*, by Miss Liza Lehmann, when the composer (following the author) had to cause Olivia in distress to get up and sing the lyrical moral on her own tragic story: "When lovely woman stoops to folly." The old Vicar was first seen bringing in his loved daughter and setting her in slow-motion sadness by his side at the home-fire, where the two grieving figures were fully enough occupied in depicting their essential part in the play. Had Olivia's lyrical comment only been made by any other means—by a voice in the wings, by a violin solo, the orchestra—had it even been left to the imagination!—the listener, simultaneously watching the silent love and sadness of the pair, the restrained tear, the comforting arm, would have experienced a perfect unity of appeal to his compassionate mind. But the conventions of Opera being flagrantly otherwise, the one figure who ought not, and should not in decency get up and voice the moral of her own folly—in touching melody, high notes and all!—Olivia herself, was expected to do so, and did so, to the alienation of all sympathy, and, in my judgment, with sadly ludicrous effect.

The whole ideal of crystallized comment in poem and music upon drama (the ideal, that is, of the Greek Chorus) has proved to be sound, and in a hundred forms revivable. One would venture again to suggest that the curtain, the very eyelid of the stage, must not fall for a vocal reflection off the stage or a choral and orchestral prologue, interlogue, or epilogue or other vocal utterance. Attention is dissipated, and *focus* of eye, ear, and mind imperilled. The scene and action, or a tableau of characters in repose, must still hold the mind, or the threads are apt to be broken to the spectator-auditor. There are so many of us to whom out of sight is truly out of mind on such occasions, that the physical eye (so apt to be caught by irrelevant sights) should be enabled to help the mind.

There seems no need at this point to enlarge further on the advantages to all partners in the music drama of adding voices to the orchestra for purposes of inward musical punctuations (when needed) of the dramatic significances, and as possible unifiers (as by prologue and epilogue) of the whole; these might be stronger even in their appeal than Shakespeare's marvellous Prologue and Epilogue in *The Tempest*, and more fittingly compared with Bach's gorgeous power of pull in the first and last choruses of the greater *Passions*.

3. Unbroken Alternation of Prominences

It is in this third and scarcely explored direction that greatest possibilities seem to lie. In the Music-drama of the future, it seems quite certain that just as four characters in a play take prominent parts in their turn and do not need to disappear from view in order to make way for a moment for a fellow-actor, so the four arts will systematically be used with alternating prominences or urgencies, without let or break to any one art, and with incalculable gain to the play. This I believe will be achievable with imperceptible ease the moment it is realized how completely acceptable it can be. At present in Grand Opera, music is *on* from Act I, Scene i, to Act last, Scene last, generally with an intensity which would make *alternation* of its prominences with one of the other three appeals sound like calculated artifice. And there, at present, lies the real crux. Reference has already been made to the chief reason for this. The mere difference of *pitch, volume, sostenuto,* and *tessitura,* as between significant song and significantly natural speech, forms, at the moment and under present unnatural conditions, so great a tonal chasm as to be only artificially bridgeable. So the alternation of speech and song, as in Opera Comique and Romantic Operas—where it is resorted to in order to get the story "through"—is often grotesque in effect, and rightly abandoned as being only fit for the frankly comic or lightly entertaining. In these the spectator-auditors thankfully get their relief, and do not resent lumpy, arbitrary artifice of transfer. At worst, it only adds to the fun. But when in serious Opera the reconcilement of *parlando* song with *cantando* speech is believed in, sought, and attained, then the marvellous interplay of the arts may be revealed. Musical interest, when at one hundred per cent., obviously demands that the interest of Scene, Action, and Words should momentarily stand at zero. Verbal interest, at one hundred per cent., does the like for music and the other arts. Zero, to music and speech, means of course, not blank deadness, but purposeful, vital silence. Zero to scenery and to action is, correspondingly, purposeful darkness and purposeful stillness respectively. It is because music has never yet sufficiently cultivated her lowlier degrees in contributing minute ratios of interest in opera ; it is because at present she leaps from zero to something round about the fifties (as it were); it is because she then dwells for the duration of the whole Opera somewhere between fifty per cent. and one hundred per cent., too wearyingly clamant upon both physical ear and attentive mind, that failures of appeal must remain still so prevalent. It seems to me an incontrovertible fact that the four arts can be expected consentingly to cultivate the power to move quite consistently from one to another percentage of prominence, given the will and skill in the collaboration. It seems reasonable to expect that, before long, this will be proved to us all in some consummate work. How fine it will be when England makes this her special contribution to the world's music; if the term "English Opera," say, in the year 1999 means to Europe something uniquely real. But any nation may achieve it. Let us in conclusion turn for illumination to Bach. For there happens to be, and this quite outside the world of opera, an example of unbroken alternation of audible styles and interests—of words and of music—so striking that it seems desirable to print it here in full for the reader's closest study.

We have previously pointed out that when two arts, running simultaneously, are merely complementaries, all is well. (Thus the Pastoral Symphony, heard to the background of a group of shepherds and starry heavens seen on a stage, raises no problem.) It is when they not only complement, but overlap—that is, when they are both communicating or depicting an identical happening—that they must synchronize and conform exactly, or there will result a blur or confusion of appeals. In saying the same things they must (as we have previously seen) be cut to measure. This disposing on the time-canvas "to measure" is illuminatingly shown, as it would seem quite by chance, in Bach's little recitative for two oboes, *continuo*, bass recitative and soprano chorus. There is, as will be noticed, *constant alternation of appeal.* But where the words are the main interest, the music is cut to their measure ; and where the *Chorale* is the thing, the words are cut to its measure ; finally, where the scene is the thing, the words cease, and the music is built to the measure of the mental picture. We should imagine the scene staged, perhaps, for children, in their Christmas Play. The curtain rises, and on the stage are discovered the beloved Babe and Mother. It is possible that a worshipping disciple may be seen watching the Babe stedfastly, from near the wings, but that is not necessary. If there, he stands for the homely present-day disciple, and may sing the *parlando* comments as he gazes on the scene. All eyes will be centred on the Child and Mother. Now the mind of Bach is, as usual, engaged on breathing (phrasing) reality into music. He has no histrionic conventions to contend with in this delicate little picture. The very last thing he could do here would be to make either of these two intimately real chief characters take *musical* parts. He could not, for example, make the Blessed Virgin rise and sing either recitative or *Chorale* to us. Why not ? For " realistic " reasons ? Such an idea is ludicrously wide of the mark. No, for real reasons. Music and her sister arts cannot prosper in company either with realism or unreality, for both are fatal to all art.

Bach's musical thought is subtly fitted to the scene and the season, devoutly viewed. Of a million right ways of speaking his thoughts in terms of the harmonic avenue (with the " metalling " of which he had so much to do), he chooses just one convincingly lovely way. Then the Lutheran Church is heard to sing one line of its hymn. It ceases ; so does the music ; the disciple speaks wonderment at the whole amazing truth. Then on goes the musical presentment, or the subjective comment of music upon it ; once more the Church's hymn is heard ; once more the disciple's reverie ; once more the musical presentment. When the end is reached we find that three essential partners have duly alternated their appeal, or message—all continuing in the musical stream, unbroken, unconfused, and rounded with the slenderest ejaculatory "Kyrie" from the Church, and a more thoughtful wondering repetition by Bach of his first gaze at the Holy Child and Mother beginning thus:

(See also pages 408 to 414.)

We may well believe that the three possible lines of advance in future efforts to solve this very formidable problem, here too briefly and quite inadequately discussed, have often been in the minds of many lovers of Music and of Drama. The simultaneous appeal to eye and ear is so powerful, and seems so right, so consistent with daily experience, that it is impossible not to cherish longing hopes for its rapid and harmonious progress in this country. Let us equally hope to escape the present appallingly lengthy probation of disastrous and pretentious Grand operatic collusion. "Fraud" was Hubert Parry's scathing word. It sounds unkind; but after much thought I, for one, am more and more led to endorse it. If this is bias, it is perhaps due to one of upbringing.

Three joys stand out in my memory, as the most real joys experienced in life from earliest childhood (apart from the indescribable joys of human companionship in the providence of God). They are those of loveliness seen, loveliness heard, and loveliness imagined. When I was about five, such things as fleecy white clouds in a blue sky above a green hill-line; or gracious phrases from a violin (for which we starved in early days); or any apt word that quickened a lovely thing in my mind

—these, above all joys, shone brightest. Now, sixty years on, the same three joys remain, and still stand out as God's best gifts, not only to childhood, but to a grown man. Is not every one in exactly the same case? "Opera," says Parry, "is pretence and fraud." Yes. If the undertaking of Grand Opera was to give to all men and to me a simultaneous consummation of these three—Beauty made audible, Beauty made visible, Beauty made imaginable by utterance of the inspiring word at the right moment, in the right relation—it has so far defrauded us and pretentiously failed to keep its promise. Personally, I believe that it has been wrecked on the rocks of miscalculated emotionalism and incompatible magnitudes, perhaps also on an excessively low estimate of the mind of the people. But future composers will yet redeem the pledge, having learnt through the already numberless and often noble miscalculations of fine minds.

Reprinted by kind permission of Messrs. Novello & Co., Ltd.

ist auf Er - den kom-men
us to earth He com-eth
arm,
poor,
Recit. Bass
Wer kann die Lie-be recht er-
Who right-ly can the love de-
Andante
-höh'n, die un-ser Hei-land für uns hegt,
-clare That fills our ten-der Sa-viour's breast?

Sopranos
mf
dass er un - ser sich - er - barm',
Our re - demp - tion to se - cure,
Recit. Bass
ja, wer vermag es ein-zu-
Yea, who can understand, or

Andante
- sehen, wie ihn der Menschen Leid be - wegt?
share His grief for man by sin op - press'd?
Sopranos
mf
uns
And
in dem Himmel ma - che reich,
rich in heaven to make us stand,

Recit. Bass
Des Höchsten Sohn kommt in die
Him-self the Son of God will
Andante
Welt, weil ihm ihr Heil so wohl ge - fällt;
give, That we may be re-deem'd, and live;

mf
und sei - ren lie - ben
All num - ber'd, num - ber'd
En - geln gleich.
with His an - gel band.
Recit.
so will er selbst als Mensch ge-bo-ren wer-den.
So now for this as Man be-hold Him born.

Andante
p
Ky - ri - e - leis!
O Lord, have mer - - cy!
tr

CHAPTER 30

MUSIC IN PHANTOM HARNESS

A VIGOROUS-MINDED philanthropist, waiting one morning in a Hampstead drawing-room for a friend to join him, was listening to some Beethoven, played for his entertainment. He was a lover of poetry (which he could read aloud thrillingly), a lover of pictures, and a would-be lover of music. Listening to the music, he stalked round the room, examining the pictures; and when Beethoven, the Bechstein, and the pianist had done their best, he said, in a judicial voice, words to this effect: "Now tell me, please, when that music dies down to a series of single notes—just a note or two, and then silence, then another note or two, and so on—*now* tell me, what does that *mean*?" (A sharp, challenging emphasis on the words *now* and *mean.*) Presumably he was referring to this passage, part of the movement played: *

And the reader, too, may return again and again to the quest of the curious: "What does it all mean?" And who can tell us? As Stevenson once exclaimed in his whimsically inquiring love for music: "Do you know

* Beethoven's Sonata No. 7, Op. 10, No. 3 in D.

a book that really tells a fellow ? " If, in the above Sonata extract, Beethoven consciously means something, then surely, says our mystified philanthropist, he, if any one, could tell us what he means. But, we reply, even if he could, ought *we* to expect or wish to mean exactly what *he* meant, every time we listen to or play it ? Ought it to mean one thing, and only that continually, to every person ? Ought it, in the programme sense, even to mean the same thing twice in succession to the same person : to Beethoven himself, to the philanthropist, to you or to me ?

Such questions should gradually tend to answer themselves ; if they do not, they cannot easily be answered. Is it not likely that our meticulous friend, the philanthropist, was (tonally) in the position of any insensitive man who, seeing furtive and curious behaviour in a fellow's downcast glances and hesitating manner, were suddenly to accost him with : " Now, what does this odd behaviour of yours mean ? " Of such social insensitivity our friend would have been quite incapable. Yet had he any better right thus to " accost " Beethoven, or the pianist, or the music itself, and to demand an explanation of its behaviour (unless, perhaps, as an intimate friend, a pupil, or the pedagogue of the composer himself) ? It is absurd to suppose that there is *not* a vivid human experience behind the passage in question, behind the whole movement. No music behaves as this does without meaning, without root cause. Even so, no one in his senses digs at a root in order to enjoy a flower, or in order to give intelligent thanks to his Benefactor for a sight of the flower. More than that, is it not impertinent and senseless to ask Beethoven to reproduce *in words* what he has already given wholly *in music* ? It is like the demand of a child to chew the string after it has enjoyed the sugar-candy.

We may go further. We have already been reminded

that even a chord may have the effect upon listeners that a word has—not, of course, any paltry defining word like *scissors*, or *artichoke*, but an "infining" word like *love*, or *grace*. In the same way we shall, I fancy, find that every fundamental attribute of a Sonata—its *intervals*, its *melodies* as well as its chords; its *rhythms*, even its graded *pianissimi*—in fact, its total behaviour may resemble corresponding fundamental attributes, or behaviours experienced and quite familiar to ordinary men in some other *genre* of life. Sonatas can resemble other vital records, such as words, gestures, postures; expressing palpably as they, though mystically and uniquely, the reaction of man's mind to all shades of human moods, hopes, fears, changing vitalities; uttering a man's attitude of mind towards life and companionship, towards death and loneliness; his faith, his seething energy, his uncanny stillness, and countless kindred experiences known to every human soul. So naturally expressive of inmost reactions can Sonata be, that we are driven to ask ourselves: why should Music alone, of all man's sublime utterances, be catechized by intellectuals—stopped in her highway, and abruptly asked, "What do you *mean* by this?"

To watch the ways of men or things long enough and intently enough is perhaps the only way to understand them. To listen often and intently to the ways of music is similarly the one clear recipe for intelligent contact and enjoyment.

Yet, when all is said, listeners and composers may hope to quicken their contact by comparing notes. With the best will in the world, not all music lovers can join with Mendelssohn in finding music "much more definite than words." Mutual concessions and interpretations are necessary. The listener must concede a more open mind and keener attention, while one of the composer's frequent concessions is to warn us verbally what set his music in action, and provoked it into a particular form. He tells us what it was, sometimes in a mere title, like *Eroica*, or *Pastoral*; but sometimes in a complete programme of thoughts or quickening events, as in Strauss's *Don Quixote*, and Elgar's *Falstaff*. Strauss and Elgar reveal their ideas—to a friend, perhaps, who tells the public, or to the public direct—either about one main string, or about all the successive fragments of string upon which his music crystallized. They sometimes write their own analyses, and not always helpfully. We listeners remain (with them) in the world of instrumental music; but we are given the composer's guide (official or unofficial) to this and that feature of the piece. What is now known as Programme music is the interesting result.

Such music, though remaining purely orchestral, can, I suppose, no longer be classed with Sonata music, though it remains akin to it. Let us think of it as music in phantom harness. Whether it be phantom poem or drama, phantom scenery or action, it is the composer's wish to harness it for our fuller sharing of his own experience. We then listen (in concert hall or in our own home) primed with his particulars, but still left free to fit or synchronize (or misfit or antagonize) such details as he gives us with the musical imaginings they have evoked in his mind. It is often difficult. But it may be an exciting and delightful experience.

Before we go further, let us notice a significant anxiety often expressed by composers of Programme music. It is the twin-anxiety with that of our intellectual listener to Sonatas, who, wanting to know what it means, says: "Please, composer, give me a programme as guide to your abstract music." The composer replies: "Here is a programme to my instrumental work, but please remember that I require my music to be heard *as music*!" Even Beethoven voiced this in his famous remark about the "Pastoral Symphony": "Mehr Empfindung als Malerei," fearing that the cuckoo, the murmuring brook, and the storm, might side-track or misdirect even the elect listener ; which fear of course should be groundless. As symptoms, surely these two anxieties bear unmistakably upon each other. Sonata aspires to communicate and Programme music aspires to attain design. Even if Sonata music only says " Contemplate this and this with me," it at least wishes to tell us something. And the most amorphous Symphonic Poem has its musical form, however loose, even though it be but the shadow cast by its phantom. It has a musical start, a finish, with something between. Like the three parts of a salmon, sold as jowl, middle, and tail, all Programme music has at least three recognizable parts or happenings to its form ; and these the composer is out to relate as effectively and unconfusedly as possible. Much more than this. In that an abstract design *is* abstract, it must be guarded from a failure to communicate ; and here the humble-minded listener may do his part. Again, in that Programme music is planned *to communicate*, it must be guarded from failure to achieve beauty of design ; and here we follow the anxious concern of the composer.

It is impossible, at this point, to consider the many forms of Programme music which may have delighted or baffled my present reader. The chief need is to give this particular order of musical enjoyment its own place in our minds, and to decide what we may expect from music linked with a phantom attendant chosen for us by the composer.

First, we realize that, as soon as we have been given the contents of his programme, our minds are left as entirely free to rove in the realms of Programme music as they are in the Symphonic realms of the classics. This is good. But if we are compelled to pull up at this and that point to find out (in words or in writing, or by effort of memory) what is supposed to be happening in the music, we merely flounder. This does not apply when the composer offers us a single title as programme. All is then well, for it is our look-out to visualize the phantom, and fit the harness to the music. If, however, we are given a page and a half of description in the book of words, all is not necessarily well; for who is to guide our listening minds to this and that chosen point in time? So young is our art, and such beginners are we, that this matter is still often left hopelessly to chance. It may be argued that it is *our* duty to study to equip ourselves beforehand, and to be ready to fit every single happening, and to seize all the points at which the several ideas pass into music. But this seems unreasonable. Imagine for a moment a play in which the audience was in continual danger of losing the drift, *unless* they had beforehand committed explanatory notes to memory as to the intention of the author *at certain points of the play!* Alternatively, imagine lights having to be turned up, in the course of the performance, in order that the public might refresh frail memory and find the author's summary of the particular scene before them. We may laugh at the absurdity of the idea. Yet is there not like absurdity in the present necessity for furtive and hasty scanning of concert programmes in the midst of a performance of some great musical work, in order to find the meaning of the composer in certain passages? I personally feel clear that this need not continue, if once it is accepted by all concerned that in Programme music, as in Sonata music, we are still living *in the world of sound,* and, as it happens, in that of instrumental music. A London critic once dared to write, wisely, perhaps playfully, "Good music should be heard and not seen." * It certainly

* This critic is one of my dearest friends on earth and seems still to love and espouse Grand Opera as intensely as I imprecate it; so the reader need have no fear that there is any suggestion in his words, or in my quotation of them, of deprecating the common joys of real Music-drama, of eye, ear, and mind at one.

should not require a carefully memorized script to make it live. We suggest that when any synchronizing of the listener's mind with the composer's intention *is* necessary at a given moment in any work—that is, if a definite thought of the phantom-partner and " conspirer " in the work is to occur to the listener (say, at bar 310 of the score)—the thing may better be done *by some audible means there and then.* Why not ? There are many ways in which this may be done. Let us here suppose a Symphonic Poem is given the title, " The Tragedy of the Triangular Duel." The necessity for the composer to give more " programme " guidance than is conveyed by the title will certainly arise. We shall need, in some way, to know when and where to expect what. This could surely be met by some such *audible* and completely self-explanatory device as that of three single tones heard in smart succession, to announce the crucial moment appointed for the three-sided duel :

while some equally obvious *audible* announcement derived from the above could notify the tragic *dénouement.* Beethoven did the like dozens of times, as we know, even in Sonata music of the highest order—not in so many words, but in so many notes.

Another audible plan seems fairly obvious. What is there to prevent the composer from framing a concise instrumental prelude (if necessary, quite distinct from the work itself), consisting of a deliberate tonal catalogue of such musical facts (or *dramatis personæ*) as are vital for the listener's comprehension of the performance ? This announcement might not only focus the ear of the audience upon the work more potently and instantly than any other device, but might give excellent and effectual play for new ingenuity and eloquence. If any good composer once devised this counterpart in the world of music to the *dramatis personæ* in the world of poetry, with masterly clearness, one can imagine every one else thinking: "Of course! Any one could tell *that* would work."

Many are the experiments continuously being made in the world of Programme music to bring each several idea audibly to mind at the compatible moment. Lines, or even whole poems, are sometimes read aloud before or with the music. Composers are coming more and more to meet the minds of listeners in such ways, and to supply what is still the gravest lack in Programme works. As in the case of Music-drama of the future, I cannot but put faith in the development of blendable interpolated *musical speech* (referred to in the previous chapter) which may be unaffectedly interjected at any quiet moment with normal and complete tonal compatibility. An unbroken musical hold upon the ear and mind could thus be preserved. How and to what extent a narrator's or interlocutor's contribution may become a convincingly integral part of the actual tonal texture in the orchestral tone-poem it is too early to guess. That it will eventually become so seems to me already proved (mostly by happy accident). Judging by analogy, from the thrill supplied by some broadcast running commentaries on exciting events, and bearing in mind the indispensability of such commentaries, it is hard to set any limit to the potentialities of such a plan properly applied to Programme music. To hear any first-rate commentator, regardful of the listener as of himself,* supplying the apt descriptive word, while the launching of a ship, a boat race, or a speed trial is heard in process, and of which literally only the *programme* is required, is not only to see through words heard the *sights* that explain the *sounds* and make the experience whole (just what Programme music desiderates); it is

* Such as Mr. Howard Marshall.

much more. It is to hear and admire deftly chosen words which interrupt no inward vision, yet which bring a flood of needed meaning into sounds that would otherwise have left listeners confusedly guessing. Even in these early days of broadcasting it has become something still more. In it we hear an artist evolving the technique of an entirely new art as he goes along. If you are in any doubt as to the significance of this, make a point of hearing (if you can) some unfortunate ego-centric and unimaginative commentator failing all along the line. By failure as well as by mastery the significance of this particular art will be brought more overpoweringly into prominence as time goes on. Strange if so different and seemingly so fortuitous a thing should suggest the one missing factor in so important a sphere of our pursuit of music.

We are now nearing the end of our inquiry. For measureless shortcomings and omissions I have to ask the reader's forgiveness. But for the consciousness of these, each chapter would have brought nothing but joy and relief in the writing. As it is, I am constrained to declare my feelings of disappointed helplessness in seeing the scanty result of my desire to be of use to friends, to beginners in music, and to that anonymous Major friend who, if he has survived the war, may still be wanting to know " what music is about." To quote Stevenson again : " Books * are of no use ; they tell you how to write in four parts, and that cannot be done by man." This book has not attempted that particular " impossible " ; yet it is destined, one knows, to be voted by one after another as of " no use. It only tells you . . ." Yet (comforting thought !) it is equally certain to kindle and refresh one here, and another there, by some sentence here, or a musical fragment there.

* (On music.)

And great is my hope that it will at least tend to send all my readers back to music itself, and to the keyboard, all ears for what purposeful sounds may evoke for contemplative regard, and especially mindful of the vital meanings we all may, *with listening connivance*, assume for ourselves. *Your* meaning for a particular phrase or movement will never specifically be *mine* ; *ours* will never be specifically the meanings of *others*, least of all, perhaps, the composer's! But *in any case do not fail to have a meaning of your very own ;* for one and the same humanly wrought piece of music has the natural power of mobilizing your meaning and mine, and a million others—all specifically different, yet all generically at one. Why at one? Because in that it is humanly devised, it irradiates a human appeal; and in that it is intuitive music, we dare to believe it has heavenly integrity.*

You may still, and rightly, ask, how are we to know *good* from *bad* in a Symphony or a Movement, in a melody or a mere phrase? Press the question further: is there no way of discerning good from bad even in a mere two-note relating; or further still, in a single tone, of this or that vibration frequency, volume, length, or calibre? "I dislike one instrument and like another," you add. "Why is it? Cannot one tone (say, that of a saxophone) be called inferior to another (say, that of a trombone)? And, at the other extreme, can we not acquire confident power to distinguish a good Symphony from a bad one?"

If we ask such conundrums with a view to settling the matter, they can do nothing but unsettle us. The search for the good in music, for criteria of judgment and of taste, leads us, I believe, along two lines. Let us take a parting glance at them.

* "Tell him the Beethoven was heaven," was the message remitted to the writer by a lady from her brother, who, dying, and suffering pain, had been unable to bear any other broadcast music than this.

Stevenson, scorning the book that would teach him to write music in four parts, moved along the first of these lines; so, sitting at his piano, he found "fourths delicious," and "consecutive fifths" like "the music of the spheres." (In books on music, of course, he had read that fourths were "discords" and consecutive fifths "forbidden"!) He stood in the nineteenth century at the beginning of the harmonic age with Hucbald of Flanders (A.D. 930) and heard an ageless glory into two so-called perfect intervals (ratios 2 : 3 and 3 : 4). And woe to the music, new or old, that fails to discover these primal values and the timeless glory which Stevenson found in his very own way in these simplest euphonies. This chapter is being written within earshot of Tchaikovsky's *1812 Overture*. The bells and a Russian chorus have just pealed out gloriously by means of gramophone and wireless in our quiet Berkshire village. If Stevenson in his early stages of acquiring musical knowledge had had these multitudinous glories thrust upon him, they might yet have been wasted until such time as he could have learnt to hear all his simpler primal values, not only unobliterated, but magically amassed into a new, manifold, yet united splendour.

We are none of us in different case either from R. L. S. on the one hand, or Tchaikovsky on the other. We are all simply at different stages of tonal sensitivity and power of apprehension. For us, as for them, the first musical good lies still in the primal evaluation of the simplest happening in the whole universe of sound, and the pure love of it at the very point-instant when, being sounded, we find ourselves able to apprehend and contemplate it fully. This applies to every tonal experience, simple and complex, if we can let the superfluous and non-apprehended parts flow away from us like the proverbial water from the duck's back.

We may be certain that many hearers only hear the

top note of all, and perhaps the bottom note of all, in nine chordal experiences out of ten. But what of that ? The rest is innocently obliviated in self-defence till such time as use makes it intelligible. Only maximum evaluation on the listener's part for what *is* joyously apprehended brings maximum good. Enter a superb flower-garden, and you will naturally enjoy only that for which you entertain the highest possible regard. Search and enjoy. This line of search for the spontaneously simple and unforced good opens up another avenue. Not only shall we seek to fill our mind with all available and intelligible glories, letting slide what is beyond us, but the more advanced mind also learns intuitively to " fill the cup " with *implied* loveliness that may not be actually heard by the ear ; if indeed there is a thirsting zeal to experience and hold implied riches. To imagine but one example: sound this chord with (let us say) Stevenson and Debussy listening :

Leave it sounding in your mind (on your keyboard *pianissimo*) and contemplate. *You* may hear it as it stands. Stevenson might find his mind full to overflowing of his beloved fifths, and so not regard even the major third as present at all :

whereas Debussy, the man of long, subtle musing upon those same fifths and fourths, in far richer measure than a mere beginner, might well hear new, unheard but implied, riches of mind such as these:

Along this line of inquiry, we find that good music, whether simple or complex, must be defined by each for himself, as that which answers Stevenson's remark: "To my ear, delicious," and (to my mind) "the music of the spheres." That, in all music, at all times, is discerned to be good which, delighting the ear, fills the mind with wonderment and makes it exclaim "of the spheres," or "from heaven, not from men," or anything else to that effect. Even a single tone, beautifully sung, may do this.

But a second criterion or standard of good music is to be found along another line, less annoying to many minds because much more tractable, more readily discoverable, and immediately agreeable. It seems in many ways the very opposite of the other. To the ear, a chord may be anything but "delicious" and yet "exactly right." To the mind, it may be anything but the "music of the spheres," and yet, then and there, exactly fitting to human requirements. This is the neighbourly goodness of all apt music, whether in double or in phantom harness. A composer puts, let us say, a conventional high note to the last syllable but one of a slenderly poised poem, and the singer sits on that note for many swaggering seconds. The *criteria* of mere aptness tells us at once that this both ruins the poem and the proportions of the music and phrases. The music and the performance are both quite *bad*. A more apt composer unexpectedly ends the poem "in the air" as it were, with no cadence, no ending in the conventional sense (as Schubert does in the *Leiermann*), and the singer in his turn lets the song die down with a *pianissimo* tremor and a complete absence of vocal display. The music and the performance are both *good.* Why ? Entire and inspired musical *fitness to purpose* has resulted in a uniquely new phase in music bringing a widened horizon to song and achieving the complete fusion, as between two arts, discussed in our four previous chapters. It is strangely true, and quite incontrovertible, that it is spontaneous *fitness* in music that makes us exclaim time after time " how perfect, just *genius* ! " This is most easily grasped, of course, when there is a known something there to be fitted. One can never say of a perfect garment seen only through a window, " What a beautiful fit ! " Yet fitness is also an attribute of the thing called abstract music. The cry for a clue to a Sonata ; the clamour for a programme ; the eagerness with which people seize upon tags such as " Fate knocking at the door " in the *Fifth Symphony*—these are the symptoms too often of unadmirable modesty, or of indolent imagination. Seeing that it fits nothing in particular to our mind, we ask, " What does this Symphony fit ? " But does it need to fit anything else if it is already Fitness in itself ? Fitness to what ? you ask. Just perfect fitness of every part to every other. We shall only find it is " to our mind " if our mind meets it. This is conspicuously true of simple things like Handel's overworked *Largo*, or Bach's almost as overworked *Melody for the G String* (falsely so-called). But the reader may expect to find it true also of a surprisingly vast number of things, the moment he decides to hear music for himself, and to meet it with his mind as fully as he can at the moment—that is, to capacity ; which capacity each day is likely to grow. Such listening begets a strange confidence in modest minds, a cock-sure humility all its own, which never fears to delight in the conventionally "wrong thing" if it is at the moment the right thing to him. The reader need have no fear that his taste will *de*grade, if only he will stoutly refuse to let his servant, the physical ear, master him, and if he also refuses to let his friend, the music-maker, tyrannize unreproved.

As I prepare to lay my pen down and carry the good news to another room that this book is finished, I still hear a reader, whom I love, but have never met, calling me back to say that, though he can understand music *with* other things, abstract music still baffles him. I hear him ask: Can you say nothing more to help me to listen to Symphonies more enjoyingly; more intelligently? The only help I can offer lies in the irritating counter-question: What, dear friend, if there is *no such thing as abstract music*?

I believe that all so-called abstract music really is ideal Programme music, as between God and the composer, and yourself (or myself); and I *suggest* to you (as the lawyers say) that this will perhaps prove a good working truth for both of us. You must try to find *the* programme. Composers are doing it, and the listener can. That dress that you saw in the window (as we agreed) could not be called a "fit"; but if you discovered loveliness in it, it was because the lines were fitting to your mind, and—never mind who is to wear it, it has achieved its first end—it has a heavenly fitness in itself before ever it is worn, whether by the earthly Mrs. Smith, or by an angel from heaven. That Sonata that you heard played was, like the dress, entirely "to your mind." It was not? Then did you not, perchance, put out all your imaginative mind to meet it? Its "programme," we may reverently suggest, was nothing less than to build a bridge (as Beethoven put it) from the mind of the Spirit to chance minds (such as yours and mine) *via* the composer's mind, who has kept Stevenson's child-values, but has also musically something more than Stevenson—the uncertain glory we call genius—genius for building tonal bridges true to spirit and to the nature of the human mind, well known to sympathetic men in all pursuits, and at the same time perpetually retaining the thing here imperfectly described as primal tonal values.

Music itself may at last prove to be the most precise language of the mind. It is delicate; it is so easily pulled out of the true. What is written on the music page for your child to practise is as unlike music as trellis-work is unlike a tree, or as a goose-step is unlike a man's free stride. What is heard from bands and in choirs is so often like the trellis and the goose-step, and so little like the tree and reality. This makes us wonder sometimes whether music is not happiest when untrammelled. There appears often a further hardship when it joins forces with other arts. For when along its own uniquely evolved harmonic avenue of meaningful distances it has become most able to throw light upon the minds of other arts, like drama, then the other art puts forward its differing claims and appeals. How can it help doing so? The position is often tense. We may so easily lose the gist. When a whole mind is needed for music, it cannot give attention shared with other claimants. For such reasons we set our hopes, perhaps not wrongly, on Sonata music intently heard and given the listener's own interpretation each time anew—Sonata music must be self-harnessed. Programmes of a heavenly order occurring to the mind (as in the case of Sonatas) may bring the listener nearer reality than earthly ones occurring to the senses. A *think* may be bigger than a *thing*.

But when all this and more is conceived and admitted, it by no means follows that the highest heaven of music may not be found in the lowliest application of it; I mean, music devised to fit earthly things and needs that surround us men, here, in travail. The finest, most thrilling lilt of poetry may seem sometimes the most commonplace—for example, Dekker's refrain of "Sweet Content":

> "Work apace, apace, apace, apace,
> Honest labour bears a lovely face."

Such a couplet may start in one man's mind a mere hackneyed tune of the threepenny Ballad, sordid kind. Or it may call out a thousand average melodies from ordinary men, a melody a day for three years, and all of them good in their way. Then, one fine day, it may send a supremely perfect melody ringing down the ages on etheric waves, worlds away, given the genius of melodic Fitness.

It is possible that our minds may find their most replenishing Harbour after this our pursuant voyage, if we turn to one of the "Revelations of Divine Love" recorded by Mother Juliana of Norwich. Her wonderful language is memorably helpful, if only we are able to include in her choice monosyllable *kinde* (her word for *humanity*) an assembly of the maximum meanings we are accustomed to give to all words such as *kindness, kinship, tact, contact, esprit de corps, humaneness,* and a dozen others; and read into the word *Grace* (her word for the Spirit) all the meanings that were ever given to to-day's words, *inspiration, genius, vision,* etc. Raise all these words to their highest power, and relate them into two conceptions of fine music—that which we call a perfect "fit" (kinde), and that which we call an "inspiration" (Grace). Here is an extract from the fifteenth "Vision":

> For Kinde is all good and fair in itself; and grace was sent out to saven kinde to the blessid point fro whence it came: that is God. For it shall

be seen afore God and of all his holy in joy without end, that kinde hath been assayed in the fire of tribulation and therein founden no lack, no default. *Thus is kinde and grace of one accord: for grace is good as kinde is good; he is two in manner of working and one in love. And neither of them worketh without other. . . .*

Musically interpreted, the last two sentences (here italicized) seem to mean that a Symphony will be good if it prove "kinde" (that is, human) to the mind of the listener, as is a perfect musical setting to a perfect poem; and that every other order of music, submitting to partnership or programme by attaining good of its own "kinde," must also manifest grace from heaven.

Shakespeare was surely not merely paying light-hearted homage to Sylvia, but giving away Art's secret, and the conclusion of the whole matter in one immortal line, when he wrote:

"*For Beauty lives with Kindness.*"

THE END

PRINTED IN GREAT BRITAIN AT
THE PRESS OF THE PUBLISHERS

SOME NELSON MUSIC BOOKS

★

MUSIC CALLING

CYRIL WINN

This book gives a pleasant and easy introduction to the art of listening, and will appeal to what the author calls "musicable readers" rather than to expert musicians. With this book, and a gramophone, groups of music lovers will find intellectual satisfaction and emotional solace.

Discussion Book No. 31 3s. 6d. net

BEETHOVEN

A. E. F. DICKINSON

The musical experience of most people to-day is made up of fleeting impressions which are confused and vague. The individuality which created the music is often obscured, if not totally ignored. This short but comprehensive study of the famous composer is intended to convert such frail recollections into a vivid personal experience. Beethoven's form is described, and the dramatic and ethical qualities of the music are pointed out. Separate chapters are given to Beethoven's craftsmanship and to the somewhat unusual circumstances of his life. The author is no blind worshipper, but he does recognize and profoundly feel those things wherein Beethoven's greatness truly lies.

Discussion Book No. 70 3s. 6d. net

NEW PATHS IN MUSIC

BASIL MAINE

Music has known thirty troublous and confused years. To deal calmly and steadily with the period is a task of considerable difficulty. Mr. Maine, the well-known broadcaster and critic, discusses Stravinsky's Opera "Œdipus Rex" and the works of other prominent European composers, the future of Symphony and of Opera, Music in America, etc., and he writes in that easy and attractive manner which immediately compels attention while satisfying serious and intellectual interest.

Discussion Book No. 75 3s. 6d. net

YOUTH AND MUSIC

DESMOND MACMAHON, D.MUS.

The first book to appear on the subject of music as applied to the Youth Club. It details the various musical activities that can reasonably be attempted in a Club and explains how to set about introducing them.

"Should prove a valuable handbook for Youth leaders. . . . The most interesting feature of the book is the refreshing treatment of jazz and swing. . . . The fruits of wide experience and sound scholarship could hardly be placed more readably at the disposal of the non-specialist musical amateur."—*The Times Educational Supplement*

5s. net

THE NATIONAL YOUTH SONG BOOK

EDITED BY DESMOND MACMAHON, D.MUS.

A collection of old and new songs, shanties, spirituals, standard operatic airs, soldier and student songs, hymns, carols, rounds, and recorder melodies, specially selected for the use of youth clubs and similar organizations, and forming a complete community song book for adults and singers of all ages who possess the spirit and joy of youth.

12s. 6d. net. Words only, 2s. net

THE NEW NATIONAL AND FOLK-SONG BOOKS

EDITED BY DESMOND MACMAHON, D.MUS.

" This collection," says *The Music Teacher*, " is excellent in that it contains something old, something new, and something new-old. The old are inevitable favourites ; the new-old include many lovely songs which are less known, but which should be better known ; and the new is concerned with fresh translations of the words and the skilful rearrangements and accompaniments." Contents range from " Black-eyed Susan " to " Robin Adair."

Part 1 contains 81 songs. 8s. 6d. net
Part 2, 100 songs and 30 rounds. 9s. 6d. net

OPERA TUNES TO REMEMBER

FLORENCE M. CLARK

" The story of eighteen famous operas, accompanied by the music of the better-known airs, motifs, and themes. The book is a delightful introduction to the great operas, and a happy thought on the part of the producer."—*Edinburgh Evening News.* 3s. 6d. net

STORIES OF GREAT MUSIC

JOHN HORTON

" What were the circumstances that inspired Handel to compose the Fireworks Music, Tartini the Devil's Trill Sonata, Haydn the Farewell Symphony, Beethoven the Eroica Symphony, Mendelssohn the Hebrides Overture ? These and other similar questions are answered by the author. His book should prove a happy introduction for many to the famous works passed under review."—*Aberdeen Press Journal.* 3s. 6d. net

THE NEW NATIONAL AND FOLK-SONG BOOKS

Edited by Geoffrey Macmahon, D.Mus.

"This collection," says *The Music Teacher*, "is excellent in that it contains something old, something new, and something new-old. The old are the inevitable favourites; the new-old include many lovely songs which are less known, but which should be better known; and the new is concerned with fresh translations of the words and the skilful re-arrangements and accompaniments." Contents range from "The Vicar of Bray" to "Robin Adair."

Part 1 contains 50 songs. 2s 6d net

Part 2, 100 songs and 30 rounds. 4s 6d net

OPERA TUNES TO REMEMBER

Frederick M. Cope

"The stories of eighteen famous operas, accompanied by the music of the better-known arias, motifs, and themes. The book is a delightful introduction to the great operas, and a happy thought on the part of the producer."—*Liverpool Evening News*. 3s 6d net

STORIES OF GREAT MUSIC

Isaac Horton

"What were the circumstances that inspired Handel to compose the Fireworks Music, Tartini the Devil's Trill Sonata, Haydn the Farewell Symphony, Beethoven the Eroica Symphony, Mendelssohn the Hebrides Overture? These and other similar questions are answered by the author. His book should prove a happy introduction for many to the famous works passed under review."—*Aberdeen Press Journal*. 3s 6d net